A HISTORY OF JEWISH LITERATURE
VOLUME V

Israel Zinberg's *History of Jewish Literature*

An Analytic Index to the *History of Jewish Literature* will appear in Volume XII.

Israel Zinberg

A HISTORY OF
JEWISH
LITERATURE

TRANSLATED AND EDITED BY BERNARD MARTIN

The Jewish Center of Culture
in the Ottoman Empire

HEBREW UNION COLLEGE PRESS
CINCINNATI, OHIO
KTAV PUBLISHING HOUSE, INC.
NEW YORK, NEW YORK
1974

Library of Congress Cataloging in Publication Data (Revised)

Zinberg, Israel, 1873–1938.
   A history of Jewish literature.

   Translation of Di geshikhte fun der literatur bay Yidn.
   Vols. 4–   published by Ktav Pub. House, New York.
   Includes bibliographical references.
   CONTENTS: v. 1. The Arabic-Spanish period.—v. 2. French and
German Jewry in the early Middle Ages. The Jewish community of
medieval Italy.—v. 3. The struggle of mysticism and tradition against
philosophical rationalism.—v. 4. Italian Jewry in the Renaissance era.—
v. 5. The Jewish center of culture in the Ottoman empire.

   1. Jewish literature—History and criticism.
I. Title.
PJ5008.Z5313   809'.889'24   72–183310
ISBN 0-87068-241-5 (v. 5)

Printed in the United States of America.

Contents

PART VI: THE JEWISH CENTER OF CULTURE IN THE OTTOMAN EMPIRE

Chapter One: THE CULTURAL FLOWERING OF TURKISH JEWRY; KARAITE SCHOLARS / 3

The favorable situation of the Jews in the Ottoman Empire—
Isaac Tzarefati's summons to the German Jews—The cultural
flowering of the Jewish community in Turkey—The disseminators
of enlightenment and their enthusiasm for Abraham Ibn Ezra's
work—The debate between Shabbetai ben Malkiel and Mordecai
Comtino—Comtino as enlightener—The cultural influence of the
Jewish scholars on the local Karaites—The Karaite scholars; Caleb
Afendopolo's poetic work—The controversy about the Karaites;
the ban as a weapon—Elijah Mizrahi and his activity—The exiles
of Spain.

Chapter Two: THE SPANISH EXILES IN TURKEY AND PALESTINE; JOSEPH KARO AND SOLOMON MOLCHO / 17

The Spanish exiles in Turkey and their influence on the local
Jews—New moods—The intensified interest in historical description—Isaac Akrish and Tam Ibn Yahya—Mystical hopes for messianic redemption—Emigration to Palestine—Public letters from
Jerusalem—The rabbinic synod literature and the messianic Kabbalah—Jacob Berab and Jacob Ibn Habib—Joseph Karo as codifier; *Bet Yosef* and the *Shulhan Aruch*—David Reubeni and his
memoirs—Solomon Molcho as a person; his sermons and his influ-

··❧[v]❧··

ence on Joseph Karo—Joseph Karo as mystic and author of *Maggid Mesharim.*

A Note on
Israel Zinberg

D<small>R. ISRAEL ZINBERG</small> is widely regarded as one of the fore-most historians of Jewish literature. Born in Russia in 1873 and educated at various universities in Germany and Switzerland, he devoted more than twenty years to the writing, in Yiddish, of his monumental *Die Geshichte fun der Literatur bei Yidn* (History of Jewish Literature). This work, published in eight volumes in Vilna, 1929–1937, is a comprehensive and authoritative study of Jewish literary creativity in Europe from its beginnings in tenth-century Spain to the end of the Haskalah period in nineteenth-century Russia. Based on a meticulous study of all the relevant primary source material and provided with full documentation, Zinberg's *History* is a notable exemplar of the tradition of modern Jewish scholarship known as *die Wissenschaft des Judentums* (the Science of Judaism).

In addition to his *magnum opus*, Zinberg, who earned his living as a chemical engineer, wrote numerous other valuable monographs and articles on Jewish history and literature in Russian, Hebrew, and Yiddish. In 1938, during the Stalinist purges, he was arrested by the Soviet police and sentenced to exile in Siberia. He died in a concentration camp hospital in Vladivostok in that same year.

The reader who wishes a fuller introduction is invited to consult the Translator's Introduction to Volume I of Zinberg's *History of Jewish Literature.*

Foreword

In 1972 the Case Western Reserve University Press began publishing an English translation of Israel Zinberg's *History of Jewish Literature*. Zinberg, an engineer by profession, was a scholar by choice and inclination. In thirty years of intensive study in the great Jewish libraries of St. Petersburg (later Leningrad), he produced eight volumes in Yiddish portraying the course of literary creativity among the Jews beginning with the Golden Age of Spanish Jewry and continuing to the end of the last century. It was not until many years after Zinberg's death that a Hebrew translation was prepared and published in the State of Israel.

There has been no work of similar scope and magnitude in the English language, despite the fact that the Jewish reading public in Britain, South Africa, Canada, and the United States constitutes about half of the Jews in the world. Now, however, the Zinberg volumes have been beautifully translated into English by Dr. Bernard Martin, Abba Hillel Silver Professor of Jewish Studies and Chairman of the Department of Religion at Case Western Reserve University in Cleveland, Ohio. All the English-speaking lands are indebted to Professor Martin for his endeavor to make accessible a literary history such as Zinberg's, a history which depicts the intellectual strivings of the Jews, their aspirations, yearnings, and spiritual search in the medieval and modern worlds, in both of which they have played a not undistinguished role.

Special gratitude is due to the Press of Case Western Reserve University which inaugurated the challenging task of publishing this handsome and very important series of books. Each volume is an aesthetic as well as intellectual delight. The Case Western Reserve Press was aided in publication by a generous grant from the Memorial Foundation for Jewish Culture. The grant is, indeed, a memorial to the martyred Zinberg, who was arrested by the Soviet police in 1938 and deported to Siberia, where he died. We, for our part, are pleased with this opportunity to express our gratitude to the Memorial Foundation for the support which made possible the publication of the first three volumes.

Unfortunately, the economic difficulties from which many universities are now suffering has led to the dissolution of the Case Western Reserve Press and made it impossible for it to continue with the remaining nine volumes. That is why the Hebrew Union College—Jewish Institute of Religion, realizing the importance and cultural implications of this work, is cooperating with the Ktav Publishing House, Incorporated, in the publication of the remaining volumes.

The completion of this series will make available to the English-speaking world a magnificent account of the literary and cultural treasures created by the Jewish people during their millennial history.

Hebrew Union College—   Alfred Gottschalk
Jewish Institute of Religion   President
Cincinnati, Ohio
January 1974

TRANSLITERATION OF HEBREW TERMS

א is not transliterated   ו = v (where not a vowel)   ל = l   פ = f

ב = b   ז = z   מ = m   צ = tz

ב = v   ח = ḥ   נ = n   ק = k

ג,ג = g   ט = t   ס = s   ר = r

ד,ד = d   י = y   ע is not transliterated   שׁ = sh

ה = h   כ = k   פ = p   שׂ = s

כ = ch   ת,ת = t

ָ = a   ֱ = e

ַ = a   ִ = i

ֹ ,וֹ = o   ֵ = ei

ֻ ,וּ = u   ֶ = e

short ָ = o   ֳ = o

יֵ = ei   ֲ = a

vocal *sheva* = e

silent *sheva* is not transliterated

Abbreviations

JQR	*Jewish Quarterly Review*
JQR, n.s.	*Jewish Quarterly Review*, new series
MGWJ	*Monatsschrift für die Geschichte und Wissenschaft des Judentums*
PAAJR	*Proceedings of the American Academy for Jewish Research*
REJ	*Revue des Étude Juives*
ZHB	*Zeitschrift für hebräische Bibliographie*

This volume is dedicated
to
Warren Wells
Stalwart American—Loyal Jew

THE JEWISH CENTER OF CULTURE IN THE OTTOMAN EMPIRE

CHAPTER ONE

The Cultural Flowering of Turkish Jewry;
KARAITE SCHOLARS

HE talented poet of *Consolaçam,* Samuel Usque, who speaks with such deep pain and burning indignation of the bloody deeds of the Inquisition, sings, with fervent sentiment, a jubilant song of praise to the brave new power—the Turkish empire which, with its stupendous victories, made Christian Europe tremble:

Turkey, great and wide as the seas that wash your shores! You gladly rescue us, like that sea whose waters receded at God's command before the newly liberated people! Jacob my people, as in those days when you left Egypt, so now cast all your sufferings and sorrows in the depths of the sea, for there, in the youthful, new land, the gates of grace, of freedom and happiness, are opened wide before you. Here you may throw off the shameful garments, the hateful mask, which through oppression and compulsion you had to wear in the land of the fanatically ruthless and vengeful people. Here you will rise to new life. Openly and freely you will return to your religion, to the faith of your fathers which your virulent enemies have compelled you through fire and sword to forsake. There, in the land of your enemies, you wandered like a stranger, despised by all, but here, under the protection of the powerful young empire, God will spread his grace over you and make you rejoice in freedom and redemption.

Proud of their great victories, the sultans, who on the ruins of the Byzantine empire built the mighty Turkish empire, realized quite well that the warlike Ottomans, who knew only how to do battle and whose hands were accustomed only to the gun and the sword, were very little suited to vitalize the land through commerce and industry. The Christian middle class residing there, the Greek and Armenian merchants and entrepreneurs, were too suspect politically to be relied on. For this reason the sultans saw in the Jews an extremely desirable element for the economic development of their burgeoning empire, and truly "opened wide the gates of grace" to the miserable Jewish wanderers driven out of the Christian lands of Europe. As soon as Muhammad II conquered Constantinople, he annulled the severe restrictions that pressed on the local Jews.

"In the first year of his reign," relates a historian of that period, "Muhammad immediately made proclamation throughout his entire land: Listen, you children of the house of Israel who dwell in my kingdom. . . . Whoever of you wishes, come to my capital city. Let every one of your people find protection and rest, and enjoy the riches of the land." And the historian further recounts:

A tremendously large number of Jews came together. The sultan gave place to all of them in Constantinople, and they settled there. . . . He also permitted them to build synagogues and houses of study, and in the royal palace he established three seats, one for the Moslem mufti, the second for the Greek patriarch, and the third for the rabbi, because each people lived under the supervision of its own judge and chief. At the head of the Jewish community was the aged rabbi Moses Capsali.[1] His seat stood in the sultan's court near the mufti's, and the sultan was very fond of him.

In the victorious Ottoman armies the Jews saw God's punishing rod, the iron hand which had been predestined to carry through the righteous judgment and destroy the "kingdom of Edom," steeped in blood and sin. They declared the Turkish sultans scions of the "righteous Cyrus," the "anointed of God," and firmly believed that at the head of the warlike Turkish hosts the angel Gabriel himself strode with sword in hand, to bring near the "end" and prepare the way for the glorious Messiah.

1. On Moses Capsali, see *infra*.

An interesting document has been preserved which gives us a clear notion of the great impression that the life of their brethren in Turkey made on the Jews who had fled from Christian Europe. Two young Jews, Kalman and David Kohen, migrated from Germany and came to Constantinople. They were so enchanted by its life that they had no doubt that, were the German Jews only to know how well and freely Jews lived in Turkey, all of them would go there, despite every difficulty and danger. They therefore requested a very respected countryman, Isaac Tzarefati, who in his youth had fled from Germany and settled in Constantinople, to compose a "summons" to the "remnant," the German Jews who were left, the communities located in Swabia and at the Rhine, in Styria, Moravia, and Hungary, and tell them how happily Jews dwell in the Ottoman empire.

Tzarefati, a scholar and a linguist,[2] was quite willing. He composed a long letter written in a unique, flowery style and circulated it among the Jewish communities in Germany.[3]

"Your cries and sobs," he writes,

have reached us. We have been told of all the troubles and persecutions which you have to suffer in the German lands. . . . I hear the lamentation of my brethren. . . . The barbarous and cruel nation ruthlessly oppresses the faithful children of the chosen people. . . . The priests and prelates of Rome have risen. They wish to root out the memory of Jacob and erase the name of Israel. They always devise new persecutions. They wish to bring you to the stake. . . . Listen, my brethren, to the counsel I will give you! I, too, was born in Germany and studied Torah with German rabbis. I was driven out of my native country and came to the Turkish land, which is blessed by God and filled with all good things. Here I found rest and happiness; Turkey can also become for you the land of peace. . . . If you who live in Germany knew even a tenth of what God has blessed us with in this land, you would not consider any difficulties; you would set out to come to us. . . . Here in the land of the Turks we have nothing to complain of. We possess great fortunes; much gold and silver are

2. Mordecai Comtino, with whom Tzarefati studied astronomy and mathematics, notes in his commentary to Maimonides' *Millot Ha-Higgayon* that he wrote this commentary especially at the request of his beloved pupil Tzarefati.
3. Concerning the time at which this letter was written there are certain differences of opinion. Jellinek, who first published Tzarefati's letter (*Kuntras Gezerot Tatnav*, pp. 14–24), believed the letter was written in the thirteenth century at the time of the Crusades. Graetz, who correctly noted that Jellinek was mistaken, believed that it was written in 1454. We think that the letter was composed several years after the Turks had conquered Constantinople, at the end of the 1450's.

in our hands. We are not oppressed with heavy taxes, and our commerce is free and unhindered. Rich are the fruits of the earth. Everything is cheap, and every one of us lives in peace and freedom. Here the Jew is not compelled to wear a yellow hat as a badge of shame, as is the case in Germany, where even wealth and great fortune are a curse for a Jew because he therewith arouses jealousy among the Christians and they devise all kinds of slander against him to rob him of his gold. Arise, my brethren, gird up your loins, collect your forces, and come to us! Here you will be free of your enemies, here you will find rest. . . .

Tzarefati's "summons" created a sensation among the German Jews, and many set out for the "blessed land." Thus in the second half of the fifteenth century the former capital of Jew-hating Byzantium, after being changed into the Moslem-Turkish Stamboul, became a major Jewish center, in which was formed, by the side of the long-settled "Greek" community, a new "German" community consisting of German and Austrian Jews. The favorable social and political circumstances contributed much to the fact that Kushta (Constantinople) soon became an important Jewish cultural center. The heyday of Jewish civilization in Turkey was inaugurated in a short time, in the course of two generations. Men of broad secular culture appeared under the banner of free, critical thought. Moses Kapuzzato Ha-Yevani, a religious poet[4] and Bible exegete, appears in his commentary to the Pentateuch as a liberal thinker who had the courage to adopt a critical attitude toward the view of the "ancients," the recognized authorities.[5] Together with him appeared the versatile Solomon ben Elijah Sharvit Ha-Zahav, who acquired a reputation with his religious poems and secular songs.[6] Many of his liturgical hymns entered the *Maḥzor* of the Romanian Rite.[7] He also translated several astronomical

4. Two of Kapuzzato's religious poems are found in the manuscript of the *Maḥzor Minhag Kaffa* preserved in the Kaufmann Collection in the library in Leningrad of the Society for the Dissemination of Enlightenment Among Jews.
5. Kapuzzato's commentary was lost. Mordecai Comtino gives a very interesting fragment of the commentary, in which Kapuzzato appears as a typical rationalist of Maimonides' school.
6. Solomon's father, a Talmudist and interpreter of Scripture, also wrote an astronomical work.
7. S. D. Luzzatto in *Kerem Ḥemed*, IV, 28; Zunz in *Literaturgeschichte*, p. 373. Some of Sharvit Ha-Zahav's religious poems are also to be found in the previously mentioned manuscript of the *Minhag Kaffa*, the Festival Prayer Book of Kaffa. Sharvit Ha-Zahav's witty poem in which the letters of the alphabet carry on a debate among themselves was published, along with three other poems of his, by David Kahana in a special collection (*Aḥiasaf*, 1893).

works from Greek into Hebrew, composed a Hebrew grammar entitled *Heshek Shelomoh*, wrote a commentary to the Torah and, in response to the request of several prominent representatives of the community in Ephesus, a commentary to Abraham Ibn Ezra's *Sefer Ha-Shem*.[8]

The fact that Sharvit Ha-Zahav wrote a commentary to Ibn Ezra's work is by no means accidental. The great Spanish scholar was at that time one of the most popular writers in the intellectual Jewish circles of Turkey. Not only Sharvit Ha-Zahav but many other learned men of that period studied Ibn Ezra's work with great reverence and composed commentaries to it. Very typical in this respect is Sharvit Ha-Zahav's contemporary Shabbetai ben Malkiel Ha-Kohen. Of his life very little is known to us. A contemporary asserts that "he came to Turkey from distant islands." Shabbetai relates of himself that he wandered over various countries and lands because of his great thirst for knowledge.[9] He diligently studied the medieval philosophical literature and himself wrote a work on logic, but his favorite author was Abraham Ibn Ezra. He believed that Ibn Ezra had no peer "from the beginning of the days of the Exile," and that for his generation he was a second Father Abraham. Shabbetai wrote a long commentary to Ibn Ezra's *Sefer Ha-Shem* and, indeed, his reverence for the memory of the famous Spanish scholar brought him into a debate with one of the most original personalities in the Jewish community of Constantinople, Mordecai ben Eliezer Comtino.

Comtino frequently begins in this manner: "Thus says Mordecai Comtino the Greek of Constantinople." He employs the title "the Greek" because Constantinople was still the capital of the "Greek empire" when Comtino was born there. He was born in the first quarter of the fifteenth century,[10] but his literary activity belonged

8. The poem in which the author tells of this, and incidentally notes the year when he came to Ephesus, has created much confusion concerning the time when Sharvit Ha-Zahav lived. Dei Rossi and Graetz read the line in question *Shenat ha-sefer golim la-goel* and came to the conclusion that Sharvit Ha-Zahav came to Ephesus in the year 1500. Steinschneider (*Hebräische Bibliographie*, VIII, 28), H. J. Gurland, and David Kahana (in his introduction to Sharvit Ha-Zahav's collection of poems) read *heasefu golim ha-goel* and obtained the date 1386. This, however, is absolutely erroneous, for Sharvit Ha-Zahav was born around 1420 (see Rosanes, *Divrei Yemei Yisrael Be-Togarmah*, I, 32) and died after 1502. It is clear that the phrase in question must be read *heasefu golim-h ralav*, i.e., 1476.

9. See the collection *Talpiot* (1895), Section "Kore Ha-Dorot," p. 2.

10. Ephraim ben Gershon speaks of him in his sermons, composed in 1455, as of an adult and prominent person.

·⋅⊰[7]⊱⋅·

to the Ottoman period and extended from approximately 1460 to 1485.[11] Very few details of Comtino's life are established. We know only (from the preface to his commentary on Ibn Ezra's *Yesod Mora*) that in the 1450's he lived in Adrianople and that one of his teachers was named Enoch Saporta. It has not been determined, however, whether Comtino owes his many-sided scientific education to Saporta. Comtino had a thorough knowledge of mathematics, philology,[12] astronomy, and other natural sciences, and was a scholar not only in medieval philosophy but also in Christian theological literature. Like many others in his generation, he was also, as Heinrich Graetz expresses it, "in love with Abraham Ibn Ezra." The clever and witty Spanish scholar of the twelfth century was for Comtino the supreme ideal and highest exemplar. Comtino not only wrote commentaries on many of Ibn Ezra's works;[13] all his literary activity is dominated by the spirit of his model, the wandering scholar of Toledo. As Ibn Ezra had been in his time, so Comtino was also an enlightener who set as his major task the spreading of culture and making accessible to the masses basic knowledge in logic, philosophy, mathematics, and the natural sciences. "Without this knowledge," he insists, "it is impossible to study the Talmud, because numerous passages will be incomprehensible; and this the sages of the Talmud themselves already indicated."[14]

Comtino wrote a popular work on mathematics entitled *Sefer Ha-Heshbon Veha-Middot*, a scientific investigation of the Persian astronomical tables entitled *Sefer Perush Luhot Paras*, various works on astronomical instruments,[15] a special work on astronomy called *Sefer Ha-Techunah*,[16] and a commentary on Maimonides' *Millot Ha-Higgayon*.[17] But just as in his day Ibn Ezra, with all

11. The year of Comtino's death has not been established. In any case he died in the 1480's, for in 1481 he published his *Sefer Ha-Middot*, and in 1487 his disciple Caleb Afendopolo speaks of him in *Keli Reva Ha-Shaot* as of one deceased.

12. Comtino also wrote religious poems. Two of his liturgical hymns, "Mi-Meonei Or Zoreah" and "Mah Mevakkesh Mi-Mecha El," were published in *Shirim U-Zemirot Ve-Tishbahot* (Nos. 124, 202).

13. Comtino's great-grandson, the well known Joseph Solomon Delmedigo, asserts that Comtino wrote commentaries to all of Ibn Ezra's works (*Melo Chofnajim*, p. 12). Comtino himself, however, notes that he wrote commentaries only to *some* of Ibn Ezra's works.

14. In his handwritten commentary to *Yesod Mora*.

15. *Maamar Tikkun Keli Ha-Nehoshet, Maamar Tikkun Keli Ha-Shaot, Maamar Tikkun Keli Ha-Tzefiyah.*

16. All the works listed are contained in manuscript in the First Firkovich Collection, Nos. 343–46, 353, 359–61.

17. Published in Warsaw in 1865.

his many-sided literary activity, had devoted particular attention to Bible exegesis, so Ibn Ezra's "lover" wrote a large commentary to the Torah as his major work.[18] In this work Comtino is
most clearly disclosed as a versatile and free-thinking investigator.
Typical is his introduction, in which he explains the motives which
impelled him to add a new commentary on the Torah to the great
number of extant commentaries:

Some commentators occupied themselves mainly with explanation of
the words and sought to translate the words according to their gram-
matical structure, but not in their logical connection with the content
of the text. Others immersed themselves in the Kabbalah, and still
others entered on the way of allusion and parable. Some believed that
the Torah is full of mysteries and hidden meanings that must be explained and illuminated. Others again were certain that everything
is according to its surface meaning, all is clear and plain, and the
commentary must be literal. Thus, each went his own way. Some
were chary of words, others diffuse and confused. One mocks the
other, but none is completely satisfactory, for they do not understand
how to separate the essential from the secondary. Seeing this, I
Mordecai ben Eliezer Comtino of Constantinople, decided to attempt
to explicate the Torah in the proper manner. In my commentary I
will employ not only the principles of grammar and the laws of logic
but also the natural sciences such as astronomy and mathematics, and
where it is necessary to throw light on the text, I will also deal with
philosophical and theological problems. All this will be done in strictest
order, and as far as possible without departing from the literal meaning.
In this connection I shall not rely on any authorities except in those
cases where a tradition hallowed by generations is involved. But when
this tradition contradicts sober, balanced judgment, I will interpret
the meaning as common sense dictates. I shall, in this connection, employ the perceptive and accurate observations of my predecessors,
and more than all others those of the sage Rabbi Abraham ben Ezra,
for he is the chief of the commentators and has no peer. But where
he too, in my view, was inaccurate, I shall go my own way. . . .

Comtino in fact appears in his commentary as a sober and free
investigator who utilizes in full measure his broad knowledge in
various fields of science. He does not seek in the text of the Bible
any allegories or allusions. He also declines to employ *midrashim*
and *aggadot* and especially avoids the mystical and mysterious.

18. This work is discussed by the bibliographers under various titles. On
the title page of the manuscript which we utilized is inscribed, in
Firkovich's hand, the title *Kelil Yofi*. This term is contained in both
of Comtino's poems found at the beginning and end of the work.
The first poem was published by H. J. Gurland in his monograph
on Comtino.

He seeks, above all, the commonsensical, the logically clear, and at times utters thoughts that are definitely inconsistent with the traditionally received views. He allows himself, for example, to express doubts about the universally accepted tradition that, before the generation of the dispersion following the building of the Tower of Babel, all men spoke Hebrew. In regard to the question of the nature of prophecy and the holy spirit and the possibility that men may see and speak with angels, Comtino rejects Naḥmanides' mystical, orthodox view and adopts Maimonides' opinion. In connection with this, he does not neglect the opportunity to remark that the Kabbalist Naḥmanides belongs, in his view, to the ignorant "multitude," who are remote from theoretical problems and about whom Maimonides speaks with such contempt in his introduction to *A Guide for the Perplexed*. Altogether in the spirit of Maimonides, Comtino also emphasizes that only the few who have attained intellectual perfection and have purified their minds through philosophical study are endowed with immortality.[19]

With all his great reverence for Maimonides and Ibn Ezra, Comtino nevertheless deems it necessary not to rely blindly on their assumptions and conclusions. Indeed, his critical attitude to ideas that Ibn Ezra expressed in his commentary to the Torah provoked a heated debate between himself and the previously mentioned Shabbetai Ha-Kohen. In the fact that Comtino allowed himself to note several errors in Ibn Ezra, Shabbetai Ha-Kohen saw an impermissible arrogance and a great insult to the "chief of the commentators," and therefore issued forth against Comtino with a special work, *Sefer Hassagot Le-Rabbi Shabbetai Malkiel*,[20] in which he poured out all of his wrath on him "who does not understand how properly to appreciate the greatest Bible exegete, who has no peer."

Comtino promptly responded with his *Teshuvot Al Hassagot Rabbi Shabbetai Kohen*, and this polemic work most clearly characterizes him as a personality. He finds Shabbatai's arguments naive and childish. He cannot imagine how it could occur to anyone that he had "shamed" Ibn Ezra's memory by allowing himself to be critical of some of his assumptions. Comtino explains:

I am enchanted by this great scholar. I know how immense are his merits in the field of Jewish knowledge. But are great men without defects? Is it utterly inconceivable that even they should be in error?

19. Manuscript *Kelil Yofi*, 91b.
20. This work has remained in manuscript. Steinschneider provides information about it in his catalogue of the manuscript collection of the library in Leyden.

And must reverence and respect for the memory of great authorities bar the way leading to free inquiry and scientific truth? Only the ignorant multitude, foolish and obscure men, believe that the ancients attained everything with their keen minds and never made mistakes, and that later generations are petty and unworthy in comparison with them. Only those who blindly follow the authority of the ancients and have not the courage to adopt their own views can see anything criminal in freely expressing one's outlook and placing strange opinions and conclusions on the scale of criticism. These little men who reside in the tents of foolishness and carry the banner of short-sighted dullness assure one another: "How do we come to this? One must not probe, one must not speculate and wish to attain with one's own mind what is beyond his understanding."[21]

Very typical also of Comtino is his attitude to the local Karaites. Here we touch on an interesting page in the cultural history of the Turkish Jewish community in the second half of the fifteenth century. The spiritual and intellectual heyday of the Karaites in the lands of the East ends with the eleventh century. Not one significant scholar appeared subsequently among them, even in the realm of religious creativity, and the spiritual and intellectual leadership of the whole Karaite community moved from the East to Byzantium. Already in the eleventh century the Karaites living there produced such a major scholar as Jehudah Hadassi who presents, in his *Eshkol Ha-Kofer*, an entire encyclopedia of knowledge—religious laws, philosophy, Bible exegesis, philology, natural sciences, and debates and polemical attacks on rabbinic Judaism and Christianity. At the end of the thirteenth century lived the famous Karaite Bible exegete Aaron ben Joseph, the author of *Sefer Ha-Mivḥar*,[22] and in the first half of the fourteenth century the most significant thinker whom the European Karaites produced, Aaron ben Elijah, lived there. Aaron ben Elijah acquired fame with his *Etz Ḥayyim*, a religious-philosophical work on the model of Maimonides' *Guide for the Perplexed*. After Elijah the intellectual decline of the Karaites commences in Byzantium also. In the course of a century there was not a single author of genuine distinction. Petty, talentless compilations, weak and pallid endeavors in the field of Bible exegesis—these exhaust the entire literary creativity of this period. From this intellectual slumber the Karaites were awakened by the local Rabbanite Jewish community. The

21. Steinschneider's Leyden catalogue, No. 204.
22. *Sefer Ha-Mivḥar* was first published in 1835 in Göslöw (Yevpatoriya). A manuscript of *Sefer Ha-Mivḥar* with a commentary and interesting supplements was located in the library in Leningrad of the Society for the Dissemination of Enlightenment Among Jews.

cultural flowering of the Jews of Constantinople as a result of the great political and social events associated with the Turkish victories, and the increased Jewish immigration had a strong influence on the Karaites. These, who found themselves in such deep intellectual decline, could not even think of any further battle with rabbinic Judaism. On the contrary, they sought intellectual and spiritual assistance from their erstwhile opponents and begged the Jewish scholars to open for them the wells of knowledge.

The scholars and spiritual leaders of Turkish Jewry at that time had attained the requisite moral height to do so. They did not reject the stretched-out hand of peace, and gladly taught the Karaite youth. Comtino's teacher, Enoch Saporta, had numerous pupils among the Karaites. He taught them not only general studies but Jewish subjects, even the Talmud and rabbinic literature.[23] Many other Jewish scholars of that period, such as Eliezer Capsali, Elijah Ha-Levi,[24] Shabbetai ben Malkiel, Elijah Sharvit Ha-Zahav, gladly instructed the Karaite youth. But more than all others Comtino participated in this activity. This Rabbanite in no way viewed the Karaites as dissidents and hostile opponents. The official representative of rabbinic Judaism, he even had the courage to declare that he considered Karaite scholars such as Sahl ben Mazliah, Benjamin Nahavendi, Japhet Ha-Levi and others as the "pillars on which the temple of Jewish wisdom rests."[25] Such words from a rabbi of the fifteenth century were completely novel and unexpected. In fact, out of Comtino's school grew a whole generation of Karaite scholars who brought with them a fresh impulse into the shrunken intellectual life of the Karaites of Europe.

Comtino's pupils were the famous Karaite communal leader Joseph Ravitzi, the well-known scholar Elijah Bashyatzi, the author of *Adderet Eliahu* and the greatest Karaite codifier, and also the versatile Caleb Afendopolo,[26] the only European Karaite who deserves to have his name noted in the history of Hebrew poetry. Afendopolo left a rather extensive collection of poems of purely secular content. He also composed an imaginative poem *Avner ben Ner*, written in *makama* style. Like Moses Dar'i in his day, Afendopolo also borrowed much from the Hebrew poets of the Spanish era. It is not difficult to find in him whole verses that are nothing more than a paraphrase of a Jewish model. For example,

23. See Elijah Mizraḥi's *Responsa*, No. 57, p. 93.
24. See *ibid.*
25. We quote according to Steinschneider's catalogue of the manuscripts in Leyden, No. 393.
26. Born in 1464, died after 1524.

one of the songs which Saul, the hero of *Avner ben Ner,* sings begins with the verse:

> Beautiful place, joy of the earth—city of the great king,
> A delight to Bathsheba, and sweeter than honey to her.[27]

This at once reminds one of Jehudah Halevi's well-known poem "Yefeh Nof Mesos Tevel." His description of a terribly ugly woman:

> They saw a woman ugly and black, like smoke in the stormwind;
> She had hair like short flax, like that of a pig

is taken almost verbatim from Alḥarizi,[28] and his love song which begins with the lines

> Turn, O pearl, dignified and delicate,
> Look upon Caleb, O white doe,
> Have pity, my friend, in the shade of my love

immediately reminds one of Dante's contemporary Immanuel of Rome.[29]

Characteristic of contemporary moods is Afendopolo's amicable attitude towards the Rabbanites. He strongly deplores the split which divided two fraternal branches of one people into hostile camps,[30] and in two elegies laments the catastrophe which struck the Spanish Jews and the expulsion of the Jews from Lithuania in 1495.

The peaceful coexistence of the Jews and the Karaites, and the large number of Karaite pupils studying with the educated rabbis and scholars, however, disturbed certain orthodox Jewish elements in Constantinople. The chief rabbi and head of the Jewish community in the Ottoman Empire, the aged Moses Capsali, a strict and stubborn zealot,[31] saw a desecration of God's name in the fact that Rabbanites taught the Talmud to Karaites who rejected the

27. We utilized the manuscript of this work which is located in the First Firkovich Collection of manuscripts, No. 818.
28. *Taḥkemoni,* Makama 6.
29. *Maḥberot,* Makama 3.
30. Very characteristic also is the reverence that Afendopolo has for the founder of the Christian faith.
31. On his controversy with the great scholar Joseph Colon, see Elijah Capsali's *Likkutim,* 6-17.

entire Oral Torah.[32] But Moses Capsali was only an ideological opponent, altogether free of any external motives, and intended merely to defend the sacred Torah. There were, however, other opponents, among them some of the leaders of the city, who in this connection had, as we shall see later on, other, purely secular and material motivations. Without the knowledge of the chief rabbi, these issued forth with a ban, and with blasts of the ram's horn and burning candles declared that whoever studies any subject whatsoever with Karaites is excommunicated. They threatened with the ban not only those who would teach Karaite youths the Bible, Mishnah, and Talmud, but even physics, mathematics, and other sciences; everything was proscribed, so that close relations with the Karaites should cease.[33] In Constantinople at that time there were a considerable number of Jewish teachers who were materially interested in maintaining friendly relations with the Karaite youth. Karaite pupils were the source of their livelihood, and the sudden prohibition was literally a disaster for them. Comtino at that time was already dead. Consequently they applied for help to his close friend Elijah Mizraḥi, who shortly after Moses Capsali's death assumed the post of chief rabbi and administrator of the Jewish community in Turkey.[34]

Elijah ben Abraham Mizraḥi, better known under the acronym Re'em, was born in Constantinople in the 1430's.[35] Before obtaining the position of grand rabbi (*hacham bashi*) he lived in great poverty. He complains in one of his *responsa*,

Sufferings and afflictions pursue me. A livelihood is as difficult for me to obtain as the division of the Red Sea. . . . With my poor health, I must spend all my time with pupils and study with them whatever their heart desires, with one Talmud, and immediately thereafter with another mathematics, with a third astronomy—and this day after day.[36]

32. Mizraḥi's *Responsa*, No. 57.
33. *Ibid.*, p. 91.
34. Around the year 1495. N. Porges endeavors to show (*REJ*, LXXVIII, 31) that Moses Capsali died around 1510. His arguments, however, are not at all convincing. Incidentally, precisely in the source on which Porges relies Capsali's name is accompanied by the words "may his memory be for blessing."
35. S. P. Rabinowitch notes in *Motzaei Golah*, p. 67 that Elijah Mizraḥi was born in 1462. This, however, is not correct. In an official document of the year 1518 (see Mizraḥi's *Responsa*, No. 15) he is called *yashish* (venerable), but this term is hardly suited to a man who was only fifty-six years old.
36. *Responsa*, end of No. 56.

Despite such an oppressive situation, Mizrahi still found time for very intensive literary activity covering the most diverse fields. He wrote a splendid commentary to Rashi.[37] His work on mathematics, *Sefer Ha-Mispar*, which was highly praised by such an expert mathematician as Joseph Delmedigo,[38] was translated by Schreckenfuchs into Latin and the translation was published by Sebastian Muenster with his own notes.[39] Mizrahi also wrote a work, *Biurim*, on Euclid's geometry, and a commentary on Ptolemy's famous astronomical work, *Biur Al Sefer Almagesti*. Mizrahi's two collections of *responsa*, *Teshuvot U-She'elot*[40] and *Mayyim Amukim*,[41] have an important cultural-historical value because in them the way of life of that era is clearly reflected.[42]

Immediately after the controversy about the Karaites erupted in the community of Constantinople, Elijah Mizrahi came forth sharply against the zealots who wielded the weapons of excommunication and the ram's horn. He took the position that in all ages, from very ancient times until Maimonides and even much later, Jewish scholars maintained the principle that Torah and knowledge must be given to *everyone* who desires them, whoever he may be, even if of another faith. The Karaites of our generation, Mizrahi insists, are not at all of those who in earlier generations fought against the Oral Torah and the rabbis. The contemporary Karaites deserve that we live with them in peace and friendship. We certainly may teach them whatever subjects they wish—not only general subjects, but even rabbinic ones. Elijah Mizrahi knew very well that the zealots who had provoked the controversy were terrorizing men with the threat of the ban not out of heavenly or religious motives but mainly for mundane and material interests, and he had the courage openly to say so. He declares,

Those who threaten "excommunication" and other severe punishments carry on warfare not for the sake of heaven but out of extraneous and petty motivations. First, out of jealousy; they are irritated by the profound respect the Karaites give to their Jewish teachers. Sec-

37. Mizrahi's commentary was so popular that there were even many eager owners who wrote their own commentaries on it.
38. See *Melo Chofnajim*, 12. *Sefer Ha-Mispar* was published in 1534.
39. Under the cumbersome title *Kitzur Melechet Ha-Mispar Asher Melukat Mi-Sefer Ha-Derashot Mi-Sifriyot Asher Rabbi Eliya Mizrahi Hibber Zichrono Le-Verachah*.
40. Consisting of one hundred numbers, it was published in Constantinople in 1560.
41. Consisting of thirty-nine numbers, it was published in Venice in 1647.
42. See, e.g., *Responsa*, Nos. 15, 25, 37–39, 46, 50–51, 53, 57, 61, 66 (with Berliner's supplement in *Kovetz Al Yad*, VII), 68, 71, 79, 84.

ondly, out of hatred for the Karaites, because the latter protest against the usurious interest that these pious zealots take from them for loans.[43]

With his authority, Elijah Mizraḥi allayed the controversy, and the Karaite youth again without hindrance studied Torah and science with Jewish scholars. At the same time, however, something occurred that produced a revolution in the entire cultural and intellectual life of the Jews in the Turkish empire. This extremely important event was the expulsion from Spain and the rush of many thousands of exiled Spanish and Portuguese Jews to the Turkish seaports.

43. Mizraḥi, *Responsa*, No. 57.

CHAPTER TWO

The Spanish Exiles in Turkey and Palestine; JOSEPH KARO AND SOLOMON MOLCHO

N the closing chapter of the third volume we noted the terrible sufferings and afflictions experienced by the Jewish exiles from Spain and Portugal in the course of the period from 1492 to 1498.[1] One shudders and finds his blood congealed in his veins when he reads the chronicles of that time, in which the record of inhuman cruelties, of fearful persecutions and oppressions which followed the unhappy wanderers who roamed over the whole world seeking a place of refuge, of shelter and rest, on their long martyr's path, is unrolled. Nine-tenths of the wanderers perished on the way, and only one out of ten managed to attain the desired goal and arrive at shores where new terrors, new persecutions and bloodshed, did not lurk for them. Among these shores of refuge the prime place was occupied by the seaports of the Ottoman Empire. It is related that the sultan Bayazid II, when King Ferdinand who expelled the Jews from Spain was mentioned in his presence, said: "How can you consider King Ferdinand a wise ruler when he impoverished his own land and enriched ours?" The Turkish sultans did, indeed, manifest broad, statesmanlike vision in welcoming the exiles in a friendly way. To the young,

1. Besides the accounts of Isaac Abravanel and Ḥayyat cited there, see also *Shevet Yehudah* (Nos. 50–60); Joseph Ha-Kohen's *Emek Ha-Bacha* (1852 edition, pp. 84–85); and Elijah Capsali's *Likkutim Shonim*, 66–91.

militant, and feudal Ottoman empire the highly educated and enterprising Sephardic Jews brought the rich seeds of civic culture, commerce, and industry. Their trade was spread over seas and continents. Thanks to them, art and industry began to blossom in the land. Even the military power of the Ottoman Empire was not insignificantly magnified by these exiles from Spain.[2] Among the Sephardic Jews were skilled technicians who familiarized the Turks with the new inventions in artillery and weaponry. They also established in Turkey factories for making gunpowder and casting cannon.

The influence of the Sephardim on their own brethren, the Turkish Jews, was of an entirely different order. We noted in the previous chapter the moods that dominated the major center of Turkish Jewry, Constantinople. Interest in secular culture was considerable. Men sought to explain the Bible in a clear, rational manner. Their attitude toward the Kabbalah was one of indifference and coldness, and such eminent representatives of the Constantinople community as Comtino and Mizrahi even considered it necessary publicly to attack mystical commentaries and endeavors to find secrets and Kabbalistic allusions in religious commandments and laws.[3] At that time such a categorical opponent of the Kabbalah as Elijah Delmedigo's disciple, Saul Cohen Ashkenazi, who read lectures on philosophy before a large audience,[4] lived in Constantinople.

Quite different moods began to prevail at the beginning of the sixteenth century, and this under the influence of the Spanish Jews who settled there. Before we proceed to these new moods, which soon occupied the entire foreground of the cultural life of the

2. About this, incidentally, testimony is given by two writers of that era, one of them a Christian, Nicolaus de Nicolay, in his account *Les Navigations en Turque*, and the other a Jew, Joseph Ha-Kohen, in *Emek Ha-Bacha* (p. 148).

3. See Comtino's above-mentioned introduction to his commentary on the Torah and Mizrahi's statement in his Responsa (No. 1): "Everything that is mentioned neither in the Babylonian Talmud nor in the Jerusalem Talmud and which was not spoken of by the decisors [*Poskim*], from whose words we live and upon whom we rely in all matters of religion in general, we cannot force upon people, even though the men of the Kabbalah spoke of it."

4. See Joseph Solomon Delmedigo, *Matzref Le-Hochmah:* "Saul Cohen . . . went down to the great city of Constantinople and there taught the flower of the land the science of philosophy and matters related to it, and the influence of his wisdom is still discernible in many writings and comments found in books by Rabbanites and Karaites which are hidden in their treasures."

Turkish Jews, we must note that at that time in the community of Constantinople, as in Italy, there was increased interest in that realm which had been so neglected in earlier times among Jews, namely, history and historical narrative. The catastrophe which struck the Jewish communities of Spain and Portugal, the sufferings which the exiles had to endure, shattered men's hearts and filled them with sorrow. They witnessed how a whole Jewish world was destroyed, how hundreds of thousands of Jews sacrificed themselves for their faith. Hence the desire to write down the tremendous events for future generations, to inscribe in their memories the heroism with which the people stood the great test, was strengthened.

It was in Turkey that Joseph Ibn Verga, who settled in Adrianople, completed the sad chronicle of persecutions and oppressions *Shevet Yehudah*. Isaac Akrish, a cripple with lamed feet but a constant wanderer, set as his task to rescue from oblivion significant historical documents. He managed to publish such important works as the letters the Jewish minister Ḥasdai Ibn Shaprut exchanged with the king of the Chazars, the biography of the well-known exilarch Bustanai, and Profiat Duran's famous tract *Al Tehi Ka-Avotecha*. One of the Spanish exiles, the physician Samuel Shullam, who after great trials arrived in Constantinople, published, with numerous abbreviations and changes, Abraham Zacuto's *Sefer Yuḥasin*, to which he added at the end a special chronicle organized from Arabic and Latin sources, as well as Sherira Gaon's famous letter which is such an important source for the history of the post-Talmudic and Geonic period.[5] The learned Spaniard Jacob Tam ben David Ibn Yaḥya[6] published in Constantinople (1510) the well-known *Josippon*, which no one at that time doubted to be an ancient work, with Joseph ben Gorion as its author. Characteristic is the introduction in which Ibn Yaḥya deems it necessary to indicate for what reasons he decided to publish *Josippon*:

5. The same Shullam also published a Hebrew translation of Flavius Josephus' *Contra Apionem*.
6. David Ibn Yaḥya was a rabbi in Lisbon. King John II condemned him to death in 1475 because of a slander that he had propagandized among the Marranos, urging them to revert to Judaism. He managed, however, to escape from prison and came to Constantinople. There in 1506 he published his Hebrew grammar *Leshon Limmudim*. The work printed at the end on Hebrew poetry, *Shekel Ha-Kodesh*, was not composed by Ibn Yaḥya but by an anonymous author. S. D. Luzzatto already called attention to this (*Iggerot Shadal*), and Steinschneider and Benjacob later confirmed it.

I witnessed with my own eyes the bitter expulsion. I saw how my brethren were pursued with venomous wrath from land to land, from one people to another, and nowhere found rest—only bestial hatred and cruel, barbarous massacre. . . . Deathly terror seized the exiled people. Cold despair filled their hearts, for the people do not remember what happened to them in former times. They do not know of the sufferings and afflictions they endured in earlier generations, and why this great misfortune occurred. And this ignorance is an immense loss, especially in our grievous day, for great would be the consolation of downcast spirits if they knew that their fathers suffered much only because they departed from God's way, and that as soon as they directed their hearts to God He manifested His great wonders and redeemed them from suffering and distress with His mighty hand.

For this reason, in order to familiarize his fellow-Jews with everything that happened in past times, Ibn Yahya decided to publish *Josippon*. Let all see that the recent events are not at all new. Let the people "see in the past a promise for the future."

This search for the cup of consolation in the tradition of the fathers, this ardent desire to find in bygone generations the firm assurance of speedy redemption, became ever more prominent among the Spanish exiles who had recently settled in Turkey after their horribly difficult wanderings. Very typical in this respect is the richly endowed and philosophically educated mystic Abraham ben Eliezer Halevi, who only in modern times has received proper appreciation, thanks to the well-known scholar of the Kabbalah, Gershom Scholem.[7] Abraham Halevi, the brother-in-law of the learned Abraham Zacuto, was born in Spain around 1460. After the expulsion he led an itinerant life, spent some time in Greece and later in Italy, and from there moved to Constantinople. The fearful events of his day strengthened his mystical-messianic moods. He saw in the triumphant Ottoman empire God's emissary and was certain that Turkey would soon conquer Rome and the entire Christian world. Like Isaac Abravanel, Abraham Halevi sought and found in the Book of Daniel assurance that in the year 1524 the beginning of the redemption would take place, and in 1530 the Messiah would reveal himself in Upper Galilee.[8] In the meantime he wished to strengthen the grieved hearts of his brethren and arouse in his generation the desire for sacrifice. Hence, he wrote his marvelous sermon "Megillat Amrafel," which is based on the verses of the Song of Songs, "Who is this that cometh up out of the wilderness" (3:6) and "For love is strong

7. See his thorough work in *Kiryat Sefer*, II, 101–41, 269–73; VII, 149–65.
8. *Ibid.*, II, 136–37.

as death" (8:6). This sermon, which unfortunately has been preserved only in fragments, is one of the most interesting literary
memorials that has come down to us from the mystics among the
Spanish exiles. It is a flaming apotheosis of martyrdom and self-
sacrifice, a passionate song of songs about the mystical, ardent love
for the Creator which is mightier not only than death but also
than inhuman sufferings and afflictions. The spirit, filled with sweet
ecstasy, vanquishes the weak bodily matter, and to all the cruel
tortures and terrible sufferings which the executioners devise, the
"saint" responds blissfully: "I am a Jew, I will remain a Jew, I
will die a Jew—a Jew, a Jew, a Jew . . ."[9] Abraham Halevi left
Constantinople, set out for Palestine, and there enthusiastically proclaimed the approaching redemption.[10]

These messianic-mystical moods occupied the dominant place
in the literary creativity of the Jews in Turkey from the beginning
of the sixteenth century on. But the chief center of literary creation
was now no longer Constantinople, as in the previous generation.
Its place was taken by Salonika, and above all by the land to which
the mystic Abraham Halevi went—the land of the fathers, Palestine, with its new cultural center, the remote town of Safed in
distant Galilee.

In the period of the Crusades, when Palestine was the battlefield
of the great struggle between the Christian and Moslem worlds,
the Jewish community there was almost entirely obliterated. The
famous traveler Benjamin of Tudela, who visited Palestine at the
end of the 1160's, relates that he found in Jerusalem only four
Jewish families, in Bethlehem twelve Jewish inhabitants, and in
Jaffa and in Jezreel both only two Jews. At the beginning of the
thirteenth century, immigration from European communities to
Palestine increased. In 1211 three hundred rabbis from England
and France set out to the land of their fathers and settled there.
In 1260, however, Palestine was attacked by large hordes of Tatars
who destroyed the land, and when Naḥmanides came there seven
years later he found in Jerusalem only two Jews, both dyers. His
efforts to enlarge the Jewish settlement and to create a cultural
center in Jerusalem had no particular success. But at the end of
the thirteenth century, when persecutions of Jews in Germany
were greatly intensified, whole groups of refugee German Jews
set out for Jerusalem.

In the Renaissance era the drive toward the land of the fathers
was also strengthened among the Jews of Italy. Their romantic

9. *Ibid.*, VII, 153.
10. Abraham Halevi died around 1530.

longing for Zion enriched Hebrew literature with a whole series of documents and public letters which have considerable cultural-historical interest. Typical, for example, is the letter which the Italian physician and scholar Rabbi Elijah sent in 1438 from Jerusalem to Italy. He had settled in 1434 in Jerusalem, where he served as rabbinic judge and head of the Talmudic academy. He lists in his letter all the trades and occupations in which the local Jews are engaged.[11] The cultured Italian physician also considers it necessary to indicate how uneducated the local Jews are and, in this connection, adds bitterly, "It is superfluous to say that in medicine they are complete asses."

Especially interesting are the letters sent from Jerusalem some fifty years later by another Italian scholar, the famous commentator on the Mishnah, Obadiah of Bertinoro, known among Jews simply as Bertinoro. Not without reason did Obadiah set as his supreme exemplars in the field of exegesis the brilliant Rashi and Maimonides. His commentary to the Mishnah is a genuine masterpiece of clarity and simplicity. Immediately upon its publication (1549) it was accepted in all the dispersions of Israel. To this day it is printed in all editions of the Mishnah. When the Christian scholar Surenhuis translated the Mishnah into Latin (1698–1703), he also translated Obadiah's commentary.

In 1486 Obadiah set out from Italy to Palestine. His journey through Greece and Egypt lasted a year and a half. A man with the keen eye of a fine observer,[12] he provides in his letter interesting information about social and cultural life in Greece, Egypt, and Palestine. Palestine was then under the rule of the avaricious Mameluke sultans, who ruthlessly oppressed the populace with heavy taxes and open robbery.[13] Hordes of thieving officials consumed the fruit of the land like locusts. The Jewish officials, the heads of the community, were no exception in this

11. The letter is published in *Divrei Ḥachamim* (1849), pp. 61–63. Of the many other letters that Italian Jews wrote from Palestine it is worth mentioning the description of Palestine by an anonymous author of the year 1522 published in *Shivḥei Yerushalayim* (1785), pp. 15–26.

12. Obadiah of Bertinoro wrote three letters from Palestine: one to his father, the second to his brother, and the third to an unknown person. Only the first two have been printed. They were first published by Adolph Neubauer in *Jahrbuch für die Geschichte der Juden*, III, 195–270. Unfortunately, the text is very corrupt (for a discussion of this, see Moses Cassuto in the collection *Ve-Zot Le-Yehudah*, pp. 296–301).

13. Obadiah of Bertinoro writes in his first letter of 1488: "It was dangerous for a Jew to go there, for the Mamelukes at that time beat and struck and robbed everyone whom they found, whether Jew or Arab."

respect. They had the duty of collecting taxes from the Jewish populace, and they stopped at no wickedness or persecution to obtain favor with the rulers. In the long letter which he sent to his father in Italy Obadiah gives a melancholy picture of how corrupt and demoralized the whole way of life of the community in the holy city of Jerusalem at that time was. Calm and sedate as the Italian scholar was, he speaks with intense indignation of the "wicked elders" who collaborate with the "informers and slanderers." These "wicked elders" attempted to place the entire burden of the taxes on the newcomers from abroad, the refugees from Germany.[14] Matters went so far that the German Jews had to flee the city and forsake their families. "In this way," relates Obadiah,

of three hundred householders there remained in the place altogether seventy. The "elders," i.e., the heads of the community, in order not to lose the favor of the rulers and to pay the taxes on time, sold the hospitals, the furnishings of the synagogues, the crowns and other ornaments of the scrolls of the Torah, and even the Torah scrolls themselves, for which there were many interested purchasers in Christian Europe.[15]

Obadiah writes:

I am certain that if an understanding and wise statesman came here, he would at once become the leader and judge not only among the Jews but also among the Ishmaelites. But the trouble is that in these regions there is not a single honorable man with an understanding of affairs who is sociable and acceptable to his fellow men. All of them are simply wild men, hate their fellows, and are interested in nothing but money.[16]

It did not at all occur to the modest Obadiah of Bertinoro that the "understanding and wise statesman" so needed by the community was himself. With his arrival in Jerusalem in 1488 a new era begins not only for that community but for the whole Palestinian settlement. He was, as it were, tailor-made for the responsible role of reviving a cultural center in the old, ruined home and

14. The greatest German rabbi of that era, Rabbi Israel Isserlein, publicly declares in his *Terumat Ha-Deshen* (no. 88): "To be sure, great praise and exceeding virtue accrue to one who lives in Palestine. Nevertheless, we have heard a number of times that there are children of the covenant from among the Arabs there who are considered completely evil, known slanderers, and these oppress and slander the Ashkenazim who are keepers of the Torah."
15. *Jahrbuch für die Geschichte der Juden*, III, 209, 213.
16. *Ibid.*, p. 213.

preparing a suitable environment for the many Sephardic Jews who would soon settle in the land. A distinguished scholar, an excellent orator,[17] an energetic communal leader, and, in addition, blessed with a noble and gentle soul, Obadiah was soon recognized by all as the leader of the generation, the grand protagonist of righteousness and justice. Even the "wicked elders" had to yield before his moral authority, and soon after he came to Jerusalem he became the spiritual leader of the community which then found itself in such a sorry condition. A letter of another Italian Jew (his name has remained unknown) who also migrated to Palestine at that time has been preserved, and this letter, written in Jerusalem in 1495,[18] presents a clear picture of the role Obadiah played and how vast his authority was not only in Jerusalem but in the entire land. "Great is this man," the unknown author writes with enthusiasm; "everything is done according to his command, nothing is undertaken without his consent. Even in Egypt and Babylonia all take account of his will, and he is also very popular among the Ishmaelites who accord him the greatest honor."[19]

The Jewish settlement at that time had already attained two hundred families, even though the Sephardic exiles for the time being still avoided Palestine and were afraid to settle there because the wild confusion which permeated the land under Mameluke rule, when no one was without peril of his life, cast a pall of fear on everyone.[20] Mass immigration first began after 1517, after Selim I had conquered Syria and Palestine from the Mamelukes and extended his sovereignty over all of Egypt. These victories made an enormous impression in Jewish circles. They saw in the Turkish sultan the "scion of Cyrus." Now the land of their fathers was under his dominion. The loveliest hopes were revived, and it is no surprise that the more mystically minded of the Sephardic exiles chose Palestine out of all of the Turkish provinces as their place of settlement. In the course of a rather short period two large Jewish communities were formed, in Jerusalem and in Safed. The

17. Bertinoro himself writes to his brother about the impression his sermons made on his listeners: "And I preach to the congregation here twice a month in the synagogue in the holy tongue, for most of them understand it, and I am to them like the song of a flute, beautiful of sound and melody, and they praise and laud my sermons." On Bertinoro's sermons, see also the letter of an anonymous writer of the year 1495 (*ibid.*, p. 282).

18. Also published in *ibid.*, pp. 273–84.

19. *Ibid.*, pp. 280–82.

20. The previously mentioned anonymous author laments in his letter: "For in all these lands there is no judgment and no judge, especially for the Jews against the Arabs."

majority of these consisted of imaginative dreamers and ardent mystics filled with burning hope for speedy redemption.

In this unique environment the two currents which occupy the entire foreground of Jewish civilization throughout the subsequent three centuries were developed most prominently. We have seen how a tremendous catastrophe broke the spiritual powers of the culturally richest Jewish community, that of Spain. After the great sufferings which they endured, the Sephardic Jews completely removed themselves from philosophical speculation, for in it they saw the source of all their troubles. Ever more melancholy became the Jewish spiritual world, ever stronger became the barrier that separated the Jews from the external world and its culture. Jews no longer attempted to create new cultural values; all their powers were applied merely to collecting and preserving with love and great diligence the entire spiritual, intellectual, and religious heritage of the previous generations, to systematizing according to the strictest order all the laws and precepts, together with their branches and further commentaries. At the same time, however, the unique blossom of the period of decline—the messianic Kabbalah with its fundamental mystical ideas on *tikkun olam bemalchut Shaddai* (improving and transforming the world into the kingdom of God) flowered richly. The world must be redeemed through ascetic abstinence, through mortifications of the flesh and fervent prayers. Souls shaken by great sufferings devoted themselves with all their fervor to the sweet dream of *kulo zakkai* (everything is to be made worthy), the idea that the redemption can be brought near by liberating the bright spark from the dark shell, "the good kernel from the sinful husk." The rigorous asceticism which the Kabbalist author of *Sefer Ha-Peliah* and *Sefer Ha-Kanah* proclaimed with such ardor veiled the Kabbalah in a melancholy garment, and this ascetic tendency was especially strengthened on Palestinian soil until it reached the extreme limit and assumed forms that were associated, as we shall later see, with some highly unfortunate phenomena in the history of Jewish mysticism.

These two currents—collecting and systematizing the heritage of rabbinic Judaism, and pathological love of Kabbalist tales—did not follow separate ways but were often fraternally interwoven and drew nourishment from the same source. In this respect the cultural center of Safed is of particular interest. This distant town of Galilee became the favorite gathering point of fervent mystics who wished to bring the "end" near with incantations and to redeem the world through prayer and mortification of the flesh. And it was precisely there that the rabbinic world, led by the celebrated rabbi Jacob Berab,[21] tried to establish a new national legislative institution that had no analogue since the Sanhedrin had ceased to exist. Because the "end" was so near and Palestine was in the hands of "the scion of Cyrus," Jews should think at once of a new Sanhedrin, for the Messiah could not come, it was believed, so long as the great court which has the right of *semichah*, i.e., ordaining rabbis and giving them full authorization to become legislators and interpreters of the Law of Moses, was not established in the holy land.[22]

Even before the new heyday of the Jewish community in Palestine began, one of the Sephardic exiles, Jacob ben Solomon Ibn Habib, had settled in Salonika. He was a respected representative of the previously noted tendency, collecting and systematizing the spiritual heritage of the earlier generations. Jacob Ibn Habib decided to assemble in a special work all the *aggadot* scattered throughout the sea of the Talmud and, at the side of the text, to give the explanations of the old commentators and add to these his own remarks (under the heading "The writer says"). "Alfasi and the later codifiers," writes Ibn Habib in the introduction, "set themselves the task of gathering and transmitting in clear and easily understandable form all the laws and rules. But it is also important to gather the *aggadot*, in which the profound thoughts of our Talmudic sages are hidden." Ibn Habib called his collection *Ein Yaakov*. He managed, however, to publish only the first two volumes, the first in Salonika (1515) and the second in Constantinople (1526). Shortly thereafter the author died, and the remaining parts of his work were completed and published by his son, Levi Ibn Habib, who later became highly renowned as a rabbi in Jerusalem. The latter parts were printed with numerous omissions, and the very essential index which the author promised to put together is also lacking. Nevertheless, *Ein Yaakov* became one of the most

21. Berab's renown while still very young is attested by the following fact: when, after the great expulsion from Spain in 1492, he escaped to Fez, the community there immediately appointed him a rabbi, despite the fact that he was then just eighteen years old. The poet of that era, Abraham Gavison, welcomed him with the following enthusiastic lines: "Say not that wisdom is lost and extinguished among Jews; it has flared up brightly again since Jacob Berab came and settled in our land" (see *Omer Ha-Shichhah*, 68b).

22. Nothing came of the Sanhedrin and the institution of *semichah*. Since Jacob Berab led the movement, the rabbi of Jerusalem, Levi bar Habib, was jealous of him, and a great controversy about *semichah* quickly arose. Several years later Jacob Berab died and his whole project was abandoned. For a discussion of the *semichah* controversy, see Graetz, Hebrew translation of *Die Geschichte der Juden*, VII, Chapter 9; S. P. Rabinowitch, *Motzaei Golah*, 218–30; *Ha-Karmel* (1873), pp. 486–94, 576–80.

popular works among the Jews. It went through an enormous number of editions,[23] and in the course of many generations served
as an inexhaustible source for all preachers. When a prohibition
was issued against the Talmud and other Jewish religious books
in Italy, *Ein Yaakov* managed to escape completely from the claws
of the censor. It had only to "change its name,"[24] and under the
title *Ein Yisrael* passed freely throughout the homes of the Italian
Jews, who only because of it had the possibility, in that era of
confusion, of possessing at least the aggadic part of the proscribed
Talmud.

As great a reputation as Ibn Ḥabib acquired with his *Ein
Yaakov*, he can nevertheless not be compared to the author of
another collection which became the actual cornerstone of all rabbinic literature in later generations. We speak of the author of
the *Shulḥan Aruch* and *Bet Yosef*, the famous Joseph ben Ephraim
Karo. Born in Spain, Joseph Karo as a four-year-old child, along
with tens of thousands of other exiles, lived through the great expulsion. Only after long wanderings did his father settle with his
family in Turkey. Karo's years of wandering were his years of
learning. He was introduced to the sea of the Talmud by his father,
who was a great scholar in rabbinic literature. The fame of the
young prodigy soon spread over the entire region, and he was soon
appointed rabbi in Nicopolis. A short while later he was invited
to Adrianople, and there in 1522 began his monumental *Bet Yosef*,
an immense collection of all the laws and religious precepts assembled and organized according to the model of Rabbi Jacob ben
Asher's *Arbaah Turim*.

Joseph Karo indicates in the introduction to his work the reasons
why he decided to compose this collection. "In the difficult years
of bitter exile," he writes,

when we are hurled from land to land and drown in seas of sorrows,
it has become particularly necessary once again critically to illuminate,
on the basis of the primary sources, and to bring into systematic order
in a special collection, all the laws and rules which rest on the Torah
of Moses and the Oral Torah and which were explained by our sages
and scholars[25]

23. The complete edition is that of Vilna of 1883. Because Jacob Ibn
    Ḥabib utilized for his work old manuscripts of the Talmud which
    escaped the censor's hand, in places a more correct text than in the
    printed editions of the Talmud has been preserved in *Ein Yaakov*
    (see *Bikkurei Ha-Ittim*, XI [1830], 97; *Iggerot Shadal*, p. 740).
24. In the Venetian edition of *Ein Yaakov* (1556) there are some pathetic
    verses about this.
25. Introduction to *Tur Yoreh Deah* (we quote according to the Venice
    edition, 1574).

Jacob ben Asher's *Arbaah Turim* served Karo merely as a point of departure, a melting pot into which he poured and created his own material, and his monumental, four-volume *Bet Yosef* is a completely independent work. With tremendous scholarship and the ability of a first-rate systematizer, Karo analyzes in the broadest fashion the sources and the course of development of each individual law. Along with this he provides a clear overview of the entire discussion which every problem in question elicited among the sages of the Talmud and among the later scholars and codifiers. Karo lays especially great weight on clarifying and bringing to a final conclusion all the questions which evoked differences of opinion among the codifiers and in which they did not arrive at the same conclusion.

But this was a generation of downcast spirits. Karo considered himself the child of an "orphaned generation," of a period of decline, and therefore did not have the strength to assume the responsible role of a final decisor. "Who can have the courage," he humbly asks,

to come forth with new arguments and demonstrations after all the iron proofs which the Tosafists, Nahmanides, Rabbi Solomon ben Adret, and Rabbenu Nissim have set forth? Who can dare raise his head among these divine mountains, refute what they have decided, or make a personal decision in questions on which they could not come to any conclusion?[26]

In all cases where there are divisions of opinion Karo therefore appeals to the "divine mountains" and considers as arbitrators three of the foremost acknowledged codifiers of the post-Talmudic era, Alfasi, Maimonides, and Asher ben Yehiel, and decides according to the majority view, i.e., determines the law according to the decision to which two of these three great scholars came.[27] Karo spent more than twenty years (1522–42) on his monumental work. He devoted twelve further years to editing his *Bet Yosef* and incidentally arranging a condensation of it, i.e., putting together a popular collection in which are given in clear, simple statements, without all the discussion but in definitive form, all the laws and rules in the same order in which they are found in the larger, original work. Thus Karo's second collection, the *Shulḥan Aruch*, arose. *Habent sua fata libelli.* Not only persons but books have their fate. *Bet Yosef* was Karo's beloved child, his true pride. The *Shulḥan Aruch* he regarded as a secondary thing, a stepchild.

26. *Bet Yosef*, Introduction to *Tur Oraḥ Ḥayyim*.
27. *Ibid.*

Nevertheless it was the *Shulḥan Aruch*, which was printed in 1550–59, that came to play the most important role in all of later Jewish culture. Not the Goliath *Bet Yosef* but its dry conspectus, the *Shulḥan Aruch*, became the cornerstone of later rabbinic Judaism, the focus around which the intellectual creativity of the major rabbinic authorities of later generations was concentrated.[28] In Karo's own lifetime[29] his *Shulḥan Aruch* went through no less than six editions.

This great dialectician and "uprooter of mountains" was not only a decisor and codifier; the strict systematizer with cold intellect and iron logicality was also permeated with the mystical-messianic tendencies of his generation. At the very time that Karo was working on his great edifice, *Bet Yosef*, he was also an ardent follower of a remarkable mystical dreamer, one of the loveliest and gentlest personalities that the Jewish Middle Ages produced, the fervent Kabbalist Solomon Molcho, whose Christian name was Diego Pires.

At the beginning of the 1520's, when the Sephardic exiles were setting out in considerable numbers for Palestine, an extraordinary figure whose name soon resounded over all of Europe suddenly appeared. The man was named David Reubeni, and he came forward wrapped in the cloak of Oriental mystery and fantastic legend. He declared himself a Jewish prince whose brother Joseph was the monarch of a powerful Jewish kingdom deep in Arabia and the populace of which stemmed from the ten exiled tribes of Israel. This small, dark-brown man, with his Oriental costume, has remained a profound enigma in Jewish history. Among the historians of the Haskalah period, who generally despised secrets and mysteries, the problem of David Reubeni was solved in a simple and clear way: he was an adventurer and swindler. Recent investigators, however, are more cautious, for they look deeper and thus confront this man as an enigma. Who knows?—perhaps we have here a unique patriot and fighter for the people who wished, in an altogether unusual but real way, with the aid of diplomacy and negotiations with kings and popes, to bring redemption to his miserable bretheren.[30] In any case this remarkable man deserves mention in the history of Jewish literature by reason of the interesting memoirs he kept in Hebrew at the time of his journey through Europe.[31]

28. For more on this, see the next volume of our work.
29. Joseph Karo died in 1575 at the age of eighty-seven.
30. In this respect Max Brod's splendid novel *David Reubeni* is symptomatic.
31. Published in Neubauer's *Seder Ha-Ḥachamim Ve-Korot Ha-Yamim*, II.

The impression made on the Jews of Rome by David Reubeni when he appeared there in February 1524, riding a white horse and surrounded by a suite of attendants, was enormous. He represented himself as the emissary of the powerful Jewish king Joseph, who had commissioned his brother to carry on negotiations with the Pope and the kings of Christian Europe to furnish the militant Jewish tribes in Arabia with cannon and weaponry so that they might, under the leadership of their king, carry on war with the Turkish sultan, expel him from the Red Sea, and wrest Palestine from him. It is difficult to describe the mystical fervor and joyous enchantment that filled the hearts of the Portuguese Marranos, whom the barbarous fanatic King Manoel had in his day dragged by force to Christian baptism, when David Reubeni came to Portugal on his richly ornamented ship, over which the Jewish national flag was waving, and the Portuguese king João III received him with great honor as an ambassador of a foreign kingdom. The hearts of the Marranos leapt up. They saw in this the promise of redemption and believed that "the times of the Messiah" were already beginning. This mood found the most enthusiastic expression in the person of an ardent young Marrano, Diego Pires.

In this extraordinary man were marvelously combined the fighter for the people and the poetic enthusiast, the sentiment of the popular propagandist and tribune and the fervor of the exalted mystic who attains the level of prophetic visions. A man of comprehensive knowledge, Diego held the post of secretary in an important government office and had frequent access to the royal court, where he was extremely popular since he was especially endowed with the remarkable gift of winning the hearts of men. It is easy to imagine the tremendous impression made on such a noble young man as Diego by the sudden appearance of the marvelous emissary from the other side of the Dark Mountains (situated, according to legend, between Asia and Africa), from the kingdom of the ten lost tribes. It appeared to him that now the great and extraordinary things of which he had dreamed were beginning. Now the magnificent miracle was taking place; one must no longer wait. Being uncircumcised, he brought himself into "the covenant of Abraham" with his own hands, since no man must know of this, and almost died from loss of blood. Then he cast off his Christian name, assumed the name Solomon Molcho, and enthusiastically devoted himself to David Reubeni's enterprise. The cautious Reubeni first of all persuaded Molcho to leave Portugal as soon as possible, before he aroused the suspicions of the Inquisition. Molcho departed for Turkey. In Adrianople he met Joseph Karo, and the young Marrano from Portugal had, as we shall presently see, a vast influence on Karo's entire outlook. From Adrianople Molcho soon travelled to Salonika and there was inducted into the *ḥochmat ha-nistar*, the hidden mysteries of the Kabbalah, by the head of the local Talmudic academy, the rigorous ascetic and Kabbalist Joseph Taytazak. It is related of Taytazak[32] that in the course of forty years he slept on a short chest with his feet hanging down, so that he should have no pleasure even while sleeping.[33] New worlds were revealed before Molcho; in moments of supreme ecstasy he would receive prophetic visions. A heavenly messenger (a *maggid*, a preacher or declarer), who lifted for him the veil covering future events, would visit him. Molcho's fiery addresses evoked great enthusiasm among his listeners and, following the suggestion of one of his admirers, he published some of them in a collection entitled *Sefer Ha-Mefoar* (Salonika, 1529).

Molcho saw in the history of the world the perennial struggle between the prince of Esau, Samael, and the bearer of the Torah, Israel.[34] Whenever the Jewish people remove themselves from the Torah, they fall into the hands of Esau and their enemies are filled with the joy of triumph. "But all the evil decrees that come upon the Jews," Molcho insists, "are sent only as a trial and not to destroy them." Molcho is certain that soon the great world struggle will end and the prince of Esau will fall. In the great catastrophe experienced by Rome in 1527, when German and Spanish soldiers arrogantly invaded the Catholic churches and mocked the priests and monks, Molcho saw the commencement of the war of Gog and Magog, the beginning of the "end of days" when the kingdom of Esau would succumb and the redeemer appear in all his glory. By way of allusion, not openly and clearly but in a disguised way, Molcho portrays the "end" and indicates that in 1540 the great miracle will occur and the Messiah reveal himself.[35]

From Salonika Molcho set out for the other major center of the Kabbalah, Safed, where his fervent preaching intensified messianic moods. There, it appears, Molcho composed his poem

---

32. See Elijah de Vidas, *Reshit Ḥochmah, Shaar Ha-Kedushah*, Chapter Seven, p. 231 (we quote according to the 1578 edition).
33. After Taytazak's death the following of his works were published: *Leshon Ha-Zahav* (a commentary to the Psalms, Venice, 1553) and *Leḥem Setarim* (a commentary to Daniel, Venice, 1608). In Baron Günzburg's collection there are in manuscript (Nos. 159 and 168) two other works by Taytazak, a commentary to the Torah and a treatise on homiletics.
34. *Ha-Mefoar*, 19b (according to the Amsterdam edition of 1709).
35. *Ibid.*, 21a.

"Yigalu Setumim."[36] The noble mystic emotively declares "that the
end of days is coming" and soon the mighty Ottoman Empire
will fall. He, the "young Solomon," is sent "from Edom" to proclaim at God's command "from Mount Carmel" the tidings that
the great day of world judgment is approaching, and he announces
that he hastens to Italy, to the capital of the world, Rome, where
God's avenging sword will first manifest itself and the great judgment commence. In this connection, one must take into consideration the powerful impression which Martin Luther's reforming activities had made in Jewish mystical circles. The mystic Abraham
Halevi circulated from Palestine in 1528 an open letter in which
he declares Luther to be a covert adherent of Judaism, a kind of
"righteous proselyte" who has declared war not only against the
pope but against all Christendom and will bring all the peoples
to the Jewish faith.[37]

Thanks to the historian Joseph Ha-Kohen, an open letter which
Molcho dispatched from Italy to his friends in Salonika has been
preserved.[38] This interesting literary memorial portrays most
clearly the unique beauty of the mystical dreamer whose sacrificial
passion then attained the supreme level. With moving simplicity
he relates the great peril in which he found himself when he returned to Italy from Turkey, for there were those who wished
to denounce him as an adherent of the most dangerous enemy of
Christendom, the Turkish sultan. Now he sees before him at dusk
on a Thursday evening the gates of the world city, millennial
Rome, which he regards as the symbol of the destruction of
Jerusalem and the degradation of his people. "The gates of weeping" were then opened in him, and he pours out his grieved heart
before the Creator of the world and begs Him to exchange His
wrath for favor, to remember His languishing people, and to accept
the ruined stones of the holy city. Ever more fervent and stormy
becomes his petition; "his eyes are like a flowing stream." In the
middle of his prayer Solomon Molcho hears a voice calling to him
from on high: "Seir [the Christian world] will fall into the hands
of its enemies. The people of Israel will reveal its power. God
will have mercy upon His servants . . . I will take vengeance and
pay to each his deserts!"

Thirty days in succession Molcho sat wrapped in rags and
rotted, torn garments in a company of cripples and beggars on
the bridge of the Tiber opposite the Vatican. His long fasting

36. Published by D. Kaufmann in *REJ*, XXXIV, 123–25.
37. *Kiryat Sefer*, VII, 161.
38. Published in his *Divrei Ha-Yamim*, pp. 91–94 (Amsterdam edition,
    1733).

and wakefulness through the nights brought the young mystic to the level of exalted cleaving to God, in which a man begins to dream while awake and the most fantastic "visions" appear to him. "In the twelfth month, the month of Adar, 1530," Molcho relates,

sleep fell upon me in the middle of the night, and the old man who had previously disclosed himself to me appeared. The old man said to me: "My son, I have come to tell you what will happen to the nations among whom you live. Come with me to the ruins of Jerusalem which you have already once visited." And he took me and brought me to Palestine to the two mountains that are between Mount Zion and Jerusalem and between Safed and Damascus. Of these two mountains, the one on the right side which is toward Safed and Damascus is the smaller one, and the one on the left side which is toward Zion and Jerusalem is the larger. And he said to me: "Lift up your eyes to the mountain on the left and tell me what you see." I said: "I see a man in white garments holding a scale in his hands." And he said to me: "Open your lips and ask him what will happen with the people from whom I have just led you forth." And I said to him: "How can I, an insignificant slave, undertake to speak with him? Who am I and what is my merit that I should be worthy to address questions to him?" The man then said: "Have no fear. Be welcome, my son. Ask and I will answer, because for this purpose have I come here." I bowed to the ground before him and said: "Now I see that I, your servant, have found grace in your eyes. Tell me, my lord, what will be the fate of the people among whom I sat there on the bridge?" And he replied: "Here in this book is noted down everything that will occur because of all the evil which has been done. Apply to the old man and he will reveal everything to you." And he handed the book to the old man. The latter looked into the book and returned it to the man in white. And the man said to the elder: "Go and tell the young man who is standing near you everything that you have read in the book." And the old man took me by the hand and brought me back to the bridge to the place where I had been sitting.

Molcho further relates at length how various creatures in the form of marvelous birds of all kinds of colors revealed themselves to him and tremendous fiery signs appeared in the heavens. The old man explained to him the symbolic meaning of everything that transpired before his eyes. "Know, my son," he said, "the great bird which you have seen is an omen of a great flood and an earthquake. The flood will occur here in this land and in another land to the north, and the earthquake will be in your native country [Portugal]." The old man further said to him: "Afterwards great wonders will take place. Then will come the great and unique day, the truly divine day, the day of the great miracle . . ."

Molcho believed so firmly in his "vision" that he gave the Portuguese ambassador in Rome, Bras Neto, a letter to King João III in which he predicted that quite soon there would be a powerful earthquake in Portugal. In the meantime he preached fervent sermons in the synagogues in the ghetto of Rome. Then the marvelous things actually happened. One can imagine the tremendous sensation created in the Christian and Jewish worlds when a short time later everything that the "dreamer," the exalted Molcho, had predicted began in fact to happen. On the eighth of October in the same year, 1530, the Tiber overflowed its banks and flooded the streets of Rome. A month later Flanders ("a land to the north") also suffered greatly from a major flood, and shortly afterwards a great earthquake took place in Lisbon and in many other cities of Portugal. At the same time "a fiery, wondrous sign"—Halley's comet—appeared in the skies above Rome. Pope Clement VII himself became an ardent devotee of this remarkable dreamer and issued a letter of protection to guard him from the fangs of the Inquisition. He also came to Molcho's aid when the latter was in great danger after his opponent, the learned translator and physician Jacob Mantino,[39] denounced him and the tribunal of the Inquisition declared him a dangerous heretic and blasphemer of the Catholic faith and condemned him to the stake on this charge. To save Molcho the pope substituted another man and, in his place, sent to the stake a criminal who had been condemned to death. The following day the "burned" Molcho was seen walking in the palaces of the Vatican. It is therefore no surprise that when a year later (1532), after his fatal audience with the emperor Charles V, Molcho ended his brief but stormy life most tragically at the stake, his followers and admirers refused to believe that the marvelous dreamer was really dead.[40] A legend was created to the effect that this time again he had been saved from the fire. Some swore that the week after Molcho was condemned to be burned he was seen in Rome. Others again declared that he went to Safed, where his bride was waiting for him. Even such a rationalistically

---

39. D. Kaufmann endeavors in his monograph "Jacob Mantino" (*REJ*, XXVII, 57) to justify Mantino's denunciation by the fact that he was apprehensive lest the agitation of the former Marrano bring the entire Jewish community of Rome into jeopardy. Against this, however, see Vogelstein and Rieger, *Geschichte der Juden in Rom*, II, 53–58.
40. When Molcho was already at the stake he was told in the emperor's name that if he would recant and were prepared to return to Catholicism, he would be allowed to live and set free at once, but Molcho proudly replied: "I am only sorry that I spent my youth in your faith; now do with me what you wish."

minded man as Joseph Ha-Kohen, when he mentions these legends in his account of the young martyr, adds, "Oh, how well it would be if I could write for certain whether all this is true or not!"[41]

Into his old age Joseph Karo regarded the memory of his young perished friend with deepest reverence. "My beloved Solomon," "my chosen Solomon"—this was Karo's highest ideal, the symbol of purity and holiness. The dearest wish and loveliest dream of Karo's life was to sacrifice himself, like Molcho, as a martyr and to praise God's holy name at the stake.[42] Molcho initiated Karo into the mysteries of the Kabbalah, and the magic and influence of the fervent young Kabbalist was so immense that even the cold-blooded codifier and keen-minded "uprooter of mountains" felt himself permeated with mystical ardor. Karo's eyes also perceived miracles. A heavenly messenger, a "proclaimer" (*maggid*), who lifted the curtain before him and revealed what is hidden in the womb of future generations to his eyes, appeared to him.

In this connection, however, we observe an extremely interesting psychological phenomenon: the mystic in Karo did not triumph over the codifier and scholar. The Kabbalist Karo, Solomon Molcho's ardent devotee, remains the author of *Bet Yosef* who spent all his days poring over the thick folios of the Talmud and its commentators. The heavenly messenger, the *maggid*, therefore reveals himself to Karo in the form of the embodied Mishnah. "I, the Mishnah, speak to you," "I am the Mishnah," the *maggid* frequently declares, "I am the soul of the Mishnah, I am the mother who reproves her children."[43] On Sabbaths and festivals in the morning, and on rare occasions also on a weekday, the Mishnah would come to him, her chosen and well-beloved son, reveal to him the hidden heavenly mysteries, give him instruction, and set before him as model "God's beloved, my chosen Solomon," i.e., Solomon Molcho. These "conversations" with the *maggid*, the personified Mishnah who visited her "chosen son" to the end of his days,[44] Karo would write down verbatim, and in this way a very unique book of memoirs, *Maggid Mesharim*, was produced.

41. *Divrei Ha-Yamim*, p. 96.
42. *Maggid Mesharim, Parashat Ve-Zot Ha-Berachah*, 50b (Zolkiev edition, 1773).
43. *Ibid.*, 13, 35, 50, and many other passages.
44. The first part of *Maggid Mesharim* was published for the first time in Lublin in 1646, the second in Venice in 1656. The historian Rosanes endeavors in his *Divrei Yemei Yisrael Be-Togarmah* (II, 201–5) to show that Joseph Karo was not a Kabbalist and that he is not the author of *Maggid Mesharim*. His arguments, however, are extremely weak.

The "soul of the Mishnah" which used to visit Joseph Karo was an extremely indignant and severe soul. Indeed, she was of those mothers "who always reprove their children." In almost every visit the *maggid* did not tire of reminding Karo that one must avoid the pleasures of this world as much as possible. One must not be eager for food, the Mishnah frequently admonishes; one must merely have a bite to maintain the body.[45] "If you observe that you have great pleasures from some dish, you should at once exchange it for another which pleases you less, for by surrendering to the desire of eating, the power of Samael, God forbid, is strengthened, and such a grievous sin demands great punishment."[46] "You ought to mortify your body as much as possible," the Mishnah warns her beloved son; "then you will have the privilege of seeing the prophet Elijah face to face. He will speak to you mouth to mouth and reveal the secrets of the Torah to you."[47] To study the Torah day and night, to be ever prepared to sacrifice oneself for the Torah—this is the major motif of the *maggid's* instructions. "Take care," the Mishnah warns Karo,

that you do not for a moment forget me or absent yourself from my Torah. If you knew how many worlds you destroyed by ceasing to think of words of Torah, you would not interrupt your study even for one second. When you walk in the street and your thoughts are occupied with me and my Torah, whole worlds go before you and proclaim, "Praise and exalt him who bears the king's form!" Innumerable hosts accompany you and whole worlds tremble before the tremendous cry, "This is the man who is favored in the sight of the King, the King of kings! This is the greatest Tanna in Palestine, this is the head of the academy of all the land of Israel!"[48]

The soul of the Mishnah promises her dear son:

Know that God Himself, as it were, and all the heavenly academy greet you. The faithful prophets, the Tannaim, Amoraim, Savoraim, Geonim, and all the codifiers—all bless you when you occupy yourself with their Torah. Entire worlds tremble when they hear how these bless you and, astonished, they ask: "Wherefore is all this?" They are then answered and told: "This is the head of all the academies in Palestine. This is the great codifier of the land of Israel, Joseph surnamed Karo, of whom the King, the King of kings Himself, desires that his name be praised!"[49]

45. *Maggid Mesharim*, 2, 20, 22, 23 ff.
46. *Ibid.*, 2, 3, 6, 11.
47. *Ibid.*, 3. Cf. *ibid.*, 16 and 24.
48. *Ibid.*, 2b. Cf. *ibid.*, 34, 55 ff.
49. *Ibid.*, "Parashah Ve-Ethanan," 45.

"Because I am so precious to you," the Mishnah says in another visit, "I will exalt you, and you will be the spiritual master of all the communities in the Exile. Because you have dedicated yourself to restoring *semichah* [rabbinic ordination] to its former glory,[50] you will have the privilege of seeing your ordination recognized by all the sages in and outside Palestine."[51] The "soul of the Mishnah" guarantees him that if he follows her paths, he will be privileged to complete his great works and see them spread throughout the dispersions of Israel. The number of his disciples will be so vast that no sage of the last five hundred years will be comparable to him in this respect, and all his disciples will shine like the stars in heaven.[52] The *maggid* promises him, "I will reveal for you the upper worlds and you, like the sages of the Talmud in their day, will also be able to perform miracles,[53] and all will know that even though prophecy has ceased in Israel, it still rests on you." But as highest reward the Mishnah promises her beloved son the crown of sacrifice and martyrdom. It assures him that he will have the privilege of ascending the pyre for the sake of God's name[54]—and this not in the lands of the exile but in the holy land of the fathers.

After Karo had become the friend of Solomon Molcho while still living in Adrianople, he began to long for the major centers of the Kabbalah, for Salonika and chiefly for Safed. The *maggid* soon came to him and commanded him to leave Adrianople, remain for a short time only in Salonika, and from there set out for Safed.[55] "I will not forsake you," the Mishnah assures him,

until I shall have fulfilled everything that I promised you. Through me you will have the privilege of coming to Palestine. There you will be in contact with many sages, and a large number of pupils will study your Torah. . . . Afterward you will merit ascending the pyre for the sanctification of God's name.[56]

It is clear that the *maggid,* who always admonishes Karo not to interrupt his study of Torah, also does not forget the Kabbalah. "You shall occupy yourself constantly with the Mishnah and the

50. When Jacob Berab wished to renew the old institution of *semichah* one of the first to be "ordained" was Joseph Karo.
51. *Maggid Mesharim,* 31.
52. *Ibid.,* 13–14.
53. *Ibid.,* 4, 9, 13, 22.
54. *Ibid.,* 53, 55.
55. *Ibid.,* 54b.
56. *Ibid.,* "Parashat Va-Yikra," 30a.

Kabbalah," the *maggid* frequently repeats.[57] "You shall set aside definite times for the study of the Kabbalah."[58] "Be diligent in studying the Kabbalah and do not under any circumstances desist from it," the *maggid* ever reminds him.[59] "You will fathom the depths of the wisdom of the Kabbalah," the *maggid* assures him; "you will surpass the great Kabbalist of Meron [Simeon ben Yoḥai], and he will learn Torah from you."[60]

This promise was in fact not fulfilled. Joseph Karo was doubtless the greatest codifier and rabbinic authority of his time, but in the wisdom of the Kabbalah he was far surpassed by his colleagues in Safed. Of these we shall speak in the chapters that follow.

57. *Ibid.*, 33, 53 ff.
58. *Ibid.*, 19, 26.
59. *Ibid.*, 49, 55.
60. *Ibid.*, 48, "Parashah Ki Tavo." Graetz concludes that by the Kabbalist of Meron is meant Rabbi Isaac Luria. This, however, is not correct. These words of *Maggid Mesharim* were written in 1569. At that time Rabbi Isaac Luria had just come to Palestine and had not yet achieved fame. Besides this, there is no doubt that "Ha-Rosh Shebe-Meron" signifies the initial letters of some Kabbalist.

CHAPTER THREE

Meir Ibn Gabbai;
THE KABBALISTS OF SAFED

E noted in the previous chapter that the *Shulḥan Aruch,* the collection of all the laws and rules which became the cornerstone of rabbinic Judaism in later generations, was completed in Safed. This Galilean town was also the cradle of the new system of Kabbalah which tyrannically laid its stamp on all later spiritual and mystical currents—indeed, on all of later Jewish cultural life. Here in this remote place in upper Galilee was built the ingenious, bizarre, fantastic structure in which are so wildly and disharmoniously mingled together exalted asceticism with morbid, importunate messianic dreams and intoxicating passion for the human ego, for the proud human personality, wrapped in the garment of incantations, whisperings and magical names, with unshakeable belief in the final victory of the good and the just—while the whole world is steeped in pitch-black uncleanness and the air is deafened by the arrogantly triumphant laughter of Samael and his hosts. All this meanders in a wild, fearful confusion without beginning or end in the depths of a narrow, dark, labyrinthine cave in which the wearied, suffering human soul trembles—the soul that has endured the terrible pangs of hell but has still not lost its belief in the intoxicating bliss of heaven, and bursts with its last powers out of the pitch blackness to the free, radiant distances of the celestial heights.

Before we proceed to the Kabbalists of Safed we must dwell on one Kabbalist who does not belong to the Safed circle but forms the connecting link between the Kabbalah of the earlier period and the Kabbalistic school of Safed. This was Meir ben Ezekiel Ibn Gabbai. Of his life virtually nothing is known. Thanks only to the indications of the author himself at the end of his two works, we know that he was born in Spain in 1480. He completed his first work, *Tolaat Yaakov*, a mystical commentary on the weekday prayers, at the age of twenty-six when he found himself in extremely difficult material circumstances,[1] and his major work was finished in the fiftieth year of his life.[2]

As an eleven-year-old child, Ibn Gabbai, along with the other Spanish exiles, set out on a difficult wanderer's way until he finally found rest in the Turkish empire. His major work, *Avodat Ha-Kodesh*,[3] on which he labored for eight years, certainly deserves far more attention than has been given it to the present time by our scholars. In this work the major problems of Kabbalist doctrine are dealt with in systematic fashion. The mystical world outlook which had developed among Jews in the course of generations here obtains for the first time a clear and unitary form, and is portrayed and explained as a completely harmonious structure.

The work is divided into four parts: *Ḥelek Ha-Yiḥud* (Section on Unity), on the oneness and uniqueness of God; *Ḥelek Ha-Avodah* (Section on Worship), on serving God with concentrated attention and devotion; *Ḥelek Ha-Tachlit* (Section on Purpose), on the goal of the world, the Torah, and man; *Ḥelek Sitrei Ha-Torah* (Section on the Secrets of the Torah), on the mysteries of the work of creation, the work of the divine chariot or throne, and the visions of the prophets.

We observed in the third volume how the first problem, i.e., God's unity, was strictly associated among the Kabbalists with a

---

1. See the end of *Tolaat Yaakov* (Cracow edition).
2. At the end of *Avodat Ha-Kodesh* the following note appears: "And my work was completed on Thursday, the second of Tevet, 1530; I began to labor on my composition when I was forty-two and completed it when I was fifty."
3. The first edition of the work was published in Venice in 1567 under the title *Marot Elohim* by the author's son-in-law Shneur Falkon.

difficult question: how could the temporal, changeable, and material develop from the absolute unity which is wholly spiritual and transcends all change whatsoever? In resolving this contradiction Ibn Gabbai relies on the arguments which Naḥmanides' teacher, Azriel, set forth in his *Perush Eser Sefirot*. Ibn Gabbai refers quite frequently to this commentary,[4] and somewhat later set its basic theses as the foundation of his subsequent work, *Derech Emunah*, in which the doctrine of the *sefirot* is especially discussed.[5]

Divinity itself, which is the source of all phenomena, is beyond all human perception, Ibn Gabbai explains, and man cannot even call it by its right name. The term *Ein Sof* (Infinite), *Rum Ha-Maalah* (Exalted Height), *Keter Elyon* (High Crown)—these are merely conventional terms by means of which we attempt to designate what is concealed from us and beyond our understanding. The name, after all, expresses the essence or nature of the thing; hence, God's name is identical with divinity itself, and as eternal and incomprehensible as the First Cause.[6] Not without reason, explains Ibn Gabbai, did our sages say, "Before the world was created, only God and His name existed." And the unexpressed and incomprehensible name contains in itself all the ten *sefirot*,[7] which are not born or created, but radiated or emanated from divinity; for the *sefirot* are the revelation of God's essence, and this essence is not altered. God does not create anything new; He merely emanates or radiates. The hidden, potential powers are disclosed and pass from potentiality to actuality.[8] Indeed, the *sefirot* are the connecting link, the mediator, between the infinite and the finite, between the First Cause and the universe. They are the vessels through which the world arises.[9] As God's emanation, the *sefirot* are of one essence with God, and they are therefore eternal and infinite, just as He is. But in the fact that they are *emanated*, that they are a disclosure of an active will, a receiver of divine influence—in this lies an element of distance and diminution, and precisely through this they are suited to create the limited and temporal.[10]

4. *Avodat Ha-Kodesh*, 12b ff. (we quote according to the Cracow edition of 1577).
5. This work was written by Ibn Gabbai especially for his pupil Joseph Ha-Levi.
6. *Avodat Ha-Kodesh*, 9.
7. *Ibid.*, 12; cf. *ibid.*, 16 and 18.
8. *Ibid.*, 10.
9. *Ibid.*, 18.
10. *Ibid.*, Part 3, Chapter 3, folio 111.

The *sefirot* are the variegated revelation of divinity, and only in their variety can man receive them; and it is to the *sefirot* (which also bear the name *middot*, "qualities") that human prayers are raised, for it is only these that mortal man can understand. It is these alone that man intends through all the praises and attributes with which he crowns divinity. The *sefirot*, however, are not to be represented as separate and independent. As emanations they are *in* divinity but not *outside* it;[11] and as man's soul reveals itself through the limbs of the body, so also divinity, the soul of all emanations, reveals itself through the *sefirot*. And just as man's soul is one, despite the fact that the activity of the organs is so varied, so also the *sefirot*, God's attributes, form an absolute unity with God, for the variety and differentiation is not in divinity and in the divine attributes (*middot*), but in us and in our concepts. We, with our limited perception, cannot otherwise receive the revelation of God's deeds.[12] In all His revelations God is one and unchangeable. There are not in Him various and opposite qualities, so that He is at one time the God of the attribute of mercy and at another time the God of the attribute of justice. He appears so to us only in our concepts, for we, with our restricted perceptions, cannot otherwise receive and grasp God's nature.[13] When we speak of God's anger or God's favor, we do not thereby disclose His true nature; we merely express and declare the attitude that *we* hold, how *we* evaluate His deeds.

One and the same ray of the sun produces the most varied results: it whitens linen and darkens man's face, it softens tar and hardens wax. The same ray, if passed through varicolored glasses, glistens with all kinds of colors. Yet we know very well that, with all its different effects and colors, it is one in essence.[14] Indeed, herein lies the deeper meaning of the Talmudic sages' dictum that before the creation of the world only God and His name existed; i.e., before the world was created the variety could not disclose itself, because there were still no creatures to receive the unitary wholeness and unchangeability of divinity according to their own categories in limited and changeable forms.[15]

But what purpose inheres in the work of creation? To what end were the world and its crown and ornament, man, created? This question is posed by the author in the preface, and to it he devotes the entire third part of his work, *Ḥelek Ha-Tachlit*.

11. *Ibid.*, 16.
12. *Ibid.*, Part 1, Chapter 11 (end). Cf. Chapter 12, folio 25.
13. *Ibid.*, 94.
14. *Ibid.*, 14–15.
15. *Ibid.*, 14.

"It is known that the deed is the end of the thought, and its perfection," declares Ibn Gabbai. Thought obtains the highest culmination only when it is incorporated in action, in an act of will, and thereby passes from potentiality to actuality. The highest perfection of God's will and of God's thought, the supreme category of their revelation, can be attained only through the deed, through their concretizing themselves in the act. And for this the *olam ha-maaseh*, the real world, was required. For the deed, the disclosure of the act of will, through which alone abstract thought attains its fulfillment, cannot occur outside space, beyond the real world. Our *olam ha-maaseh* is therefore the necessary link which brings the upper worlds to their perfection and provides for the possibility that God's will be disclosed in all its glory.[16] And at the midpoint of the *olam ha-maaseh* stands its pride and crown, man, whose body is a reflection of the heavenly "chariot"[17] and whose soul unites in itself the rays of all the *sefirot*.

Ibn Gabbai strongly assails Maimonides because the latter believed that man's soul is endowed merely with the preparation for, or possibility of, perfection, and that the distinction between man and the beast consists only in the fact that the beasts do not even have such a possibility. Only through the sharpening and enriching of the intellect with scientific problems and philosophical ideas does the potential pass, according to Maimonides, from mere possibility into actuality, and only then does man's soul become united with the "active intellect."[18] But the Kabbalist Ibn Gabbai is firmly convinced that man's soul is by nature higher even than the heavenly "spheres," for it is the emanation of God's light, the reflection of the divine *Shechinah*. And union with the lowest of the spheres, with the "active intellect," is not the task of the human soul; its role, Ibn Gabbai assures us, is a much loftier one—to actualize the consummate goal of the world, the unity of divinity with its emanation.[19]

Ibn Gabbai correctly notes that in this point the utter difference between the world view of Greek philosophy and Judaism is disclosed most clearly. According to Aristotle, God is the absolute, unlimited, thinking First Cause, the influence of which on the order of the world does not at all consist in the fact that the world is ruled through divine, creative, and effective will power. God influences the world not through His activity and work but only by

16. *Ibid.*, 2b; cf. *ibid.*, 58.
17. *Ibid.*, 57.
18. See the first volume of our work, Chapter 6.
19. *Avodat Ha-Kodesh*, 42a.

the fact that He *is* and *thinks* and is filled with the consciousness of His essence. The God of Aristotle is not the ruler of the world; He is merely *thought*, eternal and infinite thought. The "intelligences," the thinking "spheres," which move in their stupendous cycle and attain the goal and cause of their eternal circling, are incomparably higher than man, who succeeds only after much searching and probing for the divine nature in uniting himself, through his philosophical thought, with the "active intellect," the lowest of the spheres, the ruler of the terrestrial, sublunar world. The God of Judaism, however, Ibn Gabbai insists, is not the distant God who transcends the world but God the Creator who comprehends the entire world and is concerned about it, the God who is the ruler of the world, the God full of compassion, the Judge of the world who accepts all prayers and considers all tears. Not with cold intellection, with arid speculative thought, can one attain the essence of the God of Judaism or rise to the primordial source of life and being. This God is the God of revelation, of great miracle, and only through profound intuition, through religious feeling and passion, can one catch a glimpse of His light. Not philosophical speculation and theoretical, logical hypotheses are the principal thing or the highest goal, but rather moral perfection, the desire to incorporate the ideal of justice in life, to disclose the will to draw near to the holy and divine through deeds. For this reason, Ibn Gabbai indicates, the righteous man, in the Jewish view, is higher than the angels, for among angels the act of will, the struggle for the good and the just, is lacking. The angels are pure and radiant by their very nature; they cannot be impure and dark. But the fate of man is different. The soul deriving from heaven is associated with sinful matter, the earthly body, and only through fearful trials and obdurate struggle does the soul manage to overcome the sinful desires of the body and raise itself to the celestial heights.[20]

Ibn Gabbai cannot forgive Abraham Ibn Ezra[21] for having "let himself be led astray by Greek wisdom" and attacks Saadiah Gaon because the latter placed man lower than the angels. For this reason, Ibn Gabbai insists, Maimonides also could not accept the view that the world was created for the sake of man. Entangled "in the net of Greek philosophy," the author of *A Guide for the Perplexed* set man on a level considerably lower than that of the angels and the spheres, and hence had to come to the conclusion that the creation of the world and its purpose remain an inexplicable

20. *Ibid.*, Part III, Chapters 1–3.
21. *Ibid.*, 58.

enigma. To the question, To what end was the world created? one must humbly answer: Such was God's will, so He in His wisdom decreed.[22]

But for Ibn Gabbai, as we have already seen, the purpose of the world is clear and comprehensible. He has no doubt whatever that man's soul is of a higher order than the spheres, that "the righteous man is the foundation of the world" and that all creatures are subject to his will.[23] But in what does this power consist? On what is the righteous man's great might based? Ibn Gabbai answers: On the Torah and its commandments. "The Torah is the emanation of the divine wisdom," "the Torah is the secret of emanation." It is the incarnate name of God; it is the sure guide showing how the divine will is to be incorporated in specific deeds. Only thanks to the Torah and its commandments does man participate in the unification of divinity with its supreme perfection and incomparable splendor.[24] *Avodah hi ha-ikkar*, the deed is the chief thing. The ceaseless performance of good deeds, the act of will in creating the good, is the most significant factor producing harmony and perfection in the whole universe. It is the thread which links man to the Creator and His divine name.[25] It is not knowledge alone that is important; knowledge not incorporated through the act of will is like a soulless monster. True perfection is attained through the deed, through the observance of the commandment.[26] Every good deed done by man obtains an echo in the higher spheres and brings one to the supreme goal: closeness to the Creator and His incomparable splendor. And the author of *Marot Elohim* insists that not only the elect few but every one of the "great multitude" can attain this supreme level of perfection.

Ibn Gabbai deems it necessary to stress that he can in no way agree with Joseph Ibn Shemtov who insists in his *Ein Ha-Kore* that man is endowed with immortality as a reward for the observance of the commandments.[27] The reward is not the major purpose, says Ibn Gabbai; there is a far higher goal, the "goal of goals"—to praise God's name and to reveal His glory.[28] And this supreme goal requires no extraneous reward whatever. Its unique and exclusive dynamic power must be boundless, sacrificial love. This love for God, Ibn Gabbai adds, must disclose itself in man

22. *Guide for the Perplexed*, III:13.
23. *Avodat Ha-Kodesh*, 16.
24. *Ibid.*, 42a.
25. *Ibid.*
26. *Ibid.* 58, 105, 106.
27. *Ibid.*, 28, 106.
28. *Ibid.*, "Ḥelek Ha-Avodah," Chapters 6–7.

in fervid, devoted love for his fellow, for every individual, who is, after all, a reflection of the heavenly "chariot" and strives, like himself, to the single highest goal: to exalt and praise God's name. This love must shatter every barrier between one man and another.[29] Man must not be content with "Thou shalt love thy neighbor as thyself"; his love must be so great and strong that his neighbor is more precious to him than himself.[30]

This sacrificial love finds its echo in the heavenly spheres. "The upper world and the lower world are like two instruments whose chords are integrally united." The love for God, the striving toward unity and harmony, awakens to the same degree in the celestial heights love for the inhabitants of earth. "The eye turned to heaven," we read in *Marot Elohim*, "is at once noticed by the heavenly heights; the eye that seeks God sees God's glance turned to it, and when these two glances meet each other the wondrous light hidden in the holy name of God that no man may bring to his lips is revealed in all its splendor and radiance."[31]

Ibn Gabbai emphasizes the universal significance that the Torah and its commandments have for the world as a whole.[32] But he admonishes, in this connection, that one cannot with the simple human mind grasp the profound mysteries hidden in the Torah and its commandments. He takes pains to point out that man cannot rely on his mind, for the mind often errs and its theories and conclusions are frequently incorrect, even in questions relating to the ordinary phenomena of life; all the more may one not rely on it when the question of the reasons for the commandments of the Torah and the mysteries concealed in them is involved.[33] Not through speculation and intellectual theories, Ibn Gabbai several times repeats, can man find the way which discloses the mysterious depths of the divine Torah, but only with the aid of the sacred tradition and the Kabbalah. Because the human intellect cannot grasp and fathom the secrets of the Torah, God disclosed them to Moses, and from him extends for many, many generations the

29. *Ibid.*, 138.
30. *Ibid.*, 139.
31. *Ibid.*, "Helek Ha-Tachlit," Chapters 36, 54.
32. It is characteristic of Ibn Gabbai that the Oral Torah is almost as important in his view as the Written Torah. "The Written Torah and the Oral Torah," he insists, "are twin brothers who cannot be parted and of whom one cannot exist without the other." "The Written Torah was revealed to the world only through the Oral Torah." An ardent Kabbalist, Ibn Gabbai nevertheless pored whole nights over the laws and discussions of the Gemara. See the end of his *Tolaat Yaakov*.
33. *Avodat Ha-Kodesh*, "Helek Ha-Tachlit," Chapter 20.

golden chain of tradition and Kabbalah that is lovingly guarded by the righteous of the generation who watch over the "true wisdom."[34] This "true wisdom" is a beacon for the entire people.[35] It is the surest guide and faithful guardian of the treasures of the sacred Torah.[36] The Kabbalah, Ibn Gabbai assures us, is the sole source of true knowledge. He therefore attacks with great indignation those who have "allowed themselves to be led astray by Greek wisdom" and allowed the whole Torah of Moses to be permeated with its "false" spirit.

To be sure, Meir Ibn Gabbai was not the first to polemicize against "Greek wisdom" and its followers, but in his angry and bitter attacks completely new tones are heard, and what in the mystics and orthodox teachers of earlier generations was still barely discernible appears in the author of *Avodat Ha-Kodesh* (*Marot Elohim*) sharply and clearly. To be sure, Ibn Gabbai manifests in the first part of *Avodat Ha-Kodesh* a certain knowledge of philosophical matters and expresses ideas bearing a pantheistic appearance, but the work carries quite obviously the stamp of a severely limited world outlook. From it is wafted arrogant self-satisfaction and contempt for everything outside its domain. The stifling air of the culturally retarded environment is discernible. Ibn Gabbai attacks philosophy not because it refuses to acknowledge the bounds of its competence and presumes to play a dominant role even in questions of faith; he regards "Greek wisdom" and other sciences with contempt because he sees no value whatever in them and declares them to be vain playthings of man's proud intellect.

Ibn Gabbai cannot forgive Maimonides and his followers[37] for the fact that, in interpreting the meaning of the Torah, they attempted to bring it into harmony with "Aristotle's follies and lies." Maimonides, he indignantly declares, believed that no one could refute Aristotle's "foolish arguments." Indeed, it is owing to Maimonides that the plague spread over the whole of Israel. Jews turned away from the sacred tradition and began to undermine the ramparts of the Torah with the silly theories of the accursed Greek.[38] Maimonides and his followers wished to show that there is no difference between the wisdom of Israel and Greek philoso-

34. Ibn Gabbai in this connection attempts to present the chain of tradition from the time of Moses; in fact, however, he gives the chain of tradition of Jewish mysticism (*ibid.*, 77–78).
35. *Avodat Ha-Kodesh*, 57.
36. *Ibid.*, 9, 26, 33, 111 ff.
37. Ibn Gabbai especially attacks Gersonides (*Ibid.*, 65, 69, 70).
38. *Ibid.*, 57.

phy and that Aristotle's views are fully consonant with the Torah of our prophets. But this is a lie, Ibn Gabbai cries out with great anger; Greek philosophy, this false and mendacious wisdom, was always alien to us, and its introduction into God's holy camp is forbidden.[39] Every pious man, he asserts, knows that one must strictly avoid philosophy, for with its heresy it undermines the foundations of the faith, and that only the "true wisdom," which was given to us on Mount Sinai and belongs to Israel and which no other nation has merited, leads one on the right path.[40]

True knowledge about nature and the creation of the world, Ibn Gabbai is firmly convinced, is to be found not in Aristotle's *Physics* but only in the story of creation revealed in the divine Torah. The author of *Avodat Ha-Kodesh* speaks with hostility and wrath of Maimonides' attempt to bring the Biblical account of creation into harmony with the assumptions of Greek science. *A Guide for the Perplexed*, Ibn Gabbai several times repeats, was the stumbling block for the whole people of Israel; his words were the fearful net that caught and entangled many innocent souls.[41]

In this enormous contempt for "foreign" sciences, for the cultural treasures located outside the boundaries of Judaism, the new tendencies which occupied the place of supremacy in the isolated Jewish life of the later era are very clearly disclosed. Characteristic also is the exhaustive attention Ibn Gabbai gives to the problem of transmigration of the soul. We have already noted the universal import that observance of the commandments has in Ibn Gabbai's view. But it is the chosen people—"my eldest-born son Israel," God's beloved child—to whom the sacred Torah has been given as the most precious gift, that fulfills the commandments of the Torah. The people of Israel, which entered into an eternal covenant with the divine Torah, is therefore indeed the *tzaddik yesod olam* (righteous who is the foundation of the world), the most faithful guardian and protector of the world.[42] Israel can change the order of creation and perform miracles, because the laws of the universe are subject to him, the bridegroom of the Torah, without whom heaven and earth can have no existence. The soul of the people of Israel descended from the highest celestial halls, from the most hidden source of "love and unity."[43] Its mind

39. *Ibid.*, 74–75.
40. *Ibid.*, 76.
41. *Ibid.*, 136; cf. *ibid.*, 134.
42. *Ibid.*, 21.
43. This view, so widespread among the Jewish mystics, to the effect that the souls of Jews derive from a higher and purer source than the souls of other peoples is already encountered in the *Zohar*. In "Parashah Emor" we read: "Israelites are worthy, for the Holy One,

is not like that of other peoples because it is illuminated with the mysteries of the Torah which endow it with extraordinary power. But when Jews depart from the right way, deny the "holy covenant" which they entered with the Torah and do not fulfill its commandments, they at once forfeit their miraculous power and are given over as slaves to slaves. If a Jewish soul has transgressed and not fulfilled its great mission, it cannot return to its source until it has been purged of its sins. It is therefore condemned to wander through the terrestrial world, to be transmigrated successively not only into men but even into beasts, until it has been completely purified and attained the supreme degree of perfection. After all souls will have been cleansed through this process of transmigration, the long-awaited redeemer, the Messiah the son of David, will appear. All the dead will rise, and their bodies which became food for worms and corruption through the "original sin," the transgression of Adam and Eve, will return to their erstwhile heavenly purity when all their limbs and members were a reflection and mirror of the divine "chariot."[44]

We have noted that Ibn Gabbai was the harbinger of the new direction that Jewish mysticism took in its major new center, Safed. Already at the end of 1521, when no more than three hundred Jewish families lived there, an Italian Jew presented the following information about Safed in his descriptions of his travels through Palestine:

The city is filled with all good things: bread, wine, oil, all kinds of fruits—everything in such great measure that if it were not for export to Damascus, it would have to be sold at half price. There are here many Jewish merchants who bring goods from Damascus. Those who have not the capital required to carry on commerce engage in artisanry and trades. Those who have vigorous hands occupy themselves with day work. Tailors also can earn a living here. Those, however, who count on finding a post in a business or hope to earn a living through teaching will find it difficult to achieve their objective. Hence, men who have no money or trade should not come here, for they will regret it and have to leave the city.[45]

Soon, however, this castaway little town in remote Galilee became the favorite center of men who had "no money or trade," men who removed themselves from the present world and were

---

blessed be He, gives them souls that are holier than those of other peoples, so that they may fulfill his commandments." In "Parashah Pineḥas" it is further emphasized: "The souls of Israel were cut from the body of a holy light."

44. *Avodat Ha-Kodesh,* "Ḥelek Ha-Avodah," Chapters 39–42.
45. *Shivḥei Yerushalayim,* 16b.

wrapped in passionate *devekut* (cleaving to God) and mystical dreams. Not artisans or merchants set out for Safed, but mystics and dreamers who felt that the "end" was very near and that the great miracles which the divine prophets and holy men, the faithful guardians of the "true wisdom," predicted would soon manifest themselves. In Safed the air was filled with old memories. There stood the cradle of the ancient Essenes who removed themselves from the world and led an ascetic life. There the spirit of the divine Rabbi Simeon ben Yoḥai hovered. Near the city lay his grave, and near the grave was the mysterious cave where the great teacher had hidden from the enemy and created the marvelous *Zohar*, the Torah of mysticism. And now—the great day was about to come! Soon the wondrous event of which this divine book prophesies was to occur! The mystics and "calculators of the end" who assembled in Safed had already heard distinctly the steps of the coming redeemer. One must therefore prepare himself betimes for the great day. One must take care that the world be fit to be redeemed. One must do penance, purify the world from sin through fasts and mortifications of the flesh. The righteous of the generation who had penetrated the depths of the "esoteric wisdom" and whose will influences the supernal worlds must take this upon themselves. The spirit of abstinence and asceticism dominated this mystical circle, which soon became the most significant center and gathering point for all the major Kabbalists of that era.

To Safed from Adrianople came Solomon Molcho's ardent admirer, the famous codifier Joseph Karo, accompanied by his ascetic and severe *maggid* who kept admonishing his "beloved son" not to let himself be led astray by the "evil inclination" and to remove himself as far as possible from the desires of the world, including a superfluous drink of water.[46] There Karo's disciple, Moses Alshech, who acquired fame with his commentary on the Pentateuch, *Torat Mosheh*, gave fiery sermons and warned the people to repent in order to hasten the redemption. To Safed also came the venerable Rabbi David ben Solomon Ibn Abi Zimra (Radbaz), the celebrated Talmudist and fervent Kabbalist who sang of the ten *sefirot* and the seven heavenly "palaces" in his well-known hymn *Keter Malchut*,[47] which he composed following the pattern of Solomon Ibn Gabriol's poem.[48]

46. *Maggid Mesharim*, 5, 11 ff.
47. *Keter Malchut* was first published in the collection *Or Kadmon* (Venice, 1703).
48. Abi Zimra also speaks of the *sefirot* and other mystical matters in the introduction to his *Magen David* in which a mystical commentary on the significance of the Hebrew alphabet is given (Amsterdam, 1713).

From Adrianople to Safed came also the enthusiastic poet and mystic Solomon ben Moses Alkabetz, who made himself famous with his hymn "Lecha Dodi." We know very few details of the life of this interesting and gifted man. Born at the beginning of the second decade of the sixteenth century,[49] Alkabetz was educated under the supervision of the well-known Kabbalist and ascetic Joseph Taytazak, and in his youth steeped himself in the mysteries of the Kabbalah. In Adrianople he became acquainted with Joseph Karo, and the two of them together occupied themselves greatly with the "secret wisdom." Evidence of this is given by an interesting document, a published announcement[50] by Alkabetz in which he relates in feeling and inspired style how he and Joseph Karo stayed awake on the first night of Shavuot and he, Alkabetz, had the privilege of seeing with his own eyes the heavenly messenger, Joseph Karo's *maggid*, who informed them that the hour had come and that they must set out forthwith for Palestine. Alkabetz at once fulfilled the *maggid's* command and, coming to Palestine, settled in Safed. He composed a considerable number of mystical works, *Berit Ha-Levi; Apiryon Shelomoh; Otzar Nehmad; Avotot Ahavah; Eser Yesodot; Hakdamot Le-Hochmat Ha-Kabbalah; Teshuvah;* and others.[51] Most of these have remained in manuscript.

A clear notion of Alkabetz' world outlook is provided by his commentary to the Song of Songs, *Ayelet Ahavim,* published in 1552. "The truly pious man in whose heart the holy commandments of the Torah are inscribed," Alkabetz here teaches,

will never lose courage, no matter what troubles and misfortunes he may encounter in life. By three things is the genuinely religious man easily recognized: he rules over his desires, all his thought is of giving aid to his neighbor and leading him to the supreme level of perfection, and he is extremely modest in his thoughts, deeds, and speech.

Man must be particularly careful, Alkabetz stresses, with the word. This is, after all, his loveliest gift; the word raises him above all

49. The year in which Alkabetz was born has not been established. It is known only that in 1529 as a bridegroom he sent his father-in-law his first work *Manot Ha-Levi,* a commentary on the Scroll of Esther, as a Purim gift. He died in ripe old age sometime after 1590.
50. First printed in the Amsterdam edition of *Shenei Luhot Ha-Berit* p. 180), later in *Hemdat Yamim* ([1731], p. 101), and later in all editions of *Tikkun Shevuot.*
51. The list of other works by Alkabetz is given by Rosanes in his *Divrei Yemei Yisrael Be-Togarmah,* II, 162.

creatures in the world. Man is "speaking spirit."[52] Like Ibn Gabbai, Alkabetz insists that in regard to the commandments of the Torah the principal thing is not thought, not understanding the utility and significance of the commandment, but the deed, the observance, the act of will embodied in the doing.[53] And like Ibn Gabbai, Alkabetz repeats that the observance of the commandments must not be associated with calculations or hopes of any reward whatever. "The recompense of a commandment is—a commandment." The fulfilled commandment is itself the best reward, for commandment and reward cannot be separated; they are identical. Commandments, good deeds—these are light, and light is the source of our soul. When we fulfill the commandment, when we do the good deed, its light illumines our soul, and this indeed is the paradise prepared for souls. But if a man violates a commandment, then the darkness of the evil deed stains the soul, and this is its punishment, its endless affliction.[54]

Solomon Alkabetz does not have as much contempt for the "external wisdoms," the secular sciences, as does Meir Ibn Gabbai. He recognizes their value but insists that they are *earthly* wisdoms; they are valid only under the sphere of the sun, and their rule is limited to the space of the earth. But the Torah, the divine word, Alkabetz exclaims with mystical fervor, "is higher than the sun."[55] The Torah, the dazzling ray of God's light, shines over all worlds, and only on its gleaming wings can man rise to the celestial heights, to the eternal source of light and life. For Alkabetz the mystic, it is obvious that man's perfection consists not in seeking and knowing God but in loving Him,[56] and that this perfection may be attained not through philosophical speculation and logical theories, but through *devekut* (cleaving to God),[57] through passionate ecstasy and fiery enthusiasm, which pierce as quickly as lightning and before which all barriers and concealing veils fall away. Man is suddenly endowed with the holy spirit of prophecy. He obtains

52. *Ayelet Ahavim*, 37a.
53. Like Ibn Gabbai, so Alkabetz frequently notes that the Oral Law is no less important than the Written Law. See *ibid.*, 54: " 'Thy two breasts'—these are the two *Torot*. . . . They are two youths that cannot exist without one another, and they came from a holy place." Not only in the Torah, Alkabetz notes in another passage (*ibid.*, 15), are profound mysteries hidden but also in the laws of the Talmud.
54. *Ibid.*, 40.
55. *Ibid.*, 41.
56. It is interesting that Alkabetz relies in this connection on Ḥasdai Crescas (*ibid.*, 36).
57. *Ibid.*, 55.

luminously seeing eyes, and what is hidden lies open and revealed before him. For a man to be able to attain such a degree of ecstasy and spirituality, he must live in solitude, remove himself to isolated, quiet fields and there, far from noisy life with its petty tumult, Alkabetz assures us, his soul unites with the higher spheres.[58]

One of his disciples and close friends testifies that Alkabetz himself would frequently retire to quiet, isolated meadows and there enter into *devekut* and mystical ecstasy. Then prophetic visions would reveal themselves to him. Alkabetz was the spiritual focus of the Kabbalist circle in Safed. Every Friday all the members of this circle would assemble, confess to each other the sins they had committed in the course of the week, then go out walking in the fields before sunset to welcome the "queen Sabbath," the mystical "bride" of Israel, and sing fervent songs about the speedy redemption, about the Messiah the son of David, whose steps could already be heard. In this exalted environment Alkabetz, the mystic and gifted poet, on one of his walks toward the heavenly "bride" created his immortal "Lecha Dodi," which to this day is sung in all the dispersions of Israel at the synagogue service on Friday evening. "Come, my beloved, to meet the bride, let us welcome the Sabbath." This refrain, which accompanies every verse of the song of praise, obtains a symbolic meaning in the poet. The mystical fervor experienced in meeting the queenly, celestial "bride" is harmoniously braided with profound sorrow over the destruction of the holy city and with yearning hope for the speedy advent of the redeemer, who *must* come, with whose steps the air is already filled. After the stormy verse "To greet the Sabbath let us go," the poet turns to "the sanctuary of the king, the royal city":

Arise, come forth from your ruins; too long have you dwelt in the valley of weeping. God will now have mercy on you. Shake off your dust, arise. Clothe yourself in the loveliest garments, my people. Redemption, the consolation of your soul, draws near. It will be brought by the son of Jesse, the Bethlehemite. Awake, awake from your sleep! Your dawn has come. Arise, illuminated in the glorious light! Let your song of joy resound! The glory of the Lord is revealed upon you. Come, my beloved, to meet the bride, let us welcome the Sabbath![59]

58. Moses Cordovero in his *Or Ne'erav*, 32–33.
59. Alkabetz' song of praise greatly pleased the eighteenth-century German scholar Johann Gottfried von Herder, who translated it into German. Also greatly charmed by "Lecha Dodi" was the poet Heinrich Heine, but he was mistaken in believing that the author of the poem was Jehudah Halevi.

The poet of "Lecha Dodi"[60] was greatly loved by the people. Various legends were woven around his name, and in the mystical circles his death was associated with the very legend created about the premature death of the famous author of *Keter Malchut*, Solomon Ibn Gabirol.[61]

We have noted the influence Alkabetz had on the mystical circle in Safed. His effect was particularly great on the most important theoretician of the Kabbalah who then lived in Palestine, Moses ben Jacob Cordovero, who was his close friend and brother-in-law.[62]

A disciple of Joseph Karo,[63] Cordovero was a great scholar in Talmudic literature, and already as a young man served as a rabbinic judge and head of a *yeshivah* in Safed. He was one of the four noted rabbis whom Jacob Berab considered suited for endowment with *semichah* (ordination). But Cordovero acquired fame not as a rabbi and dialectician in the sea of the Talmud but as a major theoretician of the wisdom of the Kabbalah, with which his brother-in-law Alkabetz familiarized him. Cordovero relates in the introduction to his *Pardes Rimmonim* that in his youth he wasted his time on "the vanities of the world" but then suddenly heard a voice calling to him: "Arise, awake from your sleep, strengthen anew God's ruined altar!" Then the "divine Kabbalist" Solomon Alkabetz Ha-Levi came to his aid, leading him into the gates of the hidden wisdom, and his eyes became seeing.

Shortly thereafter, Cordovero became a member of the society of mystics organized around Alkabetz, and indeed it was at the latter's suggestion that he wrote the ordinances for this society.[64] Not long afterwards Cordovero completed his major work *Pardes Rimmonim*,[65] which promptly made his name known throughout the Jewish world. In the thirty-two "gates" of his work Cordovero attempts to give a complete portrait of the doctrine of the Kabbalah insofar as it is reflected in the *Zohar* and later Kabbalist books. In order, however, properly to appreciate the significance

---

60. Besides "Lecha Dodi," Alkabetz wrote other poems and liturgical hymns. Some of them entered the Sephardic festival prayerbooks and some have remained in manuscript.
61. See *Kav Ha-Yashar*, Chapter 86.
62. Cordovero married Alkabetz' sister (see the introduction to his *Or Ne'erav*).
63. Cordovero writes in his *Pardes Rimmonim*: "My teacher, my master, the pious Rabbi Joseph Karo."
64. The ordinances, which consist of thirty-six points, were first published by Solomon Schechter in his *Studies in Judaism*, II, 292–94.
65. First published in Venice in 1586.

of this work, one must take into consideration one important point
with which scholars up to the present have reckoned very slightly.
Cordovero does not even mention his predecessor Meir Ibn Gabbai
in *Pardes Rimmonim*. But if one compares Ibn Gabbai's *Avodat
Ha-Kodesh* with *Pardes Rimmonim*, it is beyond doubt that
Cordovero made extensive use of Ibn Gabbai's work, indeed, that
he took entire pages from it almost verbatim.[66]

The central place in *Pardes Rimmonim* is occupied by the problem discussed in the fourth "gate"—"Shaar Atzmut Ve-Kelim,"
concerning the real nature of the *sefirot*—whether they are separate, independent existences (*atzmut*) or are to be considered
merely as vessels of the divine emanation. This problem, which
is intimately associated with the most difficult question posed by
the Kabbalah—how the limited and finite arise out of the infinite,
how the bodily and material come from the spiritual—was explored
not only by whole generations of Jewish mystics but also by the
neo-Platonists of the ancient world and the theologians of early
Christianity. On one side, the "powers" and "ideas" were considered merely instruments and vessels through which God created
the world. These powers and ideas, however, are also the models
and patterns according to which God created the whole variety
of the world. Thus it was not possible to come to a final conclusion
concerning the nature of the *logos*—whether it must be regarded
as merely the revealing form of divinity in its creative process,
or as an independently existing power. Cordovero attempts to
effect a compromise between these two views. As God's emanations, the *sefirot* are dynamic, creative powers which are all bound
together in a complete unity in God. But the *sefirot* are also the
soul, the dynamic power, of their outward garments, of the "vessels" which are the bearers of the name by which we designate
each *sefirah* individually. It is these "vessels" and external "garments" that reveal themselves to man's eye in finite and bodily
forms. And just as the integrity and unity of the soul can disclose
themselves to us only through the various actions and movements
of the limbs of the body, so the *sefirot*, which are the essence and
emanation of God, disclose themselves through their external garments, the "vessels," in the most varied forms.[67]

Cordovero also dwells at length, in connection with this problem, on the question of God's qualities and attributes. He formu-

66. See, for example, *Avodat Ha-Kodesh*, Part III, Chapter 26; *ibid.*, Part
I, Chapters 11–12; *Pardes Rimmonim*, Gate 20, Chapter 1; and *ibid.*,
Gate 4, Chapters 4 and 9.
67. *Pardes Rimmonim*, 18a.

lates clearly and distinctly the thought expressed in the *Zohar* about the complete identity between *thinking* and *being*, between the *ideal* and the *real*, i.e., that that which *is* and that which *must be* are identical, that there is no distinction whatever between them. As far as God is concerned, in His essence the three concepts—the thinker, thinking, and what is thought—are merged into a complete unity. God cannot be clothed with any attributes or designated by any name; only the *sefirot*, through which He discloses Himself in His deeds, have names.[68] One cannot say that God is wise; He Himself, after all, is the source of wisdom and understanding, which are His "vessels." He is the source of all lights, the soul of all souls.[69]

But Cordovero was not only a mystic; he was also a rabbinic judge and head of a *yeshivah*. This is recognizable in the fact that he frequently insists that one must devote much attention to Talmudic dialectics and codes. He also complains of the Kabbalists that "the light of dialectic has never shone on them, and hence they have come to false conclusions."[70] Before one steeps himself in the mysteries of the Kabbalah, Cordovero teaches, he must study the Gemara, become proficient in the Talmudic codes, and sharpen his mind with dialectics.[71] Only then can he devote himself successfully to the theoretical Kabbalah and not stumble through the sin of anthropomorphism.[72]

Cordovero was the first as well as the last major theoretician of the Kabbalah who arose on Palestinian soil. Even in the last years of his own relatively brief life,[73] he could see how within the mystical circle of Safed interest in purely theoretical and religious-philosophical problems became progressively weaker and the dominant place was occupied ever more by the practical Kabbalah and the questions of active morality associated with it. Typical in this respect is the literary activity of Cordovero's most faithful disciple, Elijah ben Moses de Vidas, whose work for generations was regarded as the *vademecum* of piety and proper conduct and served as the pattern for popular ethical literature. After his teach-

---

68. *Ibid.*, 12; *Or Ne'erav*, 34–35.
69. *Pardes Rimmonim*, 20.
70. *Or Ne'erav*, 16a.
71. *Ibid.*, 19–20.
72. *Ibid.*, 28.
73. Cordovero died at the age of forty-eight. Nevertheless, he left a very extensive literary legacy. A considerable part of his works, however, remained in manuscript, among them an enormous six-volume commentary on the *Zohar* entitled *Or Yakar* (see *Kore Ha-Dorot*, Venice edition, 36a)

er's death, de Vidas set himself the task of producing in systematic form a compendium of practical morality on the foundation of the *Zohar* and its interpreter, Cordovero.[74]

"Not for ignoramuses nor for those who have not even smelled the odor of wisdom," declares de Vidas in the introduction, "did I write my work, but for those who have already enjoyed the first elements of the inner wisdom, the true knowledge, the wisdom of the Kabbalah." *Reshit Hochmah* (The Beginning of Wisdom)—this is the name of de Vidas' extensive composition. "I have called my work *Reshit Hochmah*," the author explains, "because it is written in the Bible, 'The beginning of wisdom is the fear of the Lord.'" Indeed, this theme—the fear of the Lord, the fear of sin, the fear of Heaven—is the fundamental motif of the ascetically severe book of moral instruction. The work begins with "Shaar Ha-Yirah" (The Gate of Fear),[75] "for fear is the chief thing." Even in the Torah, the author insists, the fear of the Lord is mentioned before "And thou shalt love the lord."[76] "Man must, above all, have fear, so that he not come to any sin,"[77] de Vidas frequently repeats. Man must remember that at every step whole armies of destroying angels, who wish to ensnare him and lead him away from the right path, lie in wait for him. In order to frighten the reader and "awaken in his heart the fear of sin," the author describes in great detail the tremendous punishments of *hibbut ha-kever* (torment of the grave).[78] To magnify the reader's terror, the author relates the following story:

To me, who write this work, there came in the month of Elul 1570 in a dream at night the soul of a friend who had died three months earlier. I asked the soul what was going on in the other world, and she told me everything about *hibbut ha-kever* and lamented that there, in the other world, sins that have been committed are punished much more severely then we men think.[79]

Only after the discussion of *hibbut ha-kever* comes "Masechet Gehinnom" (The Treatise on Hell), in which de Vidas gathers out of the ancient literature all its information about the fearful seven departments of hell and describes at length all the tortures and

74. De Vidas completed his work on the eighteenth of Adar in 1575. It was first published in Venice in 1578.
75. The work consists of five "Gates": Fear, Love, Repentance, Holiness, and Humility.
76. *Reshit Hochmah*, 6b (we quote according to the first edition).
77. *Ibid.*, 24.
78. *Ibid.*, 45.
79. *Ibid.*, 46.

punishments which sinners there have to suffer.[80] Man must therefore repent betimes and regret each sin he has committed. Repentance, however, consists not only in confessing one's sin before the entire community; one must also take upon himself a strict penance and afflict the sinful body. *Reshit Hochmah* lists quite specifically the penance for each individual sin and violation. If one has sinned with a married woman, he must as punishment sit for a whole winter naked in the snow or on ice every day for an hour, and afterward for an entire summer sit naked among the ants or bees for a full hour every day. Throughout all this time he must also sleep on the bare ground without a pillow. For a false oath one must for a certain time confess each day before the entire community and allow himself to be flogged frequently. For a false denunciation (slandering one's fellow) one must for two years observe fast days, allow himself to be lashed, and throughout his entire life beg forgiveness from those whom he has slandered. Etc., etc.[81]

In order that a man not come into temptation and fall into the net of sin, he must remove himself from earthly pleasures, from the sinful world which is, after all, "like a passing shadow." "Let a man remember that to laugh and mock is a sin." "The pleasures of this world," the author of *Reshit Hochmah* further warns, "derive from the *kelipot* [the "shells" of Kabbalist doctrine]."[82] "Where you have pleasure and enjoyment, there is the accusing Satan."[83] "The desire for eating brings to sin."[84] "Fasts weaken the material body but strengthen the soul."[85] One must avoid idle words, and one of the loveliest qualities is silence. "Once," de Vidas relates,

a righteous man who had died not long before came in a dream to my teacher [Cordovero]. This man shone like the sun in summer and every hair of his head was illuminated like a candle. My teacher asked him for what good deeds he had merited this great favor. The righteous man answered: "This is for the quality of silence; I never violated the precept forbidding idle words."[86]

It would be erroneous, however, to conclude from this that Elijah de Vidas was veiled in melancholy and that for him the

---

80. *Ibid.*, 47–54.
81. *Ibid.*, 185–86.
82. *Ibid.*, 200.
83. *Ibid.*, 281.
84. *Ibid.*
85. *Ibid.*, 167, 168, 171.
86. *Ibid.*, 102.

world was a vale of sorrow and the life-path of man a source of sadness and tears. "Three things," we read in *Reshit Hochmah*, "a man must possess in order to be truly pious and to love his Creator with his whole heart: faith, trust, and joy."[87] "The *Shechinah* only rests where true joy reigns."[88] "The spirit of prophecy can be awakened not through sadness or despondency but through joy."[89] "The Torah can be obtained only through the source of joy."[90] God also may be served only through joy, as is written in the Bible, "Serve the Lord with gladness." The author of *Reshit Hochmah* is very ill-disposed to the love songs "that women sing," because they cause "the separation of the soul from the source of life." But words of praise and glorification in remembrance of God's gracious acts may be sung at weddings and banquets with joyous melodies,[91] for such songs elevate and bring one close to God.

Elijah de Vidas is not concerned with removal from life but with hallowing life, exalting the profane and weekday to the "completely Sabbath." Man's life in the world is, in view of the Kabbalist of Safed, not petty and vain. On the contrary, immensely important is the role of man in the cosmos, for his soul is, after all, a part of God in heaven.[92] It wanders about here below, but its root is the Throne of Glory, the divine light.[93] Through every false step, every sin which man commits, he therefore brings evil not only on himself and his soul but on all the worlds. The human soul is the golden thread uniting all the worlds into one harmonious whole, imbuing them with the divine spirit.[94] The sin of one who sunders this bond, who does not endeavor to spin this golden thread further, is therefore vast. We are intimately associated with God, for "our soul is a part of Him," and when a man hallows himself he hallows his soul and thereby also hallows the heavenly root from which it derives.[95]

The surest way of hallowing the soul, of hallowing life, Elijah de Vidas is firmly persuaded, is the way of observing the commandments. He perceives in every commandment a divine mystery, a marvelous revelation of the divine radiance. And because the priest

87. *Ibid.*, 142.
88. *Ibid.*, 131.
89. *Ibid.*, 146.
90. *Ibid.*, 284.
91. *Ibid.*, 127.
92. *Ibid.*, 77.
93. *Ibid.*, 79, 80.
94. *Ibid.*, 83.
95. *Ibid.*, 190.

and faithful guardian of the divine commandments is Israel, this people bears the fate of all the worlds. God sanctified Israel, and indeed only through this people is His holiness disclosed. "Thus God said to his people Israel: 'Israel, in whom I will be glorified! You sanctify yourselves in Me and I sanctify Myself in you.' "[96] Indeed, because of this, de Vidas insists, God the Creator of all the worlds is called *Elohei Yisrael*, the God of Israel, for His glory is revealed through Israel, and if Israel did not exist the world also would not exist, and God's glory and greatness would not be revealed to His creatures.[97] Therefore, he insists, we must take care to be fit to fulfill what the Creator demands of us—to be the pure vessel of divine holiness, to be worthy of bearing the radiance of the *Shechinah*. We must remove ourselves from everything that can diminish holiness, we must avoid the corporeal and petty weekday. The loveliest symbol of holiness in life is, in the eyes of the author of *Reshit Hochmah*, the Sabbath day, the divine "bride" whom the mystics of Safed would welcome every Friday with enthusiastic songs. "The Sabbath," de Vidas exclaims fervently, "is the revelation of absolute holiness. The holiness of the Sabbath is the wondrous light, the emblem of divine harmony which is incorporated in the attribute of beauty and which discloses itself through the holiness of the Sabbath in all the worlds."[98] The Sabbath is the symbol of the pure and hallowed life, the pattern of everything beautiful and exalted; and every man should strive that the radiance of the Sabbath illumine all the days of his life, in order that the gray week days be elevated to what is completely Sabbath, to be merged into one endless holy Sabbath day.[99] "One must waste as little time as possible on weekday concerns about a livelihood and the petty needs of life." In this connection de Vidas makes a characteristic and, from the cultural-social point of view, very interesting remark: "How good it is that at the present time the disciples of the wise need not worry about a livelihood, for the rich men of the generation support them. . . . These scholars who need not engage in any work ought certainly to hallow their speech on weekdays, just as on the Sabbath day."[100]

Finally it is worth pausing on one other characteristic feature of *Reshit Hochmah*. We have noted in the earlier parts of our work how among the Kabbalists, as among the mystics and ro-

96. *Ibid.*, 189.
97. *Ibid.*
98. *Ibid.*, "Shaar Ha-Kedushah" (The Gate of Holiness), 191.
99. *Ibid.*, 194–95.
100. *Ibid.*, 197–98.

mantics of other nations, mystical religious experiences often obtain
a definite erotic coloration. This is discernible also in Elijah de
Vidas. He is not content with repeating the simile of the *Sefer
Hasidim* to the effect that the love of God must disclose itself
with the same ardor and passion as the desire of a youth for his
beloved.[101] He also considers the sexual act between man and
woman a holy mystery. He speaks not only of the "mystery of
union" but also of the "holiness of union," which he considers
the highest sacred prayer and song of praise to the Creator.[102] The
Torah relates how woman was created out of man's rib. Thus the
two separated bodies constantly yearn for the disrupted harmony.
The Torah further relates that in the beginning men were created
harmoniously whole, bi-sexual: "Male and female He created
them" (Genesis 5:2). So the divided souls always strive toward
their former harmony, and this is attained in *kedushat ha-zivvug*
(the holiness of union), when the body strives to attain its supreme
perfection and the two souls yearn to disclose their harmony and
unity in bodily completeness. "When a man unites with his wife
in holiness, the *Shechinah* rests between them." This is the supreme
mystery—when the two sexes come together in their passionate
drive to attain the highest perfection, to draw near their Creator.[103]
"Three things," *Reshit Hochmah* asserts, "provide us with some
notion of the pleasure we shall be privileged to enjoy in the next
world: the hot and radiant sun, the sacred Torah, and the union
between man and wife."[104] "He only can attain the state of *devekut*
[cleaving to God] who lives with a woman."[105] "He who has had
no desire for a woman is like an ass."[106]

Reshit Hochmah was, as we have already noted, intended for
those familiar with the foundations of the "inward wisdom," the
wisdom of the Kabbalah. For them it wished to point out the way
to hallow life and to light up the weekday and profane with the
marvelous radiance of the "heavenly bride," the Sabbath queen.
But those who had already fathomed the hidden depths of the
"true wisdom" refused to be content with this. They determined,
with the aid of the marvelous and limitless power with which this
wisdom endowed them, to bring the "end" near. Let the earthly,
weekday world cease! Let the world of twilight, with its constant

101. *Ibid.*, 98.
102. "The holiness of sexual union . . . is like the unification that a man
makes in the Shemoneh Esreh prayer."
103. *Ibid.*, 302.
104. *Ibid.*, 103.
105. *Ibid.*, 135.
106. *Ibid.*, 93.

struggle between life and darkness, between good and evil, come to an end! And let the new, long hoped-for world of divine glory and heavenly beauty appear! Indeed, at the very time that Elijah de Vidas wrote his *Reshit Hochmah*, the star of the creator of the practical Kabbalah, the "holy Ari," Rabbi Isaac Luria Ashkenazi, flared up incandescently.

CHAPTER FOUR

Isaac Luria and His Disciples

RIGINATOR of the practical Kabbalah, Isaac Luria, who is known by the acronym Ari (*Elohi Rabbi Yitzḥak*, "the godly Rabbi Isaac"), was born in Jerusalem in 1534 into a prominent Ashkenazic family.[1] Orphaned at a very early age, young Isaac went to Egypt where he was raised and educated at the home of his wealthy uncle, Mordecai Francis, a tax farmer of Cairo, who married him to his daughter when he was fifteen. The youth carried on Talmudic studies under the supervision of the famous Rabbi David Ibn Abi Zimra (Radbaz) and Bezalel Ashkenazi, who also inducted him into the mysteries of the Kabbalah. The "esoteric wisdom" literally intoxicated the sensitive, dreaming soul of the young Luria. The profoundest impression was made upon him by the recently published *Zohar*. He began to lead an ascetic life, secluded himself, and later settled on the banks of the Nile in a tent in which he spent two whole years and from which he would return home on the Sabbath only. Even then he would speak merely a few words, and these in Hebrew alone.

There, on the banks of the mysterious Nile, under the shadow of the sphinxes and pyramids, the ardent mystic wished to unveil the profound enigma of the world, to reveal the mystery of life. His dreaming soul, aroused by the imaginative images and symbols of the *Zohar*, saw an enchanted, mysterious world all around itself.

1. For this reason Luria is also called Ashkenazi, and many understand *Ari* as Ashkenazi Rabbi Isaac.

In every sound and movement, in the rise of a wave, in the tremble of a leaf, in the quiet whispering of reeds on a riverbank, in the speechless stones—everywhere Isaac Luria perceived the mighty breath of immortal life, everywhere experienced living souls languishing under the heavy burden of "sin" and pleading for *tikkun* (improvement), begging to be freed from the narrow prison, to be redeemed from the fearful magic, from the choking bonds in which lifeless and formless material held them captive.[2] To liberate the captured spirit from rigid, motionless matter—this idea, which was the glorious, effervescent credo of the ancient Greek sculptors, the ardent sentiment of the Renaissance artists, and the dynamic power of the tragic and wrathful drive in the stupendous works of Michaelangelo—also evoked the fervent ecstasy that flared in the romantic soul of the Jewish mystic, living near the silent, frozen sphinxes and the colossal pyramids.

Matter as a wicked enchanter, as a symbol of evil and sin which hold the living spirit striving toward the heights in captivity—this central idea dominated all of Luria's spiritual being. In the rushing of the waves of the Nile his ear perceived a sorrowful epic telling how an enormous number of worlds perish in the nets of evil. Our world is also in deadly peril, for on all sides it is assailed by the magical powers of sin and evil. The dangerous circle of magic must be broken, the captive spirit freed from the material *kelipot* (shells) which enclose it on all sides. And he, the solitary ascetic on the banks of the Nile, must accomplish this; he must be the redeemer.

The years spent in solitude, apart from men, and the constant fasting and mortification of the flesh—these brought the youthful mystic to complete transcendence of corporeality, to feverish hallucinations. In moments of ecstasy visions were revealed to him. Voices from the distant heavens were carried to his ears, and with open, wakeful eyes he saw marvelous dreams. Elijah the prophet would frequently come to visit him and disclose deep and terrible secrets. The godly Tanna, Rabbi Simeon ben Yoḥai, the author of the *Zohar*, also carried on long conversations with him. He would assure him that in the hours of sleep his soul rose to the heavens and there conversed with the prophets and righteous men of former generations.

2. See *Taalumot Ḥochmah*, 34, 44; *Sefer Ha-Gilgulim*, 39–40; *Ḥemdat Yamim* (1731 edition), 6a: "And once the master, may his memory be for blessing, went to teach Torah on the meadow and he lifted up his eyes and saw all the trees of the meadow filled with innumerable souls. So it was on the field and on the waters; there were tens of thousands of them."

At last Isaac Luria decided that the time had come for him to return to his birthplace, to the land of his fathers. In 1569 he set out for Palestine, spent some time in his native city of Jerusalem, and then settled in Safed, where he soon became a member of the local mystical circle. At first he studied the theoretical Kabbalah with Moses Cordovero, and with great humility called the author of *Pardes Rimmonim* nothing other than "our master and our teacher."[3] Soon, however, his mystical fervor and his own way in the Kabbalah brought it about that many in the mystical circles became his ardent followers and acknowledged him as their teacher and guide. The number of Luria's followers grew very quickly. His circle, which soon developed into a religious congregation in which the manner of life and all details of conduct were defined according to the order and ordinances of the master and his mystical system, became ever larger.[4] On the Sabbath Isaac Luria would wrap himself in four white garments, intended to symbolize the four letters of the Ineffable Name of God. There, in the castaway little town of Galilee, images of ancient times were revived. Surrounded by his beloved disciples,[5] Luria would wander over the environs of Safed, across isolated meadows and cemeteries, revealing the profound mysteries of the world and proclaiming tidings of great events soon to come. His disciples were certain that their teacher was none other than the Messiah the son of Joseph, the harbinger and messenger of the redeemer, the Messiah the son of David. They would visit the graves of prophets and saints,[6] and with trembling hearts perceive how their teacher and miracle-worker carried on conversations with the inhabitants of the holy graves. On certain days they would make pilgrimages to the nearby village of Meron and there, at the grave of the "godly" Rabbi Simeon ben Yoḥai, mystical ceremonies full of fervor and spirituality were conducted. They would sing songs permeated with ardent enchantment and tell of the approaching "end"; soon now the great miracle will occur. One must prepare to welcome the redeemer. They were already standing at the boundary. They were, after all, the "last" ones, the "final generation."

Every Friday before sunset Luria and his disciples would leave the city clothed in white garments and in the open fields welcome the "queen Sabbath," singing Alkabetz' "Lecha Dodi," of which

---

3. See *Etz Ḥayyim*, p. 20 (Warsaw edition, 1890).
4. *Taalumot Hochmah*, 46a.
5. The legend tells of ten such pupils or disciples. See *Taalumot Hochmah*, 43. *Sefer Ha-Gilgulim*, 32–33, tells of two degrees of Isaac Luria's disciples.
6. *Taalumot Hochmah*, 38; *Shivḥei Vital*, 34–35.

Luria himself testified that it is the best and loveliest of all religious hymns. "Once," relates a legend,

when the disciples on the eve of the Sabbath were singing the stanzas of "Lecha Dodi," the holy Rabbi Isaac suddenly posed a question: "Do you wish, my friends, to go at once to Jerusalem and there welcome the Sabbath?" The disciples looked with astonishment at their master, for the distance from Safed to Jerusalem is a long one and it was already close to sunset. Nevertheless, some of the disciples immediately replied that they were willing. Others, however, declared that they must first inform their wives that they were setting out on the way. Then Rabbi Isaac Luria clapped his hands and cried out, "Woe to us who have not the merit! If all of you had joyfully agreed to my proposal, an immediate end would have come to the exile and the Messiah would have appeared in Jerusalem!"

Rabbi Isaac's disciple, Ḥayyim Vital, relates:

Once we stood with the rabbi near the grave of Shemaiah and Avtalyon. The rabbi said to us, "My children, Shemaiah and Avtalyon command me to request that you pray for the Messiah the son of Joseph, that he may not die." But we did not understand and did not dare ask who the Messiah the son of Joseph really is. But the Messiah the son of Joseph was our rabbi himself. A few days later he died.[7]

Isaac Luria perished of the Black Death on the fifth day of Av, 1572, at the age of thirty-eight.[8] The sudden death of the master made a tremendous impression on his disciples and admirers. The deceased was referred to as a new Biblical Enoch who "walked with God" and of whom the Bible declares "and he was not, for God took him." This new Enoch was also taken by God, for if he had lived three years longer in Palestine, the Messiah would have *had* to come. But the generation was still not fit for this.[9]

Luria left behind no literary legacy aside from three Sabbath hymns[10] (a hymn for each meal of the day) and a few heartfelt prayers which Nathan Hannover published in his *Shaarei Tziyyon*.[11] He was accustomed to transmit his teaching orally,

7. *Taalumot Hochmah*, 38, 47.
8. See *Shivḥei Vital*, 24, 35.
9. *Taalumot Hochmah*, 44b.
10. These hymns, "Azamer Be-Shevaḥin," "Asader Le-Seudata On," and "Benei Heichla Dechesifin," were first published with a large commentary in *Ḥemdat Yamim*, II, 68–72, 124–25, and 146–47.
11. Also published in Hannover's *Shaarei Tziyyon* is a Kabbalist prayer of Isaac Luria entitled "Ve-Attah Adonai Magen Baadi."

walking with his disciples over meadows and fields outside the city.[12] One of Luria's favorite disciples, Ḥayyim Vital, became the interpreter and emissary of his system of Kabbalah. Vital energetically collected[13] all the notebooks and notes to be found among Luria's surviving disciples and, on the basis of these and of his own notes and recollections, wrote a whole series of works in which he reports Luria's Kabbalist system in great detail. But there is no doubt—and investigators must take account of this—that the disciple and interpreter placed many of his own ideas into the mouth of his master.

Vital, whose name is so closely associated with Luria's Kabbalah, was born in Safed in 1543 into the family of a scribe who came to Palestine from the Italian province of Calabria. The young Vital studied the Gemara and rabbinic codes with the celebrated Rabbi Alshech. The arid *halachah*, however, gave little pleasure to the future Kabbalist. At the age of fourteen Vital became acquainted with the Kabbalist and wonder-worker Lapidot Ashkenazi, and the young man devoted himself with great enthusiasm to the "secret wisdom." Vital had too little Talmudic knowledge to become a rabbi or rabbinic judge, and in order to support his family sought his fortune in alchemy, hoping that he would become rich all at once. Achieving no success in this field, he turned again to his "hidden wisdom," steeped himself in the *Zohar*, and began to write a large commentary on it. Marvelous dreams began to appear to the young mystic. Once Elijah the prophet came to him in a dream and led him into an amazing garden in which he saw many righteous men of various ages, all of them flying around in the form of birds. They were enjoying all kinds of sweet things and

12. *Taalumot Hochmah*, 38: "And he disclosed most of his secrets to them in the fields and deserts, and he had no need of any book."

13. More correctly, *took*. As the oldest and most distinguished disciple he declared that he was obliged to gather everything that was written of Luria's Torah, for the present generation was not fit for the fearful mysteries hidden in it. The Kabbalist Solomon Shlumal, whom we have frequently quoted, tells of this (*Taalumot Hochmah*, 46): "After the death of Rabbi Isaac Luria, may his memory be a blessing, Rabbi Ḥayyim took all the notebooks from the hands of all the colleagues and did not leave anything of this wisdom; and he did not return them to them, saying that it was no longer given to reveal the great light in this world, for those wells of wisdom were stopped up." Ḥayyim Vital himself puts forth another reason, namely, that none of Luria's disciples aside from himself properly understood the master's profound teaching. See *Etz Ḥayyim*, 8, 11: "And do not look at the notebooks that were written in the name of my teacher, may his memory be for blessing, except what we have written for you in this book."

diligently studying the laws of the Mishnah. Further on, in the center of the garden, Vital saw the Holy One Himself in the form of a mighty old man, and around Him, reclining on the richest couches, were the righteous, the sages of the Kabbalah, listening to the sacred and mysterious wisdom from the mouth of God Himself.[14]

The turning point in Vital's life was his meeting with Isaac Luria in 1570. The first encounter of the two mystics has been embroidered with many marvelous legends. One of these relates that Luria, while still living in Egypt, had a prophetic "revelation" in which he was informed that he would soon have to leave this world and must therefore set out at once for Palestine where he would meet a disciple by the name of Ḥayyim, who alone would be worthy of having the mysteries of his doctrine disclosed to him, and appoint him his successor.[15] Another legend relates that the first meeting of the two mystics occurred on the banks of the Sea of Galilee. Both of them were sailing on a little boat, and when it came to an old walled synagogue whose windows looked out to the sea, Luria gave Vital some water to drink out of Miriam's well, which is located near the river of Tiberias, and along with this revealed to him many mysteries of the Kabbalah.[16]

From that moment on the fate of these two mystics was constantly and inextricably intertwined. Isaac Luria owes the tremendous success of his system entirely to Vital, but it was Vital who contributed most to the fact that the "practical" Kabbalah took on such fearful, obscure forms and had such a negative influence on the subsequent development of Jewish culture. These two mystics, who were so close to each other in their moods and attitudes, were extremely different in their character and moral nature. Isaac Luria was a man "not of this world," a dreaming, imaginative person who always aspired to the heavens but in whom the loveliest and noblest idealism was mingled, as in Cervantes' hero, with madness and fantastic hallucinations. Ḥayyim Vital, however, was the complete antithesis of Don Quixote; he was the Sancho Panza of mysticism. A genuine mystic in his world outlook, Vital nevertheless managed to introduce into the imaginative mystical world much of the earthly and banal, as well as the empty and bombastic. Obviously, he was not an outright charlatan and fraud, as the fanatical David Kahana with his *maskil*-like rantings portrays

14. See *Shivḥei Ḥayyim Vital*, 28 (we quote according to the Lemberg edition, 1882).
15. *Taalumot Ḥochmah*, 43, 45.
16. See the introduction to *Nagid U-Metzavveh*.

him.[17] But there is no doubt that this unsuccessful seeker of fortune in alchemy was a terribly boastful man who was not ashamed to make use of screaming advertisements. To be sure, he lauds his master to the skies, relates feelingly that Rabbi Isaac Luria was a saint, a man of God, who could perform the greatest miracles. But, along with this, he exploits his master's greatness and holiness to make a name for himself. He is not content with stressing a number of times that Isaac Luria's mission consisted in revealing his secrets to his chief disciple, Ḥayyim Vital;[18] he also explicitly asserts that he is far greater than his teacher.[19] He did not have the patience to wait for his disciples and admirers to recount his praises and embroider his life with legends and miracle stories.[20] He himself wrote with his own hand the *Shivḥei Vital* (Praises of Vital), in which it is extremely difficult to distinguish the fantastic dreams of the exalted mystic from the outright deceptions of the ordinary swindler. Vital's extraordinary "autobiography" has, in fact, no analogue. It is difficult to read without a feeling of disgust Vital's exaggerations—how three years before his birth a holy man prophesied to his father that a son would be born to him who would have no peer, that the child would be not lesser than the Messiah the son of Joseph, and that "he would undoubtedly rule over all Israel."[21] Vital recounts further that a woman "who had never in her life told a lie" saw with her own eyes how over his head a fiery pillar shone with marvelous radiance,[22] and that some night watchman saw how he, Vital, flew in the air.[23] He does not tire of reminding the reader what a holy soul he possesses[24] and of asserting that with his prayers he can annul the worst decrees and that the redemption of Israel is dependent entirely upon him. With all his "holiness" and moral purity, of which

17. See his *Even Negef.*
18. *Shivḥei Vital,* 48: "For he came into the world only to teach me." See also *ibid.,* 36, and *Sefer Ha-Gilgulim,* Chapter 32.
19. *Shivḥei Vital,* 45: "You do not know how important you are before the Holy One, blessed be He, for you are a great man before Him; you are as great a man as Rabbi Akiba and his colleagues, and you will understand what no man of this generation understood, even Rabbi Yitzhak Ashkenazi your teacher."
20. Actually this happened after his death. See, for instance, *Nagid U-Metzavveh,* Introduction.
21. *Shivḥei Vital,* 4.
22. *Ibid.,* 5, 21.
23. *Ibid.,* 5.
24. *Ibid.,* 4. Vital's autobiography also has a certain ethnographic interest, for many details of the contemporary way of life are incidentally given in it.

he constantly speaks, Ḥayyim Vital nevertheless finds it necessary to settle accounts in his autobiography with his personal opponents, whom he declares wretches and utterly wicked men, and he promises that the city of Damascus, where he spent some time and enjoyed very little success with his preachments, will have an end similar to that of sinful Sodom.[25]

The exalted mystic Rabbi Isaac Luria believed with perfect faith that, aided by incantations and combinations of letters, he could perform miracles, that holy souls of former and very ancient times came to visit him and carry on conversations with him. He was certain that he could read the faces of men like an open book, and that at the first glance he could determine the "spark" of every man and recognize from the soul of what person of past generations this "spark" derived. Under the crude hands of Luria's disciple, however, his doctrine obtains the gross and clumsy forms of primitive magic, with barbaric incantations and formulas about demons and destroyers. Luria's noble drive toward spirituality and an ascetic, hallowed life, undertaken to merit becoming the pure and chosen sacrifice fit to redeem the world steeped in "sin," is drowned by Vital in a sea of thousands of practical regulations and monotonous details. In addition to all this, Vital had, from the literary point of view, an enormous lack of talent which made him absolutely incapable of rendering his thoughts in writing in anything like systematic and comprehensive form. His thick, heavy volumes are a veritable chaos, in which everything is mixed up in a confused lump.[26] Vital's vast *Etz Ḥayyim* is a tortuous, obscure labyrinth in which one stumbles at every step against hard stones. Terrible, dark shades lurk in all corners in this pitch blackness, which is rarely illuminated by a spark of true inspiration or by the lightning of creative sentiment and mystical fervor. One must have great fortitude and patience to plow through all fifty "gates" of *Etz Ḥayyim* to obtain a general notion of the plan or, more correctly, the planlessness of Vital's assemblage of "halls."[27]

As far as one may conjecture from Vital's unsystematic work, Luria bases himself in the theoretical part of his system on the fundamental principles of the *Zohar* and its interpreters, but along with this greatly alters several extremely important elements.

25. *Ibid.*, 16.
26. This is acknowledged also by the editor and publisher of Vital's work, the Kabbalist Meir Papirush, in his introduction to *Etz Ḥayyim* where he remarks: "And I studied his works and saw a great number of holy books to which there is no order, no beginning and no end."
27. *Etz Ḥayyim* is divided into seven "halls" or "palaces."

Luria's own contribution is particularly noticeable in his description of how the *sefirot* were created, especially in his doctrine of the so called *partzofin* or "faces." Before God radiated the *sefirot* out of Himself, Luria teaches, the light of the *Ein Sof* (Infinite) filled all the endless spaces, and nothing existed beside this light.[28] When the *Ein Sof* decided to create worlds in order that His names and deeds might be revealed, He contracted (*tzimtzem*) His infinite light in the center. At the midpoint a vacuum or empty space was formed, and in this space God "radiated, created, completed, and brought forth all the worlds." There, into the empty space, flowed, "in the form of a thin channel" (*tzinor dak*), the bright ray of the *Ein Sof*. The divine ray did not penetrate the lightless, empty space in the form of a straight line but in the form of rings or circles. In this fashion ten rings or circles were radiated out of the *Ein Sof*. These are the ten *sefirot* which, with Isaac Luria as with Moses Cordovero, bear a double character: inwardly, the divine light, the soul of the *sefirah*, and from the outside, the garment, the "vessel."[29] But the light of the *Ein Sof* was so tremendous even in the form of a very thin *tzinor* or channel that only the "vessels" of the first three *sefirot*, i.e., of the upper three circles which are located nearer the divine source and whose nature is therefore of a higher order, were able to endure its dazzling power. The vessels of the other seven *sefirot*, which are in the middle of the space, however, could not endure the mighty influx of the divine light. They cracked; the light which flowed in them returned to its source, and in the "broken vessels" only sparks of the holy light (*nitzotzei ha-kedushah*)[30] remained. A special barrier to separate them from the blinding, divine source of light had to be created in order that "the worlds be able to endure." Thus the *sefirot* were transformed into *partzofin*, the forms of faces. The first *sefirah* known as *Keter* (Crown) was transformed into the three-headed *Arich Anpin* (Long Face). The second, *Hochmah* (Wisdom) became the primordial source of the active and masculine and is therefore called *Abba* (Father). The third *sefirah*, called *Binah* (Understanding), is the foundation of the passive and feminine and bears the name *Imma* (Mother). The next six *sefirot*, whose "vessels" were broken, are merged into one form, the *Ze'er Anpin* (Small Face). This is the son, the child, of the

28. *Etz Hayyim*, 22: "Know that, before the emanations were emanated and the creatures were created, the supernal light filled all existence and there was no place void of it" (we quote according to the Warsaw edition of 1891).
29. *Etz Hayyim*, 22, 24, 25.
30. *Ibid.*, "Shaar Shevirat Ha-Kelim," 79–83.

previous two *partzofin* or faces, the "Father" and the "Mother." The last *sefirah* obtained the form of a young woman—*Bat* (Daughter).[31]

Precisely this order of "the work of creation"—through the "broken vessels" to the rise of the *partzofin*—was absolutely essential, Luria insists, for the existence of the world. The Jewish mystics exercised themselves greatly over the difficult problem of the *Sitra Aḥara* (the Other or Left Side), the source of evil in God's world. We have seen how as early as the thirteenth century the mystic Isaac Kohen occupied himself with this question in his *Maamar Al Ha-Atzilut Ha-Semolit*[32] and, concluding that the kingdom of wickedness also derives from the good source, confessed that he did not understand this profound, hidden mystery and gave the reader the pious advice: "Be silent and do not entertain impure thoughts. What is too wonderful for you do not investigate, and what is hidden from you do not search out." Moses Cordovero[33] also sought, but without success, to resolve this contradiction—the existence of evil in God's creation, which is entirely good. Indeed, for this reason Rabbi Isaac Luria indicates that if the *Ein Sof* had at the beginning immediately created the *partzofin*, instead of the *sefirot* and the "vessels," no evil could have existed in the world, for the divine light is completely good; the source of evil is the "broken vessel," from whose shell or husk (*kelipah*) the light has removed itself. Without evil, if good alone reigned in the world, reward and punishment could not exist, for man would have no choice of doing good through his own free will and removing himself from evil.[34] Through his good deeds the "holy sparks" that remained in the *kelipot* or "shells" obtain "improvement." Sinful men, however, cause the divine light to sink into the material *kelipot* through their wicked deeds.

The major part of Luria's Kabbalah, however, is the practical. This rests on the foundation of a very unique psychological system that is intimately associated with his doctrine concerning transmigration of the soul. At the center of Luria's system is the human soul, which is the connecting link between the finite and the infinite. As a reflection of the five *partzofin*, man's soul consists of

31. *Ibid.*, "Shaar Ha-Partzofin." The Kabbalist Abraham Herrera lists in his *Shaar Ha-Shamayim* (Part II, Chapter 12) not five but six *partzofim*. Above the Long-Faced One (*Arich Anpin*) is the Holy Ancient One (*Atika Kadisha*) who is, however, merged with the *Arich Anpin* in one form (*ibid.*, Part III, Chapter 9; Part VIII, Chapter 8).
32. Our work Volume III, p. 16.
33. *Pardes Rimmonim*, 161–62 (Koretz edition).
34. *Etz Ḥayyim*, 10.

five "roots": *nefesh, ruaḥ, neshamah, ḥayah,* and *yeḥidah.*[35] The first of these, *nefesh,* is of the lowest level, the last, *yeḥidah,* of the highest. All human souls derive from one root, from the primal man, Adam. Every limb and organ of Adam's body is a source of millions upon millions of human souls ("sparks" or *nitzotzin,* as they are called by Luria). The organs of man, however, are of various values and levels; hence the souls are also of different values. Some are "sparks" of the thinking mind, others of the seeing eye, still others of dumb hands or feet, etc.[36]

Here Luria's basic idea concerning Adam's "sin," which is regarded as pressing like a heavy burden upon man throughout all generations, appears with special clarity.[37] Through the "sin" which Adam committed, all worlds were corrupted and degraded. Good and evil, the souls of exalted levels and those of low levels, were mingled. Even the purest soul was stained through admixture with evil, sullied through contact with the *kelipah* or shell, which is the source of evil.[38] And the higher and more valuable the soul, the more the *kelipah* endeavored to stain it and immerse it in the depths of sin.[39] According to Ḥayyim Vital's report, Luria even repeated quite frequently the idea that the soul of Cain was of a higher level than that of his brother Abel; and just because Cain's soul was of a very exalted category, it had to endure far greater trials, for the *kelipot* were especially desirous of leading it astray and bringing it under their domination.[40] To regain the former harmony, to restore the *olam ha-tikkun* (the righted or ordered world) is possible only when an end is made to the chaos, to the constant struggle between good and evil, when the dominion of the *kelipot* is overcome, when all the scattered sparks of holiness are gathered together and raised to their source. Then, when the confusion and mixture of both elements, good and evil—the con-

35. *Etz Ḥayyim,* I, 49, 51–58; II, 52; *Sefer Ha-Gilgulim,* pp. 14, 18 (we cite according to the Zolkiev edition of 1744).
36. *Sefer Ha-Gilgulim,* pp. 3, 4. Isaac Luria also distinguishes between "old" and "new" souls. "New" souls are those that have not yet wandered on earth and do not derive from Adam and are therefore of a higher level than the "old." The role of these "new" souls in Isaac Luria's Kabbalah is, however, not altogether clear (see *Sefer Ha-Gilgulim,* Chapter 7).
37. *Ibid.,* pp. 14, 15.
38. *Ibid.,* Chapter 1: "At the beginning of the creation of Adam all the good souls were included in him and dependent on him, but after he sinned he mixed the good with the evil. Then the good and the evil were mingled."
39. *Ibid.,* p. 3: "The greater in value a soul may be, the more they wish to make it sin and bring it into the depths of the shells [*kelipot*]."
40. *Ibid.,* pp. 19, 21, 27, and 37 ff.

fusion which causes the temptation of sin—will come to an end in the world, when the shell of evil will be separated from the kernel of good, then the redeemer will come and the *Shechinah* will be freed from exile.[41]

The way of *haalat nitzotzin* (raising the sparks), of redeeming the world, is carried on, in Luria's view, through transmigration of the soul (*gilgul ha-nefesh*), through long wanderings of human spirits over the sinful world. Every soul enters the world with the definite task of gathering the scattered "sparks of light," separating and liberating the good from the evil, and until it has completely fulfilled its mission it cannot return to its source; it must always wander, be transformed not only into men and beasts but also into trees and stones and flowing brooks. In this connection Luria even gives a whole roster of *gilgulim*, in which the transmigrations the soul must endure for each individual sin are systematically listed. For denunciation and slander, for example, the soul is transformed into a barking dog; for sexual intercourse with a married woman, into a donkey; for gossip, into a stormy little brook; etc.[42]

The doctrine of *gilgul ha-nefesh* or transmigration of the soul, which was already long known in Jewish mysticism, was connected by Isaac Luria with his teaching concerning *sod ha-ibbur* (the secret of impregnation) and the association or union of two souls.[43] It sometimes happens, Luria teaches, that the soul has already fulfilled its mission; it is purified of sin but, through an oversight, has not fulfilled a certain commandment in its earthly life. Then it must return and unite with the soul of a living person in order to fulfill this commandment. It also sometimes happens that two separate souls are individually too weak to fulfill their mission. Providence then unites them into one body, and the one complements the other. At times, souls that are without the least defect and have already perfectly fulfilled their mission are transmigrated. These return to the terrestrial world in order to aid other souls and to give them the power and support necessary to purify themselves of their sin.[44] The perfect and purified soul impregnates another soul which requires assistance; it becomes its "mother," nourishing it and empowering it with its perfection.

41. *Ibid.*, Chapter 2 ff.
42. *Ibid.*, pp. 37, 40. This list is strikingly similar to a certain passage in Plato's *Phaedo*. It is, however, difficult to determine the transmogrifications this ancient Greek myth sustained before it was obtained by the mystics of Safed.
43. *Ibid.*, Chapters 5, 6, 7, 11, and 13.
44. *Ibid.*, p. 12: "There is a transmigration that is not needed by that soul but by the community."

On the basis of this idea Isaac Luria constructed his doctrine about the great "mission" which providence has appointed for the Jewish people. The dispersion, the fact that Israel is scattered among all the peoples, he teaches, is an immensely important factor in the liberation and redemption of the entire world. Israel fulfills its great mission in exile by the fact that, through it, all the souls of all the nations of the world, in which the holy sparks are located, obtain improvement, and through their proximity to the people of Israel these souls free themselves from the influence of the impure husk (*kelipah*) and unite with the *Shechinah*.[45]

Isaac Luria was firmly convinced that the souls of great saints of former times live again in later generations in the form of chosen individuals who are appointed by providence to do great deeds. There are also saints and righteous men who are able, through certain signs known only to themselves, to recognize at once whose soul or whose "spark" has been transmigrated into this or that righteous man, to what level this man has already attained, and with whose soul his own soul must still come together in order to attain the supreme level of perfection. When all souls have become completely pure, without the least defect, the redeemer, the Messiah the son of David, will come. But the advent of the Messiah can be hastened; this depends entirely on man's strong will and religious fervor. "If only we willed it and repented with all our hearts," asserts Isaac Luria, "we could redeem all souls from the *kelipot* and the Messiah would at once come."[46] Luria and his disciples were thoroughly persuaded that theirs was the "last generation."[47] They must therefore bring the "end" near, produce the redemption as quickly as possible. To hasten the day of the Messiah's advent, to redeem the world all the more quickly—this can be done through repentance, fervent prayer, ascetic abstinence, mortification of the flesh, and fasting.

It must, however, be noted here that Isaac Luria's asceticism and abstinence is very different from the Christian asceticism of the Middle Ages. To be sure, both Luria and Christian asceticism proceed from the view that evil, the *kelipah* or shell, dominates this sinful world. But they come to opposite conclusions. Christian asceticism renounces earthly life, refuses to recognize it and removes itself from it, because it believes that life is in the net of Samael and that man's powers are incapable of liberating it and redeeming it from sin and evil. Luria, the Jewish mystic, however, sets forth the diametrically opposite principle: not to renounce

45. *Ibid.*, p. 3.
46. *Ibid.*
47. *Ibid.*, pp. 3, 27.

the world and not to despair of it. He firmly believes that the world can be renewed, that it can be liberated from sin and evil through man's strenuous will, through his moral energy and feeling. In man's hands lies the fate of the world. Luria teaches that the world steeped in sin must be renewed through repentance and an ascetic, pure life. The "sin" of Adam gave birth to evil and transmitted great power to the *kelipot*. This power must be overcome as quickly as possible. To carry on this struggle, Luria has in his arsenal, besides mortifications of the flesh and fasting, still other weapons—incantations, magical formulas, tremendous powers of enchantment hidden in "names" and "combinations of letters."

According to the report of Ḥayyim Vital, Isaac Luria taught that a prayer or a commandment performed with a definite concentration or intention (*kavvanah*) can make a tremendous impression on the upper worlds, and that certain formulas employed at the appropriate moment can change a man's fortune and turn aside his previously determined fate. With incantations one can drive away hostile powers and exorcise *dybbukim*. For Luria the whole world is a nest of hostile spirits, and man must constantly carry on a strenuous and obdurate struggle against them. Mystical symbolism, which already played a very significant role in the early mystics, increases immensely in Luria and Vital. The whole world, man's life, his action—all are regarded as symbols and allusions under which deep mysteries are hidden. Luria and his disciples composed a very unique *Shulḥan Aruch*, in which every commandment and custom is interpreted as the external vestment of mysteries and secret symbols. All of Jewish ritual is transformed by Luria into an extraordinary mystery. Every commandment, every festival and holy day, has its own mystical significance. The Sabbath and the commandments associated with it are considered by Luria and his disciples a mystery, a mystical union between man and divinity. At the Sabbath meals, one of Luria's Sabbath songs indicates, the "Atika Kadisha" (the Ancient Holy One) Himself sits surrounded by hosts of angels.

Thus in Safed, where Joseph Karo wrote his compendium of rabbinic Judaism for later generations, the *Shulḥan Aruch*, another, mystical *Shulḥan Aruch* was created by Isaac Luria's followers. It was later published by a mystic of Safed as a supplement to Karo's compendium under the title *Shulḥan Aruch Shel Ari*.[48] In

48. Also very popular was the mystical religious code *Nagid U-Metzavveh* by the Marrano Jacob Ḥayyim Tzemaḥ, Ḥayyim Vital's ardent disciple. *Nagid U-Metzavveh*, which went through numerous editions, was responsible for the fact that many customs associated with the name of the "holy Ari" entered Jewish religious life.

this connection the following characteristic feature is discernible. Hayyim Vital endeavors to show that the mystical Torah is higher than the rabbinic Torah. He regards the author of the *Shulḥan Aruch*, Joseph Karo, with contempt and openly declares that the words of Karo's *maggid* are false and incredible.[49] From Vital also derives the legend that Joseph Karo is supposed to have begged Isaac Luria to induct him into the mysteries of the practical Kabbalah, but Luria refused because Karo's soul was suited to receive the esoteric wisdom only to the level to which Moses Cordovero had led it. Karo, however, did not cease importuning Luria, who finally agreed to fulfill his wish. But whenever Luria began to reveal the deep mysteries of the Kabbalah sleep would fall on the author of the *Shulḥan Aruch*, and Karo himself was finally persuaded that he was not fit to penetrate into the sanctuary of the "true wisdom."[50]

While the modest Isaac Luria speaks with great reverence of Moses Cordovero and calls him "our master and our teacher," Vital mentions the author of *Pardes Rimmonim* with a certain scorn and declares very arrogantly that this work is only for beginners[51] and that, in general, the works of the Kabbalists who lived after Naḥmanides are not worth taking in hand, for the true way of the Kabbalah's wisdom was hidden from them.[52] Vital speaks even more contemptuously of the rabbinic authorities who did not devote themselves to the Kabbalah. We have noted the great respect with which the Kabbalists Meir Ibn Gabbai and Moses Cordovero speak of the Talmud. The same is true of Cordovero's disciple, Elijah de Vidas.[53] Quite different is the attitude of Ḥayyim Vital, who was himself only slightly familiar with Talmudic literature. The hostile tone in regard to the Talmud noticeable in some sections of the *Zohar*, which appear to derive from the hands of Abraham Abulafia,[54] is also quite marked in Vital's introduction to his

49. *Sefer Ha-Gilgulim*, p. 42: "What the *maggid* told Rabbi Joseph Karo, may the memory of the righteous be for blessing . . . he taught him falsehood."
50. *Taalumot Hochmah*, 47.
51. See *Shivḥei Vital*, 35.
52. *Etz Ḥayyim*, 8: "And as far as all the later Kabbalist books that came after Rabbi Moses ben Naḥman, may his memory be for blessing, are concerned, do not go near them, for after Rabbi Moses ben Naḥman the way of this wisdom was hidden from the eyes of all sages; and there was left among them only a bit of the branches of ancient things, not their roots, and upon them the later Kabbalists, may their memory be for blessing, constructed their words through human reason."
53. See *Reshit Hochmah*, 5 ff.
54. See our work, III, pp. 27–39.

Etz Ḥayyim. "Man," he there explains, "was created only in order that he might study the wisdom of the Kabbalah." Further on we encounter the simile in which the Kabbalah is likened to the "mistress" and the Mishnah to the "handmaiden," and a statement to the effect that the meaning of the Mishnah, in comparison with the wisdom of the Kabbalah, is like chaff in comparison with heavy-weighted, full kernels of wheat. He who studies merely the discussion of Abbaye and Rava and is interested only in questions about what is permitted and forbidden stumbles like a blind man in the darkness. Of him it has been said, "He has made me to dwell in dark places—this means the Babylonian Talmud." The true and only source of light, Vital asserts, is the wisdom of the Kabbalah, and outside it is Egyptian darkness. He therefore divides men into three classes: (1) the ignorant multitude, (2) those who occupy themselves with the Talmud, and (3) the highest class, the sages of the Kabbalah. Vital even ventures to express the thought (to be sure, in somewhat veiled form) that he who does not study the Kabbalah is like an ass.

In the person of Ḥayyim Vital mystical Judaism manifests the tendency not only to set itself on an equal plane with rabbinic Judaism but also to replace it. This must be noted here, because we shall see, further on, the sad consequences that this tendency later called forth.

Luria's Kabbalah, which his followers and disciples (the *Gurei Ari* or "cubs of the lion," as they called themselves) propagandized so energetically, made the atmosphere in the melancholy Jewish ghetto even more oppressive. It contributed greatly to the strengthening in the consciousness of the people of ascetic moods and the tendency to regard earthly life as a "vale of weeping" in which demons and destroying spirits, with which man must carry on an obstinate and indefatigable struggle, lurk on every side. The entire milieu was filled to overflowing with fearful legends about *ḥibbut ha-kever* (the torment of the grave), about tortures in the seven departments of hell, about incantations, migrations of souls, *dybbukim*, and the pangs of the Messiah. A unique mystical-apocryphal literature, following the pattern of the previously quoted *Shivḥei Vital*, was created. Vital himself, for example, recounts, among other miracles which he performed, how a dead man came to him in a dream and begged him to have mercy on him and "improve" his sinful soul as soon as he appeared before him. "In the morning," relates Vital,

I informed the pupils of the academy about this. The same day some farmers brought a calf into the city to be slaughtered. When the wagon came into the city, the calf broke away from the farmers and ran to the house of study where I sat with my colleagues over open books. The calf leaned with its hind feet against the bench on which we were sitting and with its forefeet on the table on which the books were lying. It looked straight at me and tears flowed from its eyes. All around the table were astonished, but I explained to them, "Here my dream is fulfilled."

Further on Vital relates how he bought the calf, which was a *gilgul* or transmigration of the dead man whose sinful soul required "improvement," from its owners. The calf itself stretched out its neck under the slaughterer's knife when the ritual blessing was recited, and only Vital and those close to him tasted of its flesh "for the sake of the commandment," in order thereby to redeem the sinful soul. "The next night," Vital further relates, "the dead man came to me again in a dream and gratefully said, 'Blessed are you for having given peace to my soul.'"

Such legends were written down by the thousands and transmitted from mouth to mouth. Typical of the unique legendary literature which was produced in the circles of Isaac Luria's followers are the letters of Hayyim Vital's enthusiastic follower, Solomon Shlumal ben Hayyim of Moravia.[55] In one of these letters, written in Vital's lifetime (in 1607), Solomon Shlumal provides a very clear picture of the manner of life in the major center of the "lion's cubs," i.e., Luria's followers, in the community of Safed. "When I came to Safed in the autumn of 1602," he relates,

I found a large and holy community filled with wisdom and piety. More than three hundred great rabbis, all pious and faithful servants of God, lived there. In the city were eighteen *yeshivot*, twenty-one prayer houses, and a large *bet midrash* where about four hundred boys and young men studied under the supervision of twenty teachers. The teachers accepted no fees from the pupils; the expenses were provided by wealthy philanthropists in Constantinople. In the prayer houses every morning after services all would sit down in groups and study under the supervision of the rabbis. Some studied the Gemara, others Maimonides' *Mishneh Torah*, others the "Ethics of the Fathers," and still others the *Zohar*, etc. In brief, no one went away immediately after morning prayers to his business before spending an hour or two in words of Torah. The same thing happened again after evening prayers. Every Sabbath day the entire community would hear sermons from rabbis and pious preachers. On Thursdays after services the representatives of the community gather in one of the large synagogues and there a great and fearful prayer [*tefillah*

---

55. These letters were first published in *Taalumot Hochmah*, 1629. They were later several times reprinted.

noraah ad meod] is recited for the entire house of Israel and in memory of the destruction of the Temple. . . . The entire congregation recites this prayer with weeping and bitter sobs. Before the prayer, the well-known and pious Rabbi Galante ascends the pulpit. He gives moral instruction and tender words of reproach to the audience and summons them with holy enthusiasm to endeavor to serve God with fear and great love. After him, two other sages, heads of academies, very pious men and devoted to good deeds, ascend the pulpit. One of them is the blind Massud, my teacher, who is renowned in all the dispersions of Israel for his holiness and learning, and the other is Shalmon Maaravi, famed for his wisdom, humility, and piety. They begin to recite the prayer with great trembling and fear and with a broken spirit. Their eyes become springs from which rivers of tears flow. Whoever stands by and listens to the prayer, the bitter sobs, the shrieks and wailings that burst forth from the broken hearts lamenting the destruction of the Temple and the exile and confessing their sins, even though he have a heart of stone, will be greatly moved and will also with much weeping repent and regret his own sinful deeds. On the day before the New Moon people conduct themselves until noon as on the day before the Day of Atonement. All work is interrupted. Men gather in the large synagogue or go outside the city where the holy graves of the prophets and saints are located, and at one of these graves they pray until noon. Sometimes the entire day is thus spent in prayers, sermons, and words of moral instruction.[56]

It is very probable that this "great and fearful prayer" of which Solomon Shlumal speaks with such emotion is the *kinah* or elegy "Ad Matai Adonai," published in Nathan Hannover's *Shaarei Tziyyon*, which used to be chanted with the melody "Shomron Kol Titen." Hannover indicates that this elegy was brought from Jerusalem. Each stanza begins with the same words, *Ad matai Adonai* (How long, O Lord?) and ends with the same cry of woe, *Elohim, ba'u goyyim be-nahalatecha* (O God, the nations have come into Thine inheritance). The elegy presents very clearly the mood of the environment about which the author of the letter previously quoted tells us. We therefore present it here in virtually literal translation:

How long, O Lord? This day Thy congregation stands before Thee and weeps bitterly because Thine enemies have burned Thine house of prayer and destroyed the children of Thy covenant. O God, the nations have come into Thine inheritance!

How long, O Lord, wilt Thou forget the tumult of Thine enemies in Thy wasted sanctuary and the exile of Thy people which is op-

56. *Taalumot Hochmah*, 40.

pressed for Thee and slaughtered for Thy name's sake? How long wilt Thou be angry when Thy people pray before Thee and lament the destruction of Thine house? O God, the nations have come into Thine inheritance!

How long, O Lord, will I roll about in dirt, in all dark corners, and mine eyes grow dim from long waiting? All burn and lie in wait for me and long for my downfall from dawn to night. How long yet will I be astonished over the double destruction? How long wilt Thou not have mercy on Jerusalem? How long will the remnant of Thy sheep mourn in distress? O God, the nations have come into Thine inheritance!

How long, O Lord, will the idolators rejoice, eat up the children of Jacob, and ever make them a mockery and shame? I turn to them in peace, and they flay and skin. They also shame and strike and curse with lying lips. How long will wicked men exult and rejoice, and Thy faithful servants cry bitterly? O God, the nations have come into Thine inheritance.

Many of the prayers which were written in the milieu of Isaac Luria's disciples and with which the Kabbalists of Safed, as Solomon Shlumal relates in his letter, used to spend every day before the New Moon "until noon" and sometimes "the whole day" have also been preserved. Nathan Hannover (of whom we will speak at length in a later part of our work), himself an ardent follower of Luria, published these prayers in his *Shaarei Tziyyon* which was extremely popular among the pious people. Several of them even passed over into the present-day prayerbooks and are still used today, e.g., "Ribbono Shel Olam" which is recited after removing the scroll of the Torah from the ark, and "Yehi Ratzon" following the Priestly Blessing. Some of these prayers created in the environment of the "lion's cubs" bear a truly mystical character, but there are also some—and their number is not inconsiderable—that are distinguished by their very matter-of-fact, literally weekday and profane content. Typical in this respect are the two prayers just mentioned. In "Yehi Ratzon," which is recited after the Blessing of the Priests, God is beseeched: "Give me and all who belong to my household our sustenance and our livelihood in generous and not scant measure, with permission and not with prohibition, with joy and not with sorrow, from Thy broad hand." In the prayer recited at the removal of the Torah from the ark, the following is asked: "And remember us for long and good life, for peace and livelihood and sustenance, and give us bread to eat and clothing to wear, and riches and honor and length of days." To be sure, it is immediately added here that length of days is requested in order that one may "study the Torah and fulfill its commandments," and understanding is asked in order to "comprehend the depths of its mysteries."

Some of these prayers doubtless also have a certain cultural-literary value. With their simple, tender style, they created a new literary genre, the so called *teḥinnah* literature, with its unique manner and flavor. The Hebrew prayers of the Kabbalists of Safed served in a certain respect as a model for the countless women's *teḥinnot* or supplications which were produced in the course of the seventeenth and eighteenth centuries. In order to acquaint the reader with the style of these prayers, we present two of them here in literal translation.

I

May it be Thy will, O Lord my God and God of my fathers, that this hour in which I stand before Thee and pray for myself and my household be an acceptable hour, an hour of compassion, of acceptance and listening. I call unto Thee; mayest Thou consent. Command the angels appointed over the affairs of men that they may be with me to aid, support and save me. Incline the hearts of the people with whom I have dealings to everything I desire, and fulfill their will according to my wish. Nullify all the thoughts of my enemies and make void the schemes of my opponents. Fulfill all my desires for good, as it is written, "He will give unto thee according to thy heart and will fulfill all thy counsel." Lead my heart in the hour of my thought and my hands in the hour of my undertakings. Instruct and inform me in all my ways, and prosper me in all my doings. Send blessing upon all the works of my hands, and let me not have need of the gifts of mortals but only of Thy generous and full hand. Raise me from the dust of poverty, and exalt me from the ash heap of distress with Thy gracious hands. Support me with the right hand of Thy righteousness and load me with gracious gifts. Blessed art Thou, O God, who dost perform loving deeds. Amen. Selah.

II

O God, who providest sustenance for every being, preparest raiment for every creature, and givest sustenance to all, satisfy and sustain me, my household, and all Israel with honorable and good sustenance, in joy and not in sorrow, in honor and not in shame. Give me a livelihood in which there shall be no dishonor and reproach, a livelihood so that I shall not have to require the gifts of mortal men but receive everything from Thy generous and full hand, a livelihood so that I may occupy myself with Thy sacred and pure Torah, and so that honorable raiment may be our clothing, with reverence and not with shame. Let us live together with the other righteous in Israel with honor and without disgrace. Let our portion be for good. Let blessing and happy fortune be in our toil and our hope with peace. Aid us in all our undertakings and in the works of our hands. Prosper us and lead us in Thy ways. Raise me and all mine to long and good life, so that I may be privileged to be among those of spiritual elevation. Have mercy upon us whenever we have need of mercy. Improve our fortune and fulfill for good all the desires of our hearts. Guard and protect us, and draw us out from darkness to light. Be Thou a support for me and for all mine and for all Israel and save us from every trouble, distress, and oppression this year and every year, every month, every week, every day and minute. All times are in Thy hands. Save me from my enemies and oppressors and help me out of every trouble and sorrow, so that I shall not be weighed down with the burdens of this world. Rescue me from all evil, from marauding bands and from every other harm, and let me live in peace, quietness and security.

In the previously quoted letters, particularly in the letter Solomon Shlumal sent to the Kabbalist Issachar Baer ben Petahiah of Kremnitz in Moravia,[57] he gives a colorful portrayal of his own mystical searchings and wanderings. In this portrait we find a reflection of that restless age with its mystical moods and strivings. Hence, we present here a rather large extract from the letter:

When I was twenty-two years old, God, blessed be He, awakened my heart and I heard a voice calling to me: "How long will you sleep in the embrace of sloth? Arise, gird up your loins, search out the Torah and its commandments." Thereupon I removed myself from the world with all its profane concerns, and with my whole heart and soul set out to seek my God, the Father in heaven. I served God with weeping and fasting. I clothed myself in sackcloth and covered my head with ashes. To familiarize myself with the wisdom of the Kabbalah I diligently studied the books of ancient and latter-day Kabbalists until there came into my hands *Pardes Rimmonim*, and my joy was then incalculable. I was certain that the logical theories and clearly delineated explanations of Moses Cordovero would give me the possibility of fathoming the depths of the *Zohar*. Relying on this skilled captain, I began to swim through the deep sea of the wisdom of the Kabbalah. Four years consecutively, removed from all worldly interests and joys, constantly fasting and doing penance, I sat and studied the *Zohar* and the *Tikkunim*. Tearfully I raised my prayers to God and begged Him to enlighten my eyes so that they might be privileged to uncover the secrets of His Torah. My soul longed greatly to penetrate all the mysteries hidden under the garment of

57. Issachar Baer composed several Kabbalist works (see Ghirondi, *Toledot Gedolei Yisrael*, 183–85).

the commandments and prohibitions, to disclose the holy secrets veiled in the prayers and benedictions, to understand the nature of transmigration of the soul and of many other deep subjects. To be sure, Cordovero's works clarified many things for me; yet my soul was still unsatisfied and its thirst unassuaged. I thought I was still wandering among shadows and had not penetrated the divine palace. . . . Then, suddenly, happy tidings reached me. I received the work of the sage Immanuel[58] who lived in Italy, *Pelaḥ Hermon*, and in the introduction to it was a report that God had revealed His great mercy and graciousness to Israel and sent to the inhabitants of the Holy Land an angel, the godly Isaac Luria Ashkenazi, upon whom He poured out His holy spirit and to whom the prophet Elijah revealed such mysteries as have been hidden since the time of Rabbi Simeon ben Yoḥai. In the same introduction the Kabbalist Immanuel indicates that if Luria's disciple, Israel Saruk, who revealed to us a small part of the mysteries which his master showed the world, had not come to us from Palestine, we would never have been privileged to see the true light of the Torah.

"When I read this through," Shlumal further relates,

I was shaken. It was, after all, well known to me that the sage Immanuel had paid Cordovero's widow a thousand golden ducats merely for her permission to make a copy of Cordovero's commentary to the *Zohar* [*Or Yakar*], exclusive of the expenses of the copyists, etc. And here in Safed I first learned that, besides this, Immanuel also sent ten or twenty ducats to the sages Karo, Alkabetz, and Alshech to persuade the widow to grant the required permission. And now he confesses that, if he had not happened to become familiar with a small part of Luria's doctrine, which for the time being is kept secret, the light of Torah would remain forever hidden to him! I then decided to set out on my way at once. I gave my wife a divorce and left with her our only eight-year-old daughter and my entire fortune, even my books and clothing, so great was my thirst for the true, living word of God. I wandered through the Jewish communities of Poland, Russia, Bohemia, and Germany in order to gather the required funds. After many tribulations I finally arrived in Safed with three and a half thalers in my pocket, and for one and a half I immediately bought a copy of the *Zohar*. I spent a whole year there in great poverty and achieved nothing. I applied to all the sages of Safed, requesting them to acquaint me with the mysteries of Luria's Kabbalah and to allow me to enjoy its sweetness. I begged them to lend me, at least, for a very short time the manuscripts through which one might familiarize himself with Luria's revealed truth. No one was willing to fulfill my request. They explained that these truths can be revealed only to well-known and trustworthy men of whom it is

58. The Kabbalist Menaḥem da Fano.

known for certain that they are fit to penetrate such profound secrets which the Master of the universe has held hidden since the time of Rabbi Simeon ben Yoḥai.[59]

Yet Shlumal managed to fulfill his wish—to be sure, in a very original fashion. A daughter of the previously mentioned Kabbalist, Israel Saruk, who was already deceased at that time, lived in Safed. Shlumal married her because she gave him as a dowry something more precious to him than everything in the world—numerous manuscripts and notes of her deceased father's in which Luria's Kabbalist system was expounded.

"There were more than six hundred pages there," Shlumal relates with joyous enthusiasm,

and I had the privilege of having them come into my hands. I studied all of them diligently with the help of my master, the blind sage Massud, who is known to all Israel by reason of his holiness and humility. I have now renounced everything in the world. I know only one thing: to study the mysteries of the Torah and to serve God.

"To serve God"—this meant, for the mystics of Safed, to be occupied with mysteries, to fight against the *Sitra Aḥara* (Other Side) with incantations and magical names, to atone for the sins of the world with mortification of the flesh and fasting, to bring near the "end," the glorious day of the advent of the Messiah, the emancipator and redeemer.

This impatient expectation, this strong consciousness that the days are already numbered, that the steps of the redeemer who is to come and must come are already heard, found a resounding echo in the creativity of the most gifted poet of that era, Israel ben Moses Najara.

59. *Taalumot Ḥochmah,* 42.

CHAPTER FIVE

Israel Najara and Shalem Shabbezi

LREADY we have observed how, under the very favorable social conditions in which the Jewish communities lived under the protection of the Ottoman empire, in certain circles interest in secular knowledge was strengthened, and free, critical speculative thought, which refuses blindly to follow the trodden paths or to accept without independent searching the forms and conceptions handed on by tradition, awakened. In connection with this development, taste for art and elegant style also manifested itself. Almost all the "enlighteners" of that era, of whom we spoke in the first chapter, devoted themselves greatly to poetry and wrote songs and poems according to the model of the Spanish poets. To be sure, poetry gained little thereby, for among all these song-writers there was not a single poet blessed with genuine talent. Even the most gifted of them, Solomon Sharvit Ha-Zahav, was no more than a very skilled versifier who, in workmanlike fashion, copied the models of the brilliant poets of the Arabic-Spanish period. This imitation of the classic patterns was intensified when, at the threshold of the sixteenth century, hosts of exiles from Spain and Portugal entered the Ottoman

provinces. While in the realm of religious poetry and hym-
nology Jehudah Halevi served as the highest pattern, in epigrams,
gnomic poems, and satirical songs those imitated were Alḥarizi,
Bonafed, and Dapiera. It is interesting, however, that it was not
only Jewish models that were copied. The exiles from Spain and
their children had a great love for the literature of their former
homeland. They were interested in every new phenomenon in
Spanish literature, and as soon as the famous romance *Amadis de
Gaula,* which was then regarded as the supreme achievement in
the realm of poetic art,[1] made its appearance, a son of the "Spanish exiles," Jacob ben Moses di Algaba, promptly translated it into
Hebrew and published it at the famous Soncino press.[2]

The motives which Jacob ben Moses indicated impelled him to
translate this knightly romance are interesting:

. . . because this work will provide even more pleasure than *Josippon*
and other historical books, as the reader will himself see. Beyond this,
the reader will benefit much from this book, for it will clarify and
sharpen his understanding and make him skilled in worldly subjects,
both in business and matters of war, as well as in social affairs. The
reader will learn from it how one ought to conduct oneself among
men and of what clever schemes one may avail oneself in difficult
circumstances. Because of its great value and utility, I decided to
translate it into Hebrew that it might be accessible to all readers.[3]

Thanks to the cultured proprietor of the Soncino press, a part
of the literary legacy which has remained from the single gifted
poet of the community in Constantinople in the first half of the
sixteenth century, Solomon ben Mazzal Tov,[4] has also been preserved. We have very little biographical information about this
poet. We know only that Solomon ben Mazzal Tov, apparently
one of the Spanish exiles, was a skilled typesetter and in 1505 established in Constantinople one of the first presses in Turkey.[5]

1. This romance was soon translated into practically all the European
   languages. Furthermore, hundreds of imitations of it appeared.
2. This work is now extremely rare. As far as we know, only two copies
   of the entire edition have been preserved. We here translate in full
   the Hebrew title page: "Amadis de Gaula: A book containing great
   and marvelous tales, such as accounts of the wars and exploits of renowned men and the love affairs and chronicles of great kings."
3. See *Literaturblatt des Orients,* 1850, p. 823.
4. In the collection of poetry entitled *Shirim U-Zemirot,* 285–87, there
   are three religious poems with the acrostic Mazzal Tov. Perhaps this
   is the father of our poet.
5. See Rosanes, *Divrei Yemei Yisrael Be-Togarmah,* I, 84.

Many books which appeared in Constantinople from 1513 to the 1530's are provided with a "closing word" by him or with his notes and *haskamot* or approbations, always in the form of poetry. He also composed two halachic works on what is permitted and forbidden,[6] and a collection of songs entitled *Yeriot Shelomoh*;[7] these, however, have not been preserved. In 1645, when Solomon ben Mazzal Tov was already long dead,[8] the printer Eliezer Soncino published a collection of 298 religious poems under the title *Shirim U-Zemirot*.[9] Besides well-known poems of Solomon Ibn Gabirol, Jehudah Halevi, both of the Ibn Ezras, and Naḥum,[10] we find in it also numerous poems by unknown authors, as well as all of sixty songs by Soncino's townsman Solomon ben Mazzal Tov. Among Solomon's songs are several of wholly secular content, e.g., a poem on chess,[11] a song of praise to the famous sultan Suleiman,[12] and a poem in which a storm at sea is described. The poem begins with the following stanza: "Hear and receive my song; I will sing of the stormy sea, the tremendous sound of its waves." Most interesting are Solomon's national poems in which he expresses his painful longing for Zion and his profound sorrow over the destruction of the land of the fathers. These are also unique in their form and rhythm. Almost all of them were adapted, in the structure of their stanzas and rhymes, to a definite melody. The poet, however, did not compose his songs only according to the model of Jewish masters and the melodies of religious hymns;[13] many of his religious poems and song of Zion are constructed according to the rhythmic form and melody of Turkish and Arabic folk songs. Solomon himself indicates this. Many of his poems contain the notation "to the melody of the Ishmaelites" or "to a differ-

6. See *Shirim U-Zemirot*, Nos. 252–53.
7. *Ibid.*, No. 272.
8. He died after 1532.
9. This edition is one of the greatest of bibliographical rarities. Only two copies have been preserved, one in the British Museum and another (a defective one) in the Asiatic Museum in Leningrad.
10. *Shirim U-Zemirot*, No. 5, is the well-known *pizmon* "Nerd Ve-Charkom."
11. *Ibid.*, Nos. 152–56. The poem is reprinted by Rosanes, *op. cit.*, II, 15–16.
12. *Ibid.*, No. 240 with the subtitle "Be-Nigun Yishmaeli La-Melech Yarum Hodo." The poem begins with the verse:

> Powerful and hidden, O living and merciful God,
> Let the great king, Sultan Suleiman, live forever!

13. In poem No. 245, is noted *Be-Nigun Avo Ve-Shir* (by the poet Elijah). At Nos. 269 and 286 is noted *Be-Nigun Shahar Avakescha* (Solomon Ibn Gabirol's well-known poem). Similar notes are to be found also at Nos. 251, 255, 258, 270, and 275.

ent Ishmaelite melody."[14] In places, indeed, the poem whose
rhythm and melody served as the pattern is indicated, e.g., in number 257, where it is noted, "to the Arabic melody 'Kolo Le-Kadi.' "

The poet expressed his heartfelt sorrow over the fate of his people
to the accompaniment of foreign melodies, but the basic motif of
his sadness is always the same: the unfortunate dove driven out
of its nest, the homeless, beloved maiden whose divinely appointed
lover has forsaken her and who must languish in exile, oppressed
by cruel enemies.

Every morning I come before Thee, my Creator, with my song;
Accept my prayer, my heartfelt cry. . . .
Before Thy holy splendor I pour out my deep woe;
Let my prayer be accepted as the best of gifts.
Almighty, Holy One! Free those who languish in chains,
Quickly send Thy help, let the year of redemption and comfort
    come!
Accept her who has not lost hope in the bitterest distress,
Return to her nest the lovely dove, the tender friend.[15]

And God accepts the one languishing in chains. The joyous tidings
are heard:

The days of your sorrow are ended, my friend and my dove. Return
to your palace; in My house will you rest. Long enough have you
dwelt at the edge of the abyss. Return to Zion to rebuild your nest.
You need no longer wander in wildernesses and waste places. Return
to the temple of your King, My only one, My beloved. Listen! The
nightingale already sings, the sound of spring resounds over our land,
little dove, beloved mine.[16]

"Return, Shulamith, return," the poet calls out in another poem;
"with the prophet Elijah ascend the mountains of Zion."[17] "Return
to Bitzaron, My beloved, My beautiful, My tender one" resounds
a song of Zion in which each stanza concludes with the same refrain: "My beloved, My beautiful, My tender one."[18] And the
poet sings with enchantment: "I will sing a song of fragrant roses,
of my friend whose lips are like fragrant roses. Already I hear
his voice: Sing and rejoice, O Zion, I come to you now."[19]

14. *Ibid.*, Nos. 233–49.
15. From poem No. 246.
16. Poem No. 247.
17. Poem No. 244.
18. No. 238.
19. No. 237.

Solomon ben Mazzal Tov's song was quiet and modest, and found only a very weak resonance in the bustling capital city at the Golden Horn. However, poetry, as we shall see presently, was soon seized by a significantly stronger voice, and song, enriched with new sounds, adorned with vivid colors and forged into more perfect forms, resounded in all the dispersions of Israel and everywhere called forth enthusiasm and tears of enchantment.

Of no lesser importance than the collection of songs published by Soncino is another remarkable collection entitled *Omer Ha-Shichḥah* on which several members of the prominent Spanish family Gavison worked diligently. Abraham ben Jacob[20] Gavison, who in the second half of the sixteenth century practiced medicine in Tlemcen in Algeria, was deeply interested in literature and the poetic art. As a connoisseur of Arabic literature he brought Arabic maxims and proverbs in rhymed Hebrew translation as parallels to the Biblical sayings in his commentary to the Book of Proverbs. He also incidentally introduced many other poems, as well as quotations from various Hebrew poets. After his death, his son Jacob considerably enlarged the number of his father's quoted poems as well as the fragments of other poets. At the end of his father's work he added a whole collection of poems and songs by his son Abraham who died young (in 1605). Several items of this collection (among them are also some love songs) testify that Abraham Gavison was indeed a gifted poet. In this way the work which, at first, purported to be merely a commentary to Proverbs was transformed, especially in its second part, into an anthology of Hebrew poetry. The work rightfully bears the name *Omer Ha-Shichḥah* (The Forgotten Sheaf), for it is only because of it that the names of a whole series of poets of that time such as Abraham Zemirah, Menaḥem Abu Zimra, etc., were not forgotten.[21]

The middle one of the Gavisons, Jacob ben Abraham, valued the poetic art so much that he declares enthusiastically that on the *baalei ha-shir* (the poets) the holy spirit rests and out of them the spirit of God speaks.[22] A member of another very prominent Spanish family, Gedaliah, the son of the well-known philanthropist and physician Moses Ibn Yaḥya,[23] was so enchanted by "beautiful

---

20. Jacob Gavison, who fled with his brother from Granada, wrote a scientific work entitled *Derech Ha-Sechel* in which he appears as a follower of Maimonides and his *Guide* (see *Omer Ha-Shichḥah*, 131a).

21. *Omer Ha-Shichḥah* was first published by Gavison's great-great-grandson Moses Gavison in Livorno (Leghorn) in 1748.

22. *Omer Ha-Shichḥah*, 125.

23. At the time of the Black Death in Constantinople Moses ben Gedaliah

literature" that he decided to form a kind of "academy of art" for the *ḥachmei ha-shir* (sages of poetry). He made his opulent villa near Salonika a center in which a circle of litterateurs and poets lived. There special assemblies were held at which everyone present would read his own new creations and listen to the critical comments of his colleagues. Poets from other cities would send in their songs so that those assembled might express their critical view of them. Poetic tournaments were also frequently arranged there. Serving as weapons in these were epigrams, madrigals, and eulogies in which the great patron and noble connoisseur of art, the hospitable master of the villa, was lauded to the skies.[24] In this poetic circle at that time great reputations were acquired by Jehudah Zarko of Rhodes, the author of the poetic collection entitled *Leḥem Yehudah*,[25] and Saadiah ben Abraham Longo who wrote, besides a collection of elegies entitled *Shivrei Luḥot* (Salonika, 1594), a considerable number of poems and songs which have remained in manuscript.[26] Both poets also wrote rather successful epigrams. "I see quite frequently in the world," Zarko declares in one of these, "that the wise are brought low and fools reign. So it always is; as soon as the sun sets, the shadows take the dominant place."[27] "No fiddle will play," we read in Longo, "if it is not hollow inside, filled only with air; indeed, because of this it apparently happens so frequently that those who sing well have empty heads."[28]

The work of a third representative of this poetic circle, Isaac ben Samuel Onkeneira, the friend of the duke Don Joseph Nasi, has also been preserved. Following the pattern of Solomon Sharvit Ha-Zahav, Onkeneira produced a poem in which the letters of the Hebrew alphabet carry on a debate. To this poem, quite weak

---

Ibn Yaḥya not only gave away a large part of his fortune to aid the needy of the city, but was also extremely helpful as a physician, risking his life. His generosity was renowned throughout Turkey. It was at his home that the famous scholar and physician Amatus Lusitanus, who out of gratitude dedicated to the hospitable Ibn Yaḥya the seventh volume of his monumental work *Centuriae*, spent his last years.

24. See Carmoly, *Divrei Ha-Yamim Le-Venei Yaḥya*, 38–42, where thirty-three members of the poets' circle are listed by name.
25. Printed in 1560. Included in *Leḥem Yehudah* are allegorical poems, epigrams, and songs.
26. See Neubauer, *Cat. Bodl. Hebr. Ms.*, No. 1986. *Leḥem Yehudah* and *Shivrei Luḥot* are both extremely rare, and we have not had the opportunity to familiarize ourselves with them.
27. *Divrei Ḥefetz*, 12.
28. *Ibid.*, 13.

from a literary point of view, Onkeneira wrote a rather long commentary in which a considerable number of anecdotes written in rhymed prose are inserted. These are in fact the only valuable part of the entire composition.[29] The extent to which this narrative part made *Ayummah Ka-Nidgalot* so popular in its time is attested by the following fact: the Kabbalist Jacob Luzzatto introduces into his *Kaftor Va-Feraḥ*, which appeared three years after *Ayummah Ka-Nidgalot*, over forty legends and anecdotes, all taken from ancient works—the Talmud, Midrashim, the *Sefer Ḥasidim*, and *Tanna De-Be Eliahu*; however, he makes a single exception and also introduces a series of anecdotes from the recently published work of Onkeneira, and each time indicates the source. At the end of *Ayummah Ka-Nidgalot* is printed, in Onkeneira's Hebrew translation, a religious disputation of Joseph Nasi's which the latter carried on (in Portuguese) with a Christian priest.[30]

Closely associated with the circle of poets in Salonika was a very unique and interesting personality, Menaḥem ben Jehudah de Lonzano. Neither the place nor year of his birth is known. It may only be conjectured that he was born around 1550, for he indicates that one of his works, published in 1572, appeared in his "youthful years."[31] Orphaned at an early age, crippled and half blind, Lonzano suffered poverty and distress and wandered from city to city.[32] Despite such difficult circumstances, he obtained wide and varied knowledge, became thoroughly familiar with Greek and Arabic, assembled a collection of extremely rare manuscripts,[33] and obtained renown with his lexicographical works, *Or Torah* (a critical investigation of the textual tradition in the Torah) and *Maarich* (explanations of foreign words occurring in the Talmud, Midrash, and *Zohar*.) Lonzano lived for a considerable period of time in Constantinople, where he composed his poetic works: *Derech Ḥayyim*, a didactic poem; *Avodat Mikdash*, a description in verse of the ritual carried on in the ancient Temple (to this

29. The complete title page of Onkeneira's work reads: *Ayummah Ka-Nidgalot, Sefer Ha-Noten Imrei Shefer, Ḥibbero Ha-Melitz Ha-Hacham Ha-Shalem Morenu Ha-Rav Rabbi Yitzḥak Onkeneira*. The author frequently mentions his philological work *Sefer Ha-Anak*, which has not been preserved. Another work that he mentions in *Ayummah Ka-Nidgalot* (p. 128: "As I wrote in the book of the genealogy of the sons of Spain, called *Mareot Elohim*") has also been lost.
30. In the copy which we utilized this debate is missing. It was apparently excised by the censor.
31. He died after 1618. In that year he issued a collection of his works under the title *Shetei Yadot* (see p. 52).
32. *Ibid.*, 2.
33. Some of them he later published.

work he later added a considerable number of prayers and hymns); and *Tovah Tochaḥat*, a didactic poem in 380 verses. All these have very slight literary value. Lonzano himself considered poetry merely a "plaything," which must, however, be utilized as an appropriate and convenient instrument for teaching and liturgical purposes.[34] Despite his extensive knowledge, he was a determined opponent of "Greek wisdom," believing that it led to heresy.[35] For him the true wisdom was Isaac Luria's Kabbalah. Lonzano spent a rather long time in Safed where, in 1587, he published the ancient Midrash *Agur*,[36] and composed his *Omer Man*, a commentary to the *Idra Zuta* (a part of the *Zohar*).[37]

Despite their rather limited literary worth, Lonzano's poems deserve mention in the history of poetry because he employs in considerably greater measure than Solomon ben Mazzal Tov the meter and melodies of Arabic and Turkish folk songs. Lonzano himself was moved to do this by the fact that "the melodies of the Ishmaelites, because of their melancholy tone, are best suited to soften hearts and arouse the mood of repentance and the sentiment of humility."[38] Still another point in Lonzano's poetry is worth stressing—the clearly erotic character that is felt especially strongly in many of the poems in which he celebrates the bond of union between the community of Israel and its divine chosen One.[39] Here the influence of the mystics of Safed, among whom Lonzano lived for a considerable time, is discernible. In these poems, however, the chief thing—genuine feeling, the flame of mystical ecstasy—is lacking. But what for the learned lexicographer was merely a mechanical mosaic of images and similes, taken ready-made from the Song of Songs, came to life in marvelously beautiful, poetic, and vivid colors in Lonzano's contemporary and acquaintance, Israel ben Moses Najara.[40]

Very slight and not always accurate information has come down to us about the life of this important Jewish poet. The year of his birth is not known. The Russian-Jewish Encyclopedia (XL, 474) notes that Najara was born "not later than 1560," but we believe this date quite inaccurate. The poet was undoubtedly born

---

34. *Shetei Yadot*, 132.
35. *Ibid.*, 87.
36. See *ZHB*, X, 93.
37. We have utilized a handwritten copy of this commentary which was in the Museum of the Jewish Historical-Ethnographic Society in Leningrad.
38. *Shetei Yadot*, 65; cf. *ibid.*, 142.
39. *Ibid.*, 71, 75, 76, 79, and 132 ff.
40. On Lonzano's acquaintanceship with Najara, see *Shetei Yadot*, 142.

much earlier, no later than the 1530's. This may be conjectured
from a number of points. The celebrated and learned physician
Amatus Lusitanus mentions Najara in the preface to the seventh
volume of his *Centuriae*, which appeared in 1561. It is also known
that Rabbi Isaac Luria, who died in 1572, spoke with great enthusiasm of Najara's religious poems. The commentary to the
Torah, *Lekaḥ Tov*, which Najara's father, Moses ben Levi, composed, appeared in 1571 with a "closing word" in acrostic form
by his son.

The poet was born in Damascus, where his father served as rabbi.
He also was proficient in the Talmud, served for a brief time as a
rabbinic judge and member of the rabbinic court in Gaza,[41] and
was in correspondence with many rabbis of his time. Najara was
also a preacher as well and compiled a collection of forty of his
sermons under the title *Mikveh Yisrael*. In addition he composed
a commentary to the Torah entitled *Maarchot Yisrael*, and one to
Job entitled *Pitzei Ohev*.[42] But Najara did not acquire his fame
with these; it was rather as a divinely gifted poet that he became
known throughout Israel.

Though we know little of the poet's life, one detail has been
established with certainty, and it is precisely this that harmonizes
ill with our customary image of a judge and member of a rabbinic
court. Najara's townsman, Ḥayyim Vital, speaks of the poet (not,
to be sure, referring to him by name) with extreme hostility and
resentment. "One cannot deny," Vital declares,

that the songs he has composed are quite good, but he himself is
not even worth speaking to, and whoever sings his religious poems
commits a great sin, for his lips constantly utter lewd talk and he
himself is always drunk. Once when he was invited during the "Nine
Days" to the table of Rabbi Jacob Mendes he threw his hat on the
ground, sang in a loud voice, ate meat, and drank much wine until
he was highly intoxicated.[43]

To be sure, Ḥayyim Vital is not a completely reliable witness.
Apparently he had some personal scores to settle with the poet.
Furthermore, the vain and arrogant Vital envied Najara, because
Isaac Luria was so enchanted by his verses. Luria used to say that
even among the "family on high" Najara's hymns are received
with great enthusiasm, and that his soul is a "spark" of no less
a soul than that of King David, the godly poet of the Psalms. But

41. The poet also died in Gaza in ripe old age (in 1605 Najara was still
alive).
42. These works have remained in manuscript.
43. See *Shivḥei Vital*, 16.

of Najara's weakness for drink, additional testimony is also given by the previously mentioned Amatus Lusitanus, as well as by the author of *Meoreot Olam*.[44] Also significant in this respect is a popular legend in which great enthusiasm for the marvelous talent of the poet as well as complaints about his frivolous life are discernible. Once, the legend relates, after the third meal on the Sabbath, Najara sat at the table and sang his songs. Rabbi Isaac Luria was present and observed how above the table thousands upon thousands of angels were hovering and with great reverence receiving Najara's hymns, all of which were created through the holy spirit. Suddenly Luria noticed that one angel began quickly to call away all the legions of angels, who at once disappeared. This happened because Najara rolled up his sleeves, and with bare elbows threw himself on the table and flung his hat from his head. Isaac Luria then dispatched two of his disciples, Vital and Kohen, to Najara and directed them to explain to the poet that entire hosts of angels had descended to listen to his songs but that he had driven them away with his improper conduct. When Najara heard this he was terrified. Filled with shame, he sat down and with holy enthusiasm began to sing his hymns and praises to God which rejoice both God and men. At once the hosts of angels reappeared and listened with enchantment to the marvelous song of the poet.[45]

Apparently Najara in his youth led the restless life of an itinerant singer and derived a livelihood from teaching young people the art of poetry and elegant style.[46] His early years of wandering, it seems, were filled with grievous illnesses. Not without reason does the young poet exclaim: "When your heart is cradled in sorrow and trouble today and tomorrow, day after day, drink the liquid of the grape, my friend; enjoy the blood-red wine under the cool shade of the paradisical fields."[47]

In his itinerant years Najara became acquainted with the circle of poets at Salonika, participated in its literary enterprises, and even carried on a correspondence in rhymed prose with several of its members. In that period also he composed all the poems which he later, in his old age, published (in 1605) in his collection *Meimei Yisrael*, consisting of six sections.

In *Meimei Yisrael* we do not yet see Najara the original poet who seeks new paths, but a faithful disciple of the old masters,

44. See Graetz (Hebrew edition), VI, 288.
45. See *Hemdat Yamim* (1731 edition) I, 101; II, 78.
46. The poet frequently mentions his youthful wanderings with bitterness in his *Meimei Yisrael*. See, e.g., the Introduction, 138. On his lectures on the art of poetry, see *ibid.*, 143, 144 ff.
47. *Ibid.*, 148.

especially Alḥarizi and Immanuel of Rome. Like Alḥarizi in his day, so Najara also undertakes "to drive away sorrow, to chase away despondency," and to provide his readers with a model of artful rhetoric and elegant style. In exaggerated, Oriental figures and similes he writes eulogies to the poetic circle. He declares one of them, Abraham Laḥmi, the foremost poet of his time, to whom all ought to give obeisance, and declares that he, Najara, is his humble servant.[48] Another poet named David he declares to be "the sweet singer of Israel" and asserts that with his song he shames all the poets of his generation.[49] Najara is also not chary of praises for himself and assures us that he is "the king of the poets" who has ascended to literary heights such as no one else has ever attained.[50]

But it was not only songs of praise and dithyrambs that the young Najara sang. Like Alḥarizi and Immanuel of Rome, he was also not parsimonious with caustic epigrams and satirical, sharply pointed arrows, which he hurled with skillful hand at "stubborn fools,"[51] talentless scribblers of rhymes,[52] shameless plagiarists,[53] and all kinds of swindlers and deceivers.[54] In these youthful poems clever technique and skillful construction of verses are apparent, but the chief things, true inspiration and poetic sentiment, are lacking. As long as Najara followed the ways of the "academics" of Salonika, he did not discover his true, his *own* way. He was an ordinary itinerant singer who wrote "occasional poems," which he would present, for stipulated payment, to rich patrons who all had, as he himself expressed it, a weakness for verse-making.

A new period in Najara's creativity was inaugurated when he became familiar with the circle of mystics in Safed. The strained mood prevalent there, the impatient waiting for the "end," the burning ecstasy and spirituality—all these completely conquered his tender, sensitive soul. He became the inspired singer, the poetic echo, of all the mystical hopes with which the "lion's cubs," the Kabbalists of Safed, were permeated. The carefree, wandering singer was transformed into the poet of national sorrow, of the despondency and yearning of the homeless people for the Messiah and redeemer. The motif heard in the humble song of Solomon ben Mazzal Tov sounded with mighty chords on the strings of

48. *Ibid.*, 140.
49. *Ibid.*, 142.
50. *Ibid.*, 153.
51. *Ibid.*, 154.
52. *Ibid.*
53. *Ibid.*, 156.
54. *Ibid.*

Najara's poetic lyre. The intimate experience of mystically-minded souls, in their prayerful drive for the Infinite, in their fervent, trembling longing for God, the beloved and desired One, found their most powerful expression in the poet of Damascus. Najara wrote more than a thousand liturgical hymns and elegies.[55] In some of them the sobbing, tear-filled chords of longing and despair are heard; in others, the radiant, joyous tones of triumphant hope. But all of them together form one great, unified poem with a single, central hero, the glorious Messiah who proclaims to the world the tidings that the bond of love between the divine loved One and the "persecuted little dove," the congregation of Israel, is renewed.

Even such poems as "A'irah Shaḥar"[56] and "Toleh Eretz Al Belimah,"[57] in which praises are chanted to the Creator of the worlds and infinite heavens, conclude with the humble petition, "Gather, O God, Thine exiles; bring near my redemption." Yet songs such as the two just mentioned are rare and exceptional in Najara's poetic creativity. Not to the Creator of the cosmos, the First Cause, the omnipotent dynamic power of the infinite universe, does the mystical poet turn, but to the God of the patriarchs and the people of Israel, to God the father and protector, the God full of compassion, the God of light and love to whom all yearning hearts pray, to whom every mystical soul strives in its fervent ecstasy. And this twofold concept of God, unified through mystical bonds—the God of Israel, the national God of Abraham, Isaac, and Jacob, and God the ardently beloved, for Whom the human soul longs and trembles—is the basic motif of Najara's poetry. In hundreds of elegies and lamentations, the poet expresses the great sorrow of the nation and its firm, still unshaken hope before God.

"Accept my tears, I call to Thee out of great misery, Thou Creator of all beings! Thou art mine only protector, my help in great distress."[58] "O God, protector of all the just, have mercy on the broken heart of the miserable wanderer."[59] "Free, O protector, the miserable captive who languishes in chains among foreigners."[60] "How long, my protector, wilt Thou be angry with me?"[61] "My friend, my guardian, my protector, tell me quickly: With whom hast Thou left the few sheep, the few sheep?"[62] "Ah,

---

55. A considerable number of them have remained in manuscript.
56. *Olat Tamid*, No. 51.
57. *Ibid.*, No. 174.
58. *Ibid.*, No. 57.
59. *Pizmonim*, No. 33.
60. *Olat Tamid*, No. 38.
61. *Ibid.*, No. 6.
62. *Pizmonim*, No. 93; *Olat Tamid*, No. 146.

how long the exile continues! Yet have I not lost my hope, and my heart longs for the living God."[63] "My longing heart knocks always on the door of hope; it hopes only for Thee, my protector."[64] "Mine enemies mock me saying, You hope always for the day of freedom and yet roll about in dust, swamps, and filth." "See how the waters rise above me; all peoples rule over me; their gardens must I tend."[65] "I dreamt that Thou didst drive away my dark night with the bright dawn. As soon as I close my eyes, the day of redemption appears before me. My king, my hope, interpret my dream for good, change the dream into reality."[66] "I dreamt of Thee in sleep; trembling, I awoke. I stand with palpitating soul before Thee, my glory and beauty. Interpret my dream speedily."[67] "I ask all the wise men, all those who have fathomed the hidden mysteries: When will the day of redemption come?"[68] "Heal the wounds of the homeless people, fulfill their hope, proclaim the name of Jesse's scion; let him descend like the dew of blessing and the refreshing balsam."[69] "Redeem Thy people from the grievous exile, the people whom Thou hast chosen from all peoples." "Speedily send healing to my heart, speedily send Elijah the Tishbite and with him the king, the Messiah."[70] "Turn my steps to Zion, shining in the radiance of the redeemer's countenance!"[71] "Jesse's scion is my best hope, my elixir and my refreshment."[72] "Proclaim the tidings to the captive: the redeemer has come."

Despite the fact that Najara saw in the expected Messiah the redeemer of the whole world, the banner of all nations, wrathful tones of vengeance—vengeance for the wicked deeds, for the terrible sufferings and degradations which his people had to endure at the hands of the surrounding nations—are not infrequently heard in his songs. The poets of the Arabic period in Spain, when lamenting the grievous exile of their people among the nations of the world, could not suppress the feeling of vengeance, which bursts through in many wrathful stanzas. "Destroy like Sodom the land of Edom which has trampled my people with its feet!" Solomon Ibn Gabirol cries out. In the view of Israel Najara, injustice

63. *Olat Tamid*, No. 125.
64. *Ibid.*, No. 174.
65. *Olat Shabbat*, No. 9.
66. *Olat Tamid*, No. 188.
67. From a still unpublished poem.
68. *Olat Shabbat*, No. 50.
69. *Ibid.*, No. 4.
70. *Olat Tamid*, No. 225.
71. *Ibid.*, No. 3.
72. From a still unpublished poem.

must be punished, wickedness and violence demand judgment and recompense, and the Messiah cannot redeem the world before the wrong is rectified and black sin extinguished through just punishment. This motif resounds in many of Najara's poems. "Require from them my blood that has been shed!" the poet exclaims.[73] "How long will mine enemies rule over me?"[74] "Raise Thy spear against mine oppressors; recompense them with double ruin!"[75] "Cast deathly terror over them; make them drink the poisonous cup."[76] "Disperse them, scatter them like the dust of the roads."[77] "Clothe Thyself in anger, Thou God my Creator, return not the sword to its sheath until mine enemy is shattered and vengeance fulfilled."[78] "Smash the heads of Jacob's enemy; let those who have destroyed Thy sanctuary be annihilated."[79] "Repay, O living God, the peoples who declare war against me each day; change them into dumb dogs that cannot bark."[80] "Give rest quickly to my people. Send me mine anointed. . . . Take vengeance of mine enemies, and let Rome and its rulers fall by the sword."[81] "Repay the enemy who persecutes the innocent dove, Thy tender loved one . . ."[82]

Here we touch upon the most characteristic feature of Najara's poetic creativity. Religious ecstasy is interwoven with the motif of love. The relationships of the individual and the people of God are veiled in an erotic garment and obtain a sexual coloration; the

73. *Pizmonim*, No. 15.
74. *Olat Tamid*, No. 142.
75. *Ibid.*, No. 181.
76. *Ibid.*, No. 162.
77. *Ibid.*, No. 6.
78. *Ibid.*, No. 63.
79. *Olat Shabbat*, No. 40; *Olat Tamid*, No. 66.
80. *Olat Shabbat*, No. 2.
81. *Olat Tamid*, No. 220.
82. We could multiply the number of such quotations greatly. Hence, it is literally incomprehensible how Saul P. Rabinowitch could come to the conclusion (*Motzaei Golah*, p. 355) that "the call to vengeance is never heard from Najara's loving harp." In Najara's still unpublished poems as well, tones of love and hope are interwoven with wrathful cries of hatred and vengeance. It is characteristic that another Kabbalist who grew up in the milieu of the Kabbalists of Safed and was a disciple of Ḥayyim Vital, Ḥayyim Kohen, also composed several poems in which chords of love and longing are combined with angry cries of hostility and revenge. In his mystical dialogue-poem "Dodi Yarad Le-Ganno Lire'ot Ba-Gannim" the divine Loved One declares to the congregation of Israel: "I will put on vengeance and the flame of the Lord, and I will burn the house of the peoples and the house of those who afflict Israel; I will repay half the blood of the slain and the captured, and this will be My consolation."

mystical experiences and spiritual currents are expressed in the language of earthly desires and human longings. We noted earlier that in the first period of his creativity Najara was the faithful disciple of the Arabic-Spanish school. His collection *Meimei Yisrael* was composed according to the strict principles of Arabic meter. In his religious lyrics, however, the poet employs altogether different forms. Aside from the preface and the introduction to his *Zemirot Yisrael*, there is only one poem (*Pizmonim*, No. 88) written according to the principles of *yated* and *tenuah*. Freeing himself from Arabic meter, Najara utilizes new forms—the forms which Solomon ben Mazzal Tov endeavored with his modest powers to introduce into Hebrew literature—very successfully. In his years of wandering over the Near East and the lands on the shores of the Mediterranean, Najara had opportunity to become familiar with the folk songs sung in the languages of these lands— Arabic, Turkish, Spanish, Neo-Greek, and Italian. The majority of these were erotic poems celebrating the magic of love and feminine beauty. The Jewish youth would also eagerly sing these love songs and create similar ones, following their pattern, in the language of the Bible. "Repugnant to me," Najara complains, "are these songs in foreign tongues. I will make an end of the great clamor; I will renew the sacred bond and replace the profligate poems of lust and desire."

Najara attempted to replace these erotic songs in a very original fashion. He wrote religious hymns and poems precisely according to the rhythm and melody of these folk-songs. Along with this, he not only utilized the rich forms and chants of the Arabic and Turkish folk songs but each time indicated precisely the foreign song, with its rhythm and motif, which served him as a pattern. Hence we encounter very frequently among his poems remarks such as these: "A lovely poem to the melody of 'Ni Akonias Dionius Turki," or "a beautiful poem to the melody of "Ya Ein Khari Saal A'niva A'ravi."[83]

There is no doubt, however, that it was not merely to remove the Jewish youth from the erotic folk songs that Najara attempted to adapt his religious poems to the rhythm and meter of the popular foreign lyrics. For the "adaptation" is not content simply with the external form, the rhythm and meter of the verse construction; it goes significantly deeper and is felt also in the images and symbols which the poet employs. Najara's religious lyric is saturated with erotic terminology. It breathes the burning speech of tem-

---

83. In several (very few) instances, a Hebrew poem, not a foreign one, serves Najara as a pattern, e.g., "Pizmon Le-Ḥen Yedid Nafshi Becha Ḥeshki." For more on this, see W. Bacher, *REJ.*, LIX, 101–5.

pestuous passion. It is in the full-blooded language of ardent desire and passion that Najara discovers the most appropriate forms for expressing his mystical-religious emotions with supreme clarity. In the long chain of hundreds of Najara's elegies and hymns a unique conversation is carried on—a dialogue between the tragic, miserable beloved, the congregation of Israel, and her divine, appointed One, who in His wrath has forsaken her. In this extraordinary, mystically beautiful epic of love the most varied tones resound, from the delicately soft, heartfelt and sad to the ardent and tempestuous in which the fiery expression of seething passion flares and the cry of unshattered hope, borne on the wings of triumphant joy, is heard.

"Tell me, Thou light of my eyes," laments the forsaken beloved one, "why hast Thou forgotten her who yearns for Thee and knocks on the doors of Thy graciousness?"[84] "How great is my pain! Will my terrible sorrows last forever? Wilt Thou forever forget Thy little dove, the one in love with Thee?"[85] "Since Thou, my beloved friend, hast forsaken me, mine eyes have forgotten sleep. Return to me, my help, my protector! Speedily redeem my soul!"[86] "Like a deer has my ardently loved One fled. He has forsaken His house and left His longing one in captivity. . . . My brethren, my loved ones, and also my friends: Tell me, how long will He be wroth with me? How long will I languish, forgotten, forsaken, oppressed, trodden by every people?"[87] "Speedily rebuild Thy ruined house! Rest there with me; I will give Thee my love and joyously sing Thee my song!"[88]

As one penetrates more deeply into Najara's poetic creativity it becomes clear that it was not only the erotic element that made him adapt his religious poems to the melody and rhythm of the folk lyrics. Other important factors that were intimately associated with the uniqueness of his literary talent contributed to this. Najara belonged to that species of poet who is first of all a singer, who creates musical *songs* rather than writes poems. For him the tune, the chord, precede the poetic words. The rhythm in Najara's poems derives primarily from the fact that he felt and created them as songs; he sang them before writing them down on paper. He constructed and formed them according to the rules of melodic rhythm, not according to the principles of poetic meter. Only when one considers Najara primarily as a singer, as a poet in song,

84. *Olat Tamid*, No. 12.
85. *Ibid.*, No. 49.
86. *Ibid.*, No. 35.
87. *Pizmonim*, No. 82.
88. One of Najara's still unpublished poems.

can one properly appreciate his marvelous sensitivity for melodic verse construction, his mastery in song technique. Najara understands how artfully to employ the unique rhythm of the folk song. Through repetition of the same closing line, through special rhythmic pauses, through the harmonious pairing of like-sounding words,[89] through fast tempo and unique assonances, the poet obtains the loveliest effects.

It is impossible to render in translation the marvelous grace of these prayer stanzas, permeated with quiet sorrow, of the forsaken loved one:

> *Yauf halomi, ve-yudad hezyoni*
> *Bintot zemami, ahar mahmad eini*
> *Borah me-immi, ve-natash meoni*
> *Lo shoafah, nichsefah gam kaltah nafshi*[90]

or

> *Tzuri goali Yah, Tzuri goali Yah!*
> *Maher ve-hahesh pedut, yaaleh yefehfiyah . . .*[91]

Like the tender tone of a flute resound these lovely elegiac lines:

> *Yah El magen le-holchei tom, holchei tom*
> *Shivhacha mi yemallel ad tom*
> *Rahem lev dal ein bo metom*
> *El becha yeruham yatom*
> *Rahem lev dal ein bo metom*[92]

or

> *Yedidi roi mekimi—mi-mirmas anshei latzon*
> *Hagidah li attah al mi—natashta meat ha-tzon?*
> *Natashta meat ha-tzon . . . ?*[93]

The tender, sorrowful tones, however, are not infrequently interrupted by tempestuous chords permeated with passion. "I know neither sleep nor rest," the homeless and longing one cries out.

89. Like Moses Ibn Ezra and Alharizi in their time, Najara also employs homonyms very skillfully.
90. *Olat Tamid*, No. 88.
91. *Ibid.*, No. 72.
92. *Pizmonim*, No. 33. The number of *pizmonim* composed in the rhythm of folksongs is especially large among Najara's still unpublished works.
93. *Pizmonim*, No. 93.

I am hurled like a little ship on the turbulent sea of passion. To Thee, my friend, my love, my pride and my glory! I would be a suckling child and have Thee for my mother; I would lie at Thy splendid breasts and still my thirst—my friend, my love, my pride and my glory! I would be a young branch and have Thee rest in the shade of my garden, and I would watch over Thy fruit—my friend, my love, my pride and my glory! I would be a tent so that Thou wouldst rest in it; happily we would enjoy bliss and love—my friend, my love, my pride and my glory! I would be a bell and Thou my echo; with my song I would still the flame of Thy Love—my friend, my love, my pride, and my glory! I would be Thy servant and have Thee my commander. I long to serve thee. Sweeter than freedom it is for me to be enslaved to Thee—my friend, my love, my pride, and my glory![94]

In another poem[95] the beloved laments:

My heart seethes like a kettle. My loved One has forsaken me. My soul longs for Him, and I languish in captivity. Wherefore hast thou forgotten me, my love, my support, my hope and consolation? I roam over all paths and ask all wanderers: Have you not seen my Friend, my loved One, the joy of all hearts? Tell Him I am sick of love. Let Him say when He will assuage the flame of my heart.

"O come quickly, my Friend, Thou light of my eyes! Enough homelessness, enough! Return to my breasts, to my breasts return, my Friend, Thou light of my eyes!"

And the "loved One" is not deaf to the sobs of His "little dove." The beloved is, after all, so enchantingly beautiful:

Weep not, My love, shed no tears, thine eyes are so wondrously lovely. With thy glance alone hast thou captivated My heart. Sweeter than the best wine is the fragrance of thy breath. Lovelier then crimson are thy lips. More precious to Me than all treasures is thy love. Quickly come to Me, My love! Enough roaming in strange lands. Return to thy home, return to Me, thou loved one, thou beauteous one! Let thy song resound with trumpets and harps—no more of misery wilt thou know.[96]

94. *Olat Tamid*, No. 97.
95. *Ibid.*, No. 102.
96. *Ibid.*, No. 11. Besides the large number of poems in which the beloved celebrates his "lovely little dove" Najara's beautiful duet poem "Yaaleh Yaaleh Bo'i Le-Ganni," in which the couple declare their mutual, free love for one another should also be mentioned.

Enough homelessness already, My little dove, enough wandering
from nest to nest. Clothe thyself in silk and brocade, My sister, My
friend, My beloved little dove! Soon will I gather the dispersed people.
Come quickly to Me, My little sister, My bride![97]

Thy days of sorrow are passed, the years of suffering forgotten,
the enemy who laid waste thy home destroyed. Return to Me, My
friend! Come to Me, My friend! Thy homelessness hath broken My
heart. Not forgotten is thy woe. Come to Me, My friend! Return
to Bitzaron, thou lovliest hope of Mine! Let song resound in My habita-
tion. Come to Me, My friend! I will fulfill thy request. I will send
thy redeemer. Sing to Me, then, My songs that are so sweet to Me.
Come to Me, My friend![98]

Soon the day of redemption, the day of redemption for innocent
blood, comes. Enough languishing among enemies. Come, rest, in My
bosom. Let Me drink thy breath of spices, thou beloved Mine. Let
Me hear thy sweet voice, sing to Me thy songs, My only beloved,
desired one. Sing thy song of joy—I come quickly to thy help, to
free thee from long exile. Faithful is My love to thee, with a crown
will I adorn thy head. I will renew thy youth, and thou wilt bloom
like the willow tree near the fresh spring.[99]

In Oriental images and similes the lover celebrates the magical
charm of his beloved.[100] A prose translation can give no notion
of the gracious, tender beauty of such harmoniously musical, play-
ful lines as the following:

> *Yafu dodaich neimah—ayummah cha-nidgalot*
> *Sefataich tzuf ve-reah—appech mor va-ahalot*
> *Rum komatech liverosh damah—shadaich le-ashkolot*
> *El mi adammech, tzeviah—bi-tzevaot o be-ayalot.*[101]

Like a sparkling beaker of the finest wine do these lines of
Najara's, with their colorful cascade of marvelous assonances,
glisten:

> *Yemimah, temimah u-neimah—adinah boi na immi*
> *Kevudah bat melech penimah—be-rinnah u-tehinnah kumi*
> *Ahoti ra'yati kedumah—ahavtich keratich immi*
> *Shezufah, hadufah u-redufah . . .*[102]

97. *Olat Tamid*, No. 16.
98. *Ibid.*, No. 66.
99. From the *pizmon* "Yayin Ha-Tov Ratov Hashkeni."
100. *Olat Tamid*, No. 55, 94, 100, 101, 104, and many others.
101. *Ibid.*, No. 159.
102. *Pizmonim*, No. 28.

One other feature of Najara's poetic creativity must finally be noted. We have observed the erotic imagery in which the poet portrays the mystical feeling of religious enthusiasm and the hope for the speedy advent of the Messiah. But, in the spirit of the Kabbalists of Safed, Najara also laments the vanity of the terrestrial world with its petty desires, and summons men to repentance and regret. In his youth Najara composed a didactic poem "Mesaḥeket Ba-Tevel" on the vanity of man's life in this world.[103] But in this poem there is far more rhetoric than feeling. Only in the later period of Najara's creativity does this motif find a powerful resonance in a series of heartfelt prayers and elegiac poems.[104] Especially characteristic in this respect is the still unpublished elegy with the melancholy opening lines, "Man dreams, man slumbers on his couch; he thinks he rests, but he is only a momentary shadow which flies without wings and quickly disappears."

The poet proudly says of himself, "I created verses that shine like the rising of the sun." And he was quite justified in holding such a belief. With their artful form the strophes of the author of *Zemirot Yisrael* and *She'erit Yisrael* attain the perfection of the great masters of the Arabic-Spanish period. Mystical fervor, an insatiable drive toward the eternal and immortal, stormy waves of deep feeling and experiences expressing themselves in colorful, lucid images—all these raise Najara's finest poems to an exalted height. Not without reason did he become the favorite poet among the Jews of the East and his songs no less popular than the religious poems of Jehudah Halevi. Najara's songs also triumphantly penetrated the Minhag Ashkenaz (German Rite). Among the German Jews, too, the poet of Damascus is revered, and his famous hymn in Aramaic "Yah Ribbon Olam Ve-Alemayya" is sung with great enthusiasm at the third meal of the Sabbath day.

Najara created an entire school. Many religious poets adopted his style and wrote poems in his manner.[105] Like their model, they also sang of the advent of the Messiah. All of them waited with strained impatience for the speedy redemption.

It was not only in Damascus and Palestine that Najara's Muse

---

103. Published in *Meimei Yisrael* (169–71).
104. See *Olat Ḥodesh*, Nos. 24, 26, 27, 38, 40, *et. al.*
105. Several such lyrics composed according to his pattern were introduced by Najara himself in his *She'erit Yisrael*. Numerous liturgical poems of Najara's followers are printed in the collections *Sefer Pizmonim* (Calcutta, 1842), *Shirei Zimrah* (Tunis, 1872) and *Yagel Yaakov* (Jerusalem, 1885). In the last collection many liturgical hymns and *pizmonim* which were already published ten years earlier in Jerusalem are reprinted. For more on this, see Bacher, *REJ*, LX, 221–34.

found such a clear echo but also in distant Yemen, at the southern end of the Arabian peninsula. For many generations the small Jewish community in Yemen was "a people dwelling alone." Until modern times virtually nothing was known of the way of life and the cultural condition of Yemenite Jewry. Only after Jacob Saphir wrote a description of his travels through Yemen[106] was interest in the Yemenite community aroused. Several European libraries soon obtained collections of handwritten poems and other manuscripts from Yemen. In this way the possibility of obtaining some notion of the cultural creativity of the Yemenite Jews emerged.

For centuries the Jews of Yemen lived in poverty and distress and suffered severe persecutions. Their entire consolation was in Kabbalist books and the singing of songs. Not only in the synagogue but at every gathering and joyous occasion—at a circumcision, a *bar mitzvah*, especially at weddings—religious and secular songs were sung by the Yemenite Jews with unique, tender melodies.[107] The classical poets of the Spanish period served as their pattern and prototype. They would write down with great love many poems of Solomon Ibn Gabirol, Jehudah Halevi, and Moses and Abraham Ibn Ezra[108] for their song collections. The songs the Yemenite Jews themselves produced are distinguished by a unique quality, their bilingualism. Jehudah Halevi and several poets of the Spanish period (Alḥarizi, Joseph Ibn Zaddik, and others) occasionally braided an Arabic line into their poems to obtain a certain effect. With the Yemenite Jews, however, it was quite different; among them Hebrew and Arabic had grown so closely together that they created in both languages simultaneously. Not only did they write both Hebrew and Arabic songs; they also produced bilingual poems in which Hebrew and Arabic lines follow one another. Until the seventeenth century, however, no truly gifted poet appeared among the Yemenite Jews. All were mere versifiers who imitated foreign models. Only in the middle of the seventeenth century did a talented poet who founded an entire school appear among the "singers of Yemen," and he and his followers were under the powerful influence of Israel Najara's creativity. The name of this poet was Shalem (Salim) ben Joseph Shabbezi.

We know very few details of Shabbezi's life. As a writer and a man he made such a colossal impression upon his generation that even in his lifetime his name was adorned with fantastic legends

106. See *Even Sappir*, I, 111–48.
107. See A. Z. Idelsohn, *Gesänge der jemitischen Juden* (1914).
108. We owe it to the Yemenite Jews that Abraham Ibn Ezra's *Diwan*, which Egers published in 1886, was preserved.

and the most remarkable miracle stories were told about him. Every Friday, it is recounted of him in Yemen, he would go to Palestine through *kefitzat ha-derech* (foreshortening of the way) and there spend the Sabbath, sometimes in Jerusalem and other times in Safed or Hebron, and after the end of the Sabbath on Saturday night he would return to Yemen again in the same miraculous way. All the angels who vex Israel had a deathly fear of him, for he used to punish them with the severest afflictions. Marvelous also was Shabbezi's power of creation. He composed so many works that three hundred asses could not carry their weight. Even after his death he remained the great miracle-worker. At his grave, relates Jacob Saphir, a perpetual light burns to this day, and from all corners of the land sick people come to pray at his grave, and when someone suffering from illness afterwards washes with the water that flows from the cave near his grave, he is at once cured. This great miracle-worker, the legend relates, was all his life a manual worker and supported himself through weaving.

Some genuine biographical details can be obtained only from the poet's works. Thanks to them, we know that his family name was Mashta[109] and Shabbezi the name of his native-place (near Ta'iz), where he was born in 1619.[110] He spent most of his life at the capital city of Yemen, San'a (in Hebrew it is called Uzal) However, it appears that he had to live for a time abroad, for he laments in one of his songs

> I listened to the wisdom of the sons of Uzal,
> But now I am among mine enemies like one robbed.

He died in Ta'iz sometime after 1679, for among his poems is a lament on the expulsion suffered by the Yemenite Jews in that year.

The poet's father, himself an ardent Kabbalist, familiarized him with the esoteric wisdom in his youth, and Shabbezi, at the age of twenty-seven, completed a mystical commentary on the Torah entitled *Ḥemdat Yamim*. The distinguished scholar of the Kabbalah, Gershom Scholem, who first acquainted us with this very rare book[111] insists that at that time Shabbezi was still not familiar

---

109. Jacob Saphir is mistaken when he declares that Mashta was the name of the poet's mother.
110. Saphir is again in error when he indicates that Shabbezi lived in the sixteenth century. We also find this false information in the *Russian-Jewish Encyclopedia*, VII, 600.
111. *Kiryat Sefer*, V, 266–72.

with the teaching of the Kabbalists of Safed. He was, however, under the strong influence of the poet who lived in the circle of ideas of the "lion's cubs" of Safed, Israel Najara, the composer of *Zemirot Yisrael*. Testimony to Najara's great popularity among the Yemenite Jews is provided by the manuscript collections of poems that were written in Yemen in the seventeenth century and that have been preserved. In each of these there are a number of Najara's poems, and in the poetry anthology of the Harkavy Collection, which we have utilized, it is even explicitly indicated that several poems are copied from *Zemirot Yisrael*. Some of these poems were so beloved that the Yemenite Jews considered them their own and were certain that a Yemenite poet had written them. This, in fact, led some scholars to erroneous conclusions: they consider, for example, Najara's lovely song "Yadad Shenat Enai" among the "songs of Yemen."[112] Najara's poems owed their immense popularity not only to their mystical-messianic mood but also to their melodic rhythm which especially pleased the Yemenite Jews, with their great fondness for melody and song. It is therefore not surprising that Najara's mystical Muse had such a powerful influence on the creativity of the finest poet of Yemen, the Kabbalist Shalem Shabbezi.

Shabbezi himself notes in one of his Arabic poems that the Muse appeared to him when he was still quite young and he then began to write poetry. Among the Yemenite Jews there is a legend to the effect that Shabbezi composed no less than fifteen thousand poems.[113] This, of course, is an enormous exaggeration, but there is no doubt that his poems are to be counted in the hundreds. W. Bacher, in his monograph *Die arabische und hebräische Poesie der Juden Jemens*, gives a list of barely two hundred of Shabbezi's poems. How incomplete this listing is may easily be conjectured from the following fact: in the abovementioned poetry anthology of the Harkavy Collection we found seventeen of Shabbezi's poems that are not included in Bacher's roster. Like all the other Yemenite poets, Shabbezi wrote not only Hebrew and Arabic poems but also bilingual ones in which Hebrew lines are interwoven with Arabic.[114]

In respect of content Shabbezi's poems are "of all species." He wrote songs of praise to various officials, Jewish and Moslem, acquaintances, and friends. In one poem he even celebrates the

112. See D. Yellin in *Ha-Shiloah*, II, 159. Jacob Saphir even believes that this poem was composed by Shabbezi (*Even Sappir*, I, 111).
113. See Idelsohn in *Reshumot*, I, 31.
114. The list put together by Bacher consists of fifty-five Hebrew, eighty-five Arabic, and fifty-two bilingual poems.

mighty acts of the Moslem warriors.[115] He also wrote a whole series of "disputation" poems. In these, debates are carried on not only between the *paterfamilias* and the bachelor but even among the coffee plant, tobacco, and the Yemenite plant *Kaat*, as to which of them is preferable and most useful. The poet compromises and decrees that best of all of them is the fruit of the vine. But it is not in these poems that the uniqueness of Shabbezi's Muse appears. Not with them did the poet of Yemen acquire fame but with his characteristically Jewish religious-national and communal songs.

Bacher divides Shabbezi's poems into various groups: prayers, praises and laudations of God, communal songs, wedding poems, religious meditations, love songs, didactic poems, etc.[116] In fact, however, it is difficult to distinguish between one group and another, for Shabbezi's uniqueness as a poet consists in the fact that in him it is virtually impossible to separate the individual from the community, the poet from the congregation of Israel, the national mood from the religious-mystical. All these groups of poems are united by one fundamental idea, one basic mood—the longing for the Messiah, the romantic hope for speedy redemption. Here, no doubt, the powerful influence of the author of *Zemirot Yisrael* is discernible. But because Shabbezi was an authentic poet, he reveals himself to us in his creativity not as an ordinary pupil of Najara's who repeats and sings after the latter's "style" and "manner" but as a gifted master who knows how to forge old material into new forms, how to place on well-known motifs, employed by others, the stamp of his own personality, how to vivify them with the intimate pulsation of his poetic soul. Certainly the influence of his unique environment, of the Yemenite Jewish community, which throughout centuries of isolated life created its own rhythm and style, of which we know so little to the present day, was also involved here.

The most characteristic feature of Shabbezi's poetry is its mystical-symbolic vesture. He has only a very few lyrical poems with a concrete, sharply defined content, e.g., "Nefesh Yeḥidah Eich Le-Sod El Titzpeni" and "Be-Yaalat Ḥen Yeḥidati Devukah." In the first of these[117] the poet encourages his soul and its striving toward God, and in the second[118] he expresses his love for the Torah

115. On the influence of the Arabic milieu and Arabic poets on Shabbezi, see Bacher, *Die arabische und hebräische Poesie der Juden Jemens*, p. 47.
116. *Ibid.*, 82–83.
117. Found in the abovementioned manuscript anthology of poems in the Harkavy Collection.
118. Published by D. Yellin, *Ha-Shiloaḥ*, II, 155.

and asserts that it makes him forget the grievous sorrows of exile. But the Yemenite poet speaks very seldom merely of his personal experiences, apart from the community. He exclaims with great feeling: "Strong is the love in my heart for my Creator; I praise His greatness and uniqueness day and night; He is my protection and my fortress . . .''[119] But Shabbezi deems it necessary to conclude this lyrical effusion of the soul by turning to the community, the "holy people," asking them to remember Zion and to wait for the happy tidings which the prophet Elijah will bring them. The lyrical poem is suddenly transformed into a fellowship song which, apparently, was sung at table on joyous occasions. Now the poet sings a song of praise to the living God who created all the worlds, but the closing stanzas are transformed into a petition that God may aid as quickly as possible the "homeless daughter" and redeem the "lioness who wanders at strange doors."[120] The same thing occurs in the lovely song "Eretz Ve-Shamayim Ve-Ḥeilom Omedim."[121] In magnificent stanzas the poet portrays how the whole cosmos, all the stars and hosts of heaven, praise the almightly God. Then suddenly the joyous paean is interrupted and concludes with the humble petitionary chord, "Redeem, my Creator, Thy holy people which wanders in exile; in love let the voice of the redeemer be heard!" In his mystical poem "Adon Ha-Kol Meḥay-yeh Kol Neshamah"[122] the poet describes how God pours out His great mercy on the first *sefirah*, noble *Hochmah* (Wisdom) which, thanks to the radiance of the divine grace, rules all worlds. But this song also ends with the characteristic closing verse "Send us, my Friend, the balm of Gilead; there in Zion shall we rejoice, both men and women."

As in Najara, so in Shabbezi tempestuous chords of vengeance often erupt amidst the motifs of messianic hope. Shabbezi himself lived through the expulsion from the Yemenite capital city of San'a, which he described in his elegy "Azil Demaot." In many other poems he laments the fearful sufferings his people had to endure at the hands of the "cruel Moslems." In his lovely "Im Ninalu Daltei Nedivim Daltei Marom Lo Ninalu" the poet complains,

For dogs have surrounded me—from all sides they have assembled; Wild asses and lions and wolves—they have terrified my heart and soul.[123]

119. In the manuscript anthology of poems in the Harkavy Collection.
120. *Ibid.,* 233.
121. *Ibid.,* 269.
122. *Ibid.,* 232; also published by Idelsohn, *Gesänge,* 39.
123. Published by Idelsohn, *Gesänge,* 53.

"Closed is my mouth in the day of homelessness," Shabbezi declares in another poem; "scattered and dispersed is my people. In vain do I seek a true friend, I am cast away and impoverished; the day of rapine has filled me with terror." And he turns in supplication to God: "For the sake of the righteous fathers, gather all the dispersed and remember the love of our youth; let us go up to Zion together; let me hear that my light is come!" "Return, my God, the remnant of Thy people, fulfill its hope, destroy and cut off its enemies, pour out Thy wrath on the wicked, break their arms, for they have inflicted so much evil on Thy children. They oppress the poor and unfortunate. Write down all their sins in a book." Especially typical of Shabbezi are the poems in which the mystical coloration removes the boundary between the poet, the congregation of Israel, the Torah, and the poet's Muse. In the poem "Maalot Galgal Ve-Ḥashmal"[124] the author addresses the celestial spheres with the petition: "Ask the beloved about me: How long will I yet languish in exile? How long will the enemy oppress me and will I, God's servant, sob as a captive amidst the sons of Kedar who hate me so?" In the second verse the "beloved" replies: "Come, my dear, and greet me!—From Him, my Friend, comes my law and my fortune. Let Him bestow His great mercy upon my people." In the third verse the congregation of Israel speaks: "Day and night I remember Him with love. Let His grace stream over me; He forgets not one who calls upon Him!" In the further stanzas the poet himself speaks. He applies to his soul to beseech God's grace. In the last verse he turns to his "beloved" asking her to rejoice with the chosen hero (the Messiah), and concludes with the wish: "Let my Rock proclaim: My lord, the scion of David, is come!"

With a very similar stanza of hope ends the bilingual poem entitled "Ayahu Alhassan Almata Asam"[125] in which the poet proudly declares;

> *Li geveret ḥen tizmon, taaroch shulḥan ve-chos.*
> *Eshmeah shirim u-fizmon, hi le-chol ḥai taamos.*
> *Shikkenah dodah be-armon, limmedah mofet ve-nes.*

In this "gracious lady" (*geveret ḥen*) who lets the poet hear "songs and hymns" (*shirim u-fizmon*) are interwoven all three of his loves—the Muse, the congregation of Israel, and the Torah. The same thing is repeated in the long mystical poem entitled "Sisi

124. In the manuscript anthology of the Harkavy Collection, 170.
125. In the manuscript anthology in the Harkavy Collection.

Geveret."[126] The "lady" rejoices his heart both day and night. With her he praises the sole Creator. She is the living word of his lips, awakens God's spirit in his soul, drives away his sorrow, and illumines all his paths. "Strengthen and arouse my spirit," the poet begs,

when I write and create poems. Satisfy and refresh the flowers of my garden. Accept, thou lovely-eyed, the poor and homeless one with grace and love. Let the end, the redemption, arrive speedily. Let us hear the glorious tidings, Come is the Messiah, accompanied by Elijah! Let the cry resound: Ascend to Zion with a song of joy!

In the tender song "Ani Ha-Dal"[127] the poet's "mistress' is called Hadassah. She hovers constantly over him with great love while he meditates and creates. "Beloved Hadassah," declares the poet, "is firmly bound in my heart when I wander in exile with my loud steps. . . . Day and night I remember her; my heart and my thoughts are captivated in love. The beautiful notes make homelessness forgotten; my friend and I rejoice in song." In other poems the author's mistress and beloved is called *ayumah* (exalted one) and *ayumati* (my exalted one.) "My exalted one arouses my love; she asks me to sing a paean to God the Almighty."[128] In the poem "Ayumah Be-Har Ha-Mor"[129] the poet requests his "exalted one" to ascend the "mountain of myrrh" and there sing a poem to the Creator. In mystical colors he portrays in the poem 'Rei'aḥ Hadas"[130] how the Muse visited him in the middle of the night. In another poem "Yeḥidah Bat Galim"[131] the poet's mistress is called *bat galim*. But here his Muse is the congregation of Israel, and the dove, the mystical symbol of the *Shechinah*, hovers and spreads its wings "over the fates" (*alei ha-goralot*) and prays before almighty God.[132]

The dove as symbol of the *Shechinah* is especially celebrated by Shabbezi in a mystical poem, "Yonah Le-Dodah Ish Emunot Taavah," in which God and the *Shechinah* are portrayed as a loving bridal pair and all ten *sefirot* illuminate and adorn the bride.[133]

126. *Ibid.*
127. Published by Idelsohn, *Gesänge*, 40.
128. In the manuscript anthology in the Harkavy Collection.
129. *Ibid.*
130. *Ibid.*
131. *Ibid.*
132. *Ibid.*
133. Idelsohn, *Gesänge*, 42. In the closing verse the poet deems it necessary to note: "This poem *was born of Joseph* for one who understands the mystery; my mouth is in this song and my hand wrote it, for my view agrees with the friend of my soul."

"Who has kissed me?" With these words a whole group of Shab-bezi's poems begin. "Who has kissed me with the kisses of love?"[134] Here the poet speaks to his soul, which yearns greatly for the love-kiss it has received in a dream. "Who has kissed me while I am exiled and driven away?" "In the land of Yemen do I groan and lament": so begins another poem. Shabbezi turns with words of consolation to the Jewish community of Yemen. It must hope that its beloved will not forsake it, that the day will come when "our Messiah will bloom like a flower." The poet is certain that "I will go up to Mount Zion and song will break forth, and I will hear from the mouth of my beloved the word: I send Yinnon [symbolic name for the Messiah] and Elijah the prophet." Again the congregation of Yemen laments: "Who has kissed me, while I am impure and filthy? I languish in the tents of Kedar. I am in Yemen, but my soul has flown thence; for the glorious land [of Israel] does she yearn like a hind." "Who has kissed me while I am hidden and concealed?" Now the congregation of Israel dreams that it is at its beloved's palace of love and that its fondest hopes are fulfilled. The poet blesses the beloved in her sweet dream and carries his song to her as a gift of a kiss.

Like Najara, Shabbezi wrote numerous dialogue poems in which the congregation of Israel pours out in the language of Shulamith its ardent love for its divine Beloved. Typical in this respect is the love poem "Kol Dodi Dofek." The Beloved declares:

> The voice of My lover resounds; I will welcome him.
> I will answer from afar, saying to My lover:
> If you desire, you will feed at My breast
> On sweet honey, on balm of Gilead.

The lover replies:

> Make haste, my friend, thou perfect beauty.
> There is no flaw in thee, my bride; thou are like the sun.
> Come now with me to thy mother's chamber.

And the beloved answers with the words of the Biblical Shula-mith "Come, let us take our fill of love."[135]

Shabbezi's wedding songs have a close affinity to these dialogue poems. We have noted a number of times the mystical vesture given by the Kabbalists to sexual intercourse between man and wife.

134. In the manuscript anthology.
135. See *Even Sappir*, I, 83; *Reshumot*, I, 37.

In the wedding ceremony, in the bridal pair, they saw a symbol of the sacred bond between divinity and the *Shechinah*, between God and the congregation of Israel. In the wedding music they heard the trumpet of the Messiah proclaiming the tidings of speedy redemption. Almost all of Shabbezi's epithalamia bear this mystical, national-messianic character. The above mentioned mystical lyric poem, "Ahavat Hadassah," is also a wedding song, as attested by the verse:

> Know, O holy congregation, the song composed.
> Bride and groom are under the marriage canopy.

Lustily and cheerfully begins one of Shabbezi's wedding songs: "Give me the cup, my friend, hand me the cup of wine!"[136] But at once the poet recalls: "I will ask of Him who dwells in the beauteous heavens, Will my people be speedily redeemed? . . . Let Him gather all my wanderers!" In another wedding song Shabbezi declares: "In the hall of joy do I remember the incomparable love of Zion." And in still another he admonishes the assembled guests to think of Zion in their rejoicing. Typical is his poem "Akaveh Ḥasdecha Shochen Meonim."[137] This is a national-religious poem in which the author beseeches God to send speedy help to the holy people in its homelessness, to assemble the dispersed with the sound of the ram's horn and bring them directly to Mount Zion. Only in the closing lines do we become aware that we have before us a wedding song:

> Proclaim a testimony to the revelers
> And make glad the afflicted poor.
> Then wilt Thou rejoice brides and grooms
> With fine wine and roses.

The nuptial poem "Ahallel Be-Siaḥ" really celebrates the bond between God and the congregation of Israel: "Sing to thy king, O daughter of Zion; His help hath come. On the mountains are heard the lovely steps of the messenger proclaiming the glorious tidings. For thus hath God said: 'I return to Jerusalem, and I will betroth thee unto Me in righteousness and justice, in lovingkindness and compassion.'"

136. Manuscript anthology, 170.
137. *Ibid.*, 274.

The happiness of the bride and groom is associated by Shabbezi with the tidings the prophet Elijah will bring:

> The rejoicing of a groom has come upon my heart;
> Arise, O Tishbite, proclaim to the bride.[138]

And in ecstasy and joy the poet of Yemen exclaims:

> I heard a song from the end of the earth,
> A voice saying: The King Messiah has arrived!

Thus to distant Yemen came the tidings: He has come, he has shown himself—the long awaited one, the ardently desired one! Over the entire Diaspora was heard the proud call: I, your Messiah, Shabbetai Tzevi!

138. *Reshumot*, I, 53.

CHAPTER SIX

The Cultural Center in Amsterdam

ORN on the banks of the mysterious Nile and raised in the quiet, remote little town of Safed in Galilee, Luria's Kabbalah soon achieved the most brilliant triumphs throughout the diaspora. The "lion's cubs" disseminated their master's mystical doctrine over all lands with great energy. It quickly obtained devoted followers in Italy and simultaneously spread its dominion over the major Jewish community in the Polish lands. Its influence was also soon felt in the new Jewish center that was established on the banks of the North Sea, in the Protestant Netherlands. In the first half of the sixteenth century Italy was for the Marranos the only place of refuge where they could hide from the Spanish-Portuguese Inquisition, with its destroyers. But after the fanatical Cardinal Carafa ascended the papal throne and the pyres on which scores of victims perished flared up in Ancona, Italy became no less of a wicked stepmother to the Marranos then the other Christian countries. Soon after the Catholic reaction embodied in the Counter-Reformation spread its wings over all of Italy, however, the Marranos found a new place of refuge in the former province of the cruel Philip II, the Netherlands, which after a stubborn and heroic struggle attained independence and quickly became a true fortress of freedom and tolerance.

At the end of the sixteenth century the refugee Marranos built in Amsterdam, the major center of Holland, a small colony which in the first decades of the seventeenth century quickly grew into a rich and flourishing Jewish community. In fact, these new inhabitants, the Marranos who had fled from Spain and Portugal, contributed not a little to the fact that commerce and industry flourished so rapidly in the Netherlands and that this small, poor state soon came to play a dominant role in the world market.

It was not, however, material wealth and financial talents only that the Marranos brought with them, but cultural treasures as well. Among the refugees from the Iberian peninsula there were also, besides bankers and entrepreneurs, many intellectual workers—doctors, scholarly investigators, litterateurs, and poets. Thanks to wealthy patrons who provided generous support, the young community of Amsterdam soon established well-organized institutes for study, rich libraries, and splendid presses, and rapidly became the chief center of Jewish culture in all of northwestern Europe. Previously, in dealing with the literary activity of Moses Zacuto, we noted that the Marranos, though filled with gratitude and love for their hospitable new home, could nevertheless not forget the land of their birth, the cruel and merciless stepmother with her rich literature which was then experiencing its period of efflorescence. Just at that time the "golden century" of Spanish national drama, which bloomed so magnificently under the rays of two great geniuses, Lope de Vega and Calderon, began. This flowering found an echo in the literary creativity of the Marranos who were saved from the bloody claws of the Inquisition by the protection of the Netherlands republic. Among the refugee Marranos a whole series of poets, who expressed in lyrical songs written in Spanish their pain and longing for their stepmotherly native land, appeared. Following the pattern of the Spanish classics, the Marrano refugees from Spain and Portugal produced heroic poems, dramas, and tragedies. Antonio Enriquez Gomez composed some twenty dramas in which the influence of his contemporary Calderon is quite clearly discernible. Among the dramas of Gomez are several Biblical ones, as well as a Purim comedy entitled *Comedia famosa de Aman y Mordechay.*

Another poet, the Portuguese Marrano Reuel Jesurun (Paul de Pina) composed an oratorio entitled *Vikkuaḥ Shivah Harim* (The Seven Mountains) which was produced on a ceremonial occasion in 1624 in the Amsterdam synagogue Beth Jaäcob[1]

It was in the Marrano literary circles that the first attempts were made to cultivate in Hebrew literature the ripest fruit of poetic

1. The names of the eight participants in this oratorio have been preserved. See Kayserling, *Die Sepharadim*, p. 20 (we cite according to the Hebrew translation). See also I. Schipper, *Geshichte fun Yiddisher Teater-Kunst*, I, 134.

creativity, drama. Of one of these attempts, Moses Zacuto's *Yesod Olam,* we have spoken earlier. But Zacuto's drama remained in manuscript; it was published only in modern times. Another Hebrew dramatic work, composed by Zacuto's younger contemporary Joseph Penso,[2] had a different fate. As a ten-year-old child, Joseph Penso came in 1660, together with his Marrano family, to Amsterdam and was educated at the model school with seven classes known as Talmud Torah under the supervision of Isaac Aboab and Moses de Aguilar. As a seventeen-year-old, Penso wrote his three-act allegorical drama *Asirei Ha-Tikvah,* which appeared in print in 1673. Such an extraordinary phenomenon—a dramatic work in verse in the language of the Bible—created a tremendous sensation in the literary circles of Amsterdam, and twenty-one litterateurs enthusiastically sang the praises of the young poet in Hebrew, Latin, and Spanish verses. One of these panegyricists declares: "Sure and proud the Hebrew Muse steps forth in cothurni for the first time."[3]

Penso's work is an allegorical drama. The central figure is "the king," abstract man, in whom the good impulse (*yetzer tov*) carries on a struggle with the evil impulse (*yetzer ra*). The "mind, "providence," "truth," and the heavenly emissary, the angel—all endeavor to make man follow the right path; but Satan and his servants, man's desires—chiefly the evil impulse in the person of the profligate woman—wish to lead man astray and snare him in the net of sin. The struggle between the agents of light and darkness, the intrigues of the "evil spirits," their temporary success and the final victory of the mind and truth—in these consists the entire "action" of *Asirei Ha-Tikvah.*

As the work of a seventeen-year-old youth, *Asirei Ha-Tikvah* is still immature; the form in places is naive and crude. Nevertheless it is to be seen that the author possessed talent, and his first work promised a future gifted poet. But Penso later entirely abandoned Hebrew literature, and his first attempt was without a successor.

As we have noted, more than twenty litterateurs celebrated the first published Hebrew drama in poems of praise. Most of these eulogies were in Hebrew. One of the Hebrew poets, Solomon de Elveiro, acquired fame with his discussion of the poetic art, *Sharsherot Gavlut,* but his own poems, as well as those of his col-

2. Known in Judeo-Spanish literature under his family name de la Vega. On Joseph de la Vega's Spanish works, see Kayserling, *op. cit.,* pp. 81–82.

3.   *Tandem Hebrae gravi procedit Musa cothurno*
       Primque Felici ter-pede pandit iter.
We quote according to the first edition of Penso's drama. In the second edition all these songs of praise are missing.

leagues, have no literary value. Only Penso's teacher, Isaac Aboab de Fonseca, who also enthusiastically celebrated his pupil's first drama, deserves mention in the history of Hebrew literature.

Aboab's life was rich in dramatic moments and experiences. As a small child[4] he fled with his parents from Portugal in fear of the Inquisition, which had already cast its eye on his Marrano family. After long wanderings the exiled family reached Amsterdam, where the young Isaac was educated under the supervision of the aged *ḥacham* Isaac Uzziel. Aboab mainfested such remarkable talents that at the age of twenty-two he was himself given the title *ḥacham*. He was also already renowned at that time as one of the most brilliant orators. In 1642 Aboab was invited to become rabbi of the new community of Pernambuco in Brazil, which was then under the sovereignty of Holland. He travelled to Brazil together with his friend, the learned grammarian Moses de Aguilar, along with several hundred other Jews. The young community, however, had a sad fate. War presently broke out between Holland and Portugal, which wished to regain dominion over Brazil. The war ended with Portugal's victory, and Brazil again became a Portuguese colony. The Jews then had to leave the country, and Aboab, together with the other exiled Jews, returned to Europe.

These sad experiences find an echo in Aboab's small collection which begins with the words, "I have made a memorial of the wondrous deeds of God, and much good to the house of Israel."[5] In pious songs Aboab describes the terror the enemy aroused in the Jewish populace when the city was beleaguered. He also quotes the prayers he composed in time of trouble for the community. With intense feeling Aboab tells of God's great mercies—how two ships by which the community was rescued from the foe arrived at the right time. In the collection are also other poems which Aboab composed in his day; these testify that in this rabbi there was a spark of the poet. In places the strong religious feeling of a deeply believing soul striving toward the heights is discernible. Aboab exclaims in one of his poems: "O give me, Thou my Creator, the wings of an eagle, that I may rise above the clouds; high in the heavens will I fly, so that I may see and hear Thy hosts of angels praising Thy glory and calling one to the other: Holy, holy, holy is the Lord of hosts!"[6]

4. Isaac Aboab was born in 1605 in the city of Castrodaire in Portugal.
5. The collection remained in manuscript and only in recent times has it been published by M. Kayserling (in *Ha-Goren*, III, 155–74). Aboab also writes in the introduction to *Shaar Ha-Shamayim* about the troubles that the Jews lived through in Brazil after the victory of the Portuguese.
6. *Ibid.*, pp. 65–66.

Aboab's significance, however, consists not merely in his poems and religious hymns. As we shall see later, he introduced into Jewish literature, in his Hebrew translation, a unique mystical work that is closely associated with the conceptions and tendencies obtained by the Lurianic Kabbalah among the followers and theoreticians of the Shabbetai Tzevi movement.

We have noted that the Jewish community in Amsterdam quickly grew into an important cultural center. The atmosphere of tolerance and religious freedom and the close intercourse with the outside world brought it about that the Jewish intelligentsia of Amsterdam commanded the heights of the European culture and science of that time. The Marranos who had fled from the Inquisition grew up on the dogmas of the Catholic Church, and the fact that they probed and searched and finally threw off the faith in which they had been raised from childhood awakened in them the power of critical, inquiring thought which cannot be satisfied with accepted tradition. These tendencies and moods brought it about that in the Amsterdam Jewish community appeared such a skeptical rationalist as Uriel Acosta and such a free thinker as Baruch Spinoza, who took no account of any tradition whatever. These tendencies, however, came into conflict with others in complete opposition to them. Catholicism, which the Marranos cast off, nevertheless laid its stamp upon them; it infected them with its fanaticism and zealous militancy. To the faith of their fathers, for the sake of which they had suffered so much, the Marranos devoted themselves with the flame and ardor of true converts. The thought of the universal, world-emancipating role of Judaism filled their hearts with pride and mystical ecstasy. Hence, the mystical ideas of the Kabbalists found a resounding echo among them. One Marrano perished at the stake of the Inquisition only because he used to sing a little song: "Has the redeemer already come? No—*this one* is not the redeemer; the redeemer is yet to come."[7] The messianic mysticism whose apostle was the Marrano Solomon Molcho necessarily enchanted with its magic these men who had just fled from the Inquisitors' claws and who themselves, or their own loved ones, had confirmed with their blood their loyalty to Judaism and their belief in the great mission of the "chosen" people. Many-sided secular, even philosophic, education was frequently interwoven, among these persons, with mystical ideas, with blind belief in the marvelous and the supernatural, with faith in all kinds of superstitious stories and legends that obscure critical thought. Very typical in this respect

7. See Kayserling, *op. cit.*, p .34.

is an important writer and communal leader of that time, Isaac Aboab's friend of his youth, Menasseh ben Israel.

As a child of a Marrano family which fled from Lisbon in 1603, Menasseh ben Israel was brought when he was quite young[8] to Amsterdam and there, together with Isaac Aboab de Fonseca, was educated under the supervision of the aged Isaac Uzziel. Blessed with rich capacities, he acquired renown in his youth with his versatile culture. Menasseh was proficient not only in Hebrew but in Latin and knew many other European languages well. As an orator and preacher he successfully sustained comparison with such an extraordinarily gifted speaker as his friend Isaac Aboab.[9] His extensive knowledge of the literature of the ancient world and Christian theological writings was manifested by the young Menasseh in his four-volume *Conciliador,* in which all the passages in the Bible which at first glance contradict each other are quoted and exhaustively explained. This work, written in Spanish, was soon translated into Latin and English and made its author's name extremely popular in the Christian literary world. Through it he entered into correspondence with the most important scholars of that time, such as Dionysius Vossius, who translated his *Conciliador* into Latin, Hugo Grotius, Anna Marie de Schurman, and many others, as well as with the patroness and supporter of science, the Swedish Queen Christina. Menasseh's extraordinary popularity was aided not a little by the remarkable grace of his personality, the nobility of his character, his brilliant talent as a speaker, and his affability as a man of society.

The Jewish scholar was in close and friendly relations with many Dutch theologians and mystics of that time. The "apocalyptic" year 1666, when the thousand-year term from the fearful number with the mystical three sixes, 666, the accepted symbol of beast and man in the Christian world,[10] would be fulfilled, was then approaching. In Christendom it was firmly believed that the year 1666 would be a harbinger of the "end." Beelzebub, or Satan, would free himself from his chains. The wars of Gog and Magog would commence, and then the great miracles would occur and the "kingdom of heaven" reveal itself in all its glory.[11] These mystical moods and messianic expectations had a significant influence on Menasseh ben Israel's world outlook. He was devoted to his

8. Menasseh ben Israel was born in 1604 in the city of La Rochelle.
9. The well-known Spanish preacher Antonio de Vieira gave the following characteristic of these two talented orators: "Menasseh says what he knows, and Aboab knows what he says."
10. See the Revelation of St. John 13:18.
11. *Ibid.,* Chapter 20.

people with all his soul and witnessed with great pain the terrible sufferings of his brethren in the Christian lands. In Portugal and its colonies pyres flared up on which the best and most faithful children of the Jewish people[12] perished in fearful agony. The Thirty Years War brought horrible destruction to the Jewish community in Germany, and Chmielnitzki's wild bands drowned hundreds of flourishing communities of the Ukraine in blood. Menasseh was certain that all these terrors were the "pangs of the Messiah;" fearful darkness precedes the dawn. With great fervor he applied himself to the messianic Kabbalah and wrote a work, *Estatua de Nabuchanassar*,[13] in which he attempts, on the basis of a certain passage in the Book of Daniel, to calculate the "end," when the bitter exile would cease and the glorious redemption come. Relying on the words of the prophet Isaiah, "And He will gather the outcasts of Israel and assemble the scattered of Judah from the four corners of the earth" (Isaiah 11:12), Menasseh was certain that the Jews would be redeemed from exile and return to the land of their fathers only after being dispersed to all corners of the world and after the ten lost tribes were recovered. There appeared a certain Marrano traveller who asserted that in America, in the mountains of Ecuador, he had found among the Indians remnants of the lost tribes. These fantastic tales made such an impression on Menasseh ben Israel that he composed in 1650 a work entitled *Esperança de Israel* (The Hope of Israel) in which he triumphantly shows how beautifully the predictions of the prophets to the effect that the people of Israel would remain indestructible in exile were fulfilled, and that the speedy advent of the Messiah must now be awaited. This work was especially popular in England and evoked a rather large number of treatises in which all of the questions touched on in Menasseh's work are discussed. At the same time Menasseh wrote his only Hebrew work, *Nishmat Ḥayyim* (published in 1652). Here is revealed most clearly his unique personality, in which encyclopedic knowledge lived together peaceably with childish notions and primitive superstitions. In the epilogue to his work the author requests the reader to consider his conclusions attentively and give fullest credit to his words.

Menasseh adds,

I endeavored to obtain as much knowledge as possible and to collect a great number of books over which I pored day and night. I know

12. To these martyrs Menasseh ben Israel devotes several lovely and moving pages in his *Mikveh Yisrael* (*Esperança de Israel*).
13. This treatise was adorned with four illustrations by Rembrandt.

that not everything in my work will please the philosophers who demand that all things be demonstrated with logical proofs. But I have already explained numerous times that my guide is Rabbi Simeon ben Yoḥai, and I will not diverge from him by a hair's breadth. I advise you too, dear reader, to believe everything taught by Rabbi Simeon ben Yoḥai, the last of the sages of the Mishnah in time but the first in value and importance, for he has virtually no peer among the sages of Israel. He ascended to the heavens and with the light obtained there illuminated the eyes of Israel.[14]

"Virtually no peer"—this qualification Menasseh ben Israel considers it necessary to insist on, for he remembers that only two or three generations before there was a great Jewish scholar who could, in his view, sustain comparison with the author of the *Zohar*. This is the "holy Ari," the "divine" Rabbi Isaac Luria. "I always follow the ways of the Kabbalists," declares Menasseh, "and believe their words, for they have fathomed all mysteries. I know very well that the wisdom of Rabbi Isaac Luria rises above the highest mountains."[15] "Blessed is the generation that was privileged to have him in its midst!"[16] he exclaims with great enthusiasm and, along with this, assures the reader that all the miracles related about Luria in *Shivḥei Ha-Ari* are pure truth.[17] It is therefore no surprise that in his *Nishmat Ḥayyim* Menasseh so frequently quotes *Gedulat Ha-Ari* and *Shevaḥ Yakar*.[18]

Nishmat Ḥayyim is, in this respect, an extremely interesting phenomenon. Its author, with his European education and encyclopedic knowledge, quotes, when dealing with the question of the immortality of the soul, many thinkers of the ancient world and numerous later philosophers, scholars, naturalists, and poets. But all of them are covered with the ascetic cloak of Luria's Kabbalah, the melancholy and superstitious dread of the old *Sefer Ḥasidim*, which is so frequently quoted in *Nishmat Ḥayyim*. Menasseh ben Israel reports as "firm truth" that as soon as a man dies he is attacked by hosts of destroying angels who mock his helpless corpse.[19] "These destroying angels," he declares, "are the most dangerous mischief-makers for men. They produce all kinds of diseases and afflictions; these do not, as the doctors naively believe, come from a chill or a draught."[20] *Nishmat Ḥayyim* describes

14. *Nishmat Ḥayyim*, 106 (we quote according to the Leipzig edition, 1862).
15. *Ibid.*, 30.
16. *Ibid.*, 66.
17. *Ibid.*, 106.
18. *Ibid.*, 57, 65, and 103–4 ff.
19. *Ibid.*, 58.
20. *Ibid.*, 87.

in detail all the genera and species of demons and evil ones (p. 71). It relates how one can predict events from the flight of birds and their cries (81) and tells also of new-born children who prophesy (75), as well as of all kinds of incantations and formulas and of terrible forms. A whole series of chapters deal exclusively with magic and exorcism, with tricks of male and female witches who disguise themselves as cats and dragons. There are also lengthy accounts of "transmigrations" and vampires that suck the blood of men, and other terrifying portraits. There is no doubt, explains *Nishmat Ḥayyim*, that the dead in their graves are extremely well informed about everything that transpires in this world among the living.[21] With incantations and combinations of letters, one can conjure the deceased to reveal what is hidden for the living.[22] Also with magic and incantations, with names of the *Tum'ah* (uncleanness) and the *Sitra Aḥara* (other side), one can perform supernatural miracles.[23] Understandably, the doctrine of the transmigration of the soul, the mystery of impregnation (*sod ha-ibbur*), and tales about *dybbukim* occupy an especially honored place[24] in the work of Menasseh ben Israel, who was such a devoted follower of Isaac Luria's teaching.

The most interesting point in this connection is the following. Menasseh always repeats that he follows the way of the Kabbalists; nevertheless he considers it necessary to rely on "common sense" and on the proofs of scientific experimentation. He endeavors, for example, to demonstrate "by way of reason and logic" the existence of spirits and demons.[25] A bit of confusion, however, occurs here: Menasseh confounds one thing with another and does not mark the distinction between childish superstition and common sense, between rigorously scientific experiment and fantastic legends and old wive's tales. He introduces, for instance, a highly fantastic story out of *Shivḥei Vital* about a woman with a *dybbuk*— how this *dybbuk*, who refused to leave the woman, tells Ḥayyim Vital the whole story of his sinful life in the world. "See, understanding reader," Menasseh triumphantly declares "how the *dybbukim* and spirits themselves testify that such things really happen and how beautifully all this accords with common sense and logical thought."[26] "The whole world knows of such deeds and all take account of them and believe in them, for common sense so obliges,"

21. *Ibid.*, 50.
22. *Ibid.*, Chapters 7 and 28.
23. *Ibid.*, 89.
24. *Ibid.*, Part IV, Chapters 6–23.
25. *Ibid.*, Part III, Chapter 13.
26. *Ibid.*, 104.

the author later repeats.[27] On the basis of such "experiments" and logical theories of "common sense" Menasseh also relates, as if it were a well-known and certain thing, that there are men who can see with their eyes how water flows deep under the earth.[28]

As a mystic and devoted follower of Rabbi Simeon ben Yoḥai and Rabbi Isaac Luria, the author of *Nishmat Hayyim* was firmly convinced that a man's soul exists before he is born and continues to lead an independent life after his death. In this connection, he often notes that Plato expressed similar ideas, and this, Menasseh ben Israel explains, is because, as is well known, Plato was a pupil of the prophet Jeremiah.[29] It should also occasion no suprise that the Greek thinker Pythagoras set forth the doctrine of transmigration of the soul considerably before Rabbi Simeon ben Yoḥai and Rabbi Isaac Luria. "It is, after all, common knowledge," explains Menasseh ben Israel, "that this Greek thinker was a pupil of the prophet Ezekiel and later became converted and joined the children of Abraham."[30] For Menasseh it is also beyond doubt that even the Brahmins of India are descended from Abraham and that the name Brahmin is a corruption of Abrahamanim.[31]

But Menasseh recalls quite well that one of the greatest of Jewish scholars denied what he, Menasseh, holds to be "true and established." This was the author of the *Mishneh Torah*, Moses Maimonides, who refused to believe in demons, transmigrations of the soul, and the like. His disbelief derived from the fact, Menasseh regretfully explains, that this great Jew stumbled along the false paths of Aristotle, who believed only in what one can see with his eyes and attain through speculative thought. The author of *Nishmat Hayyim* therefore admonishes the reader not to let himself be led astray on the ways of Aristotle and his disciples, for "their words are false and their doctrine is false." Let the pious reader follow only the God-fearing Jewish sages, the true shepherds, whose Torah is spread over the whole world.[32]

Nishmat Hayyim, which was so enthusiastically received in its own day, most clearly characterizes the moods which then dominated the Sephardic community of Amsterdam. This work explains why Menasseh ben Israel's townsmen responded with such tremendous ardor to the Shabbetai Tzevi movement. Three years after Menasseh ben Israel's work appeared, another mystical work

27. *Ibid.*, 105.
28. *Ibid.*, 106.
29. *Ibid.*, 22, 105.
30. *Ibid.*, 105, 106.
31. *Ibid.*, 105.
32. *Ibid.*, 72–106.

came off the press in Amsterdam, a work closely associated with Menasseh ben Israel's colleague, Isaac Aboab, and with the views of the mystics who led the Shabbetai Tzevi movement. The work in question is Abraham de Herrera's *Shaar Ha-Shamayim* (*Puerta del Cielo*).

The Marrano Abraham (Alonzo) de Herrera occupied a high position at the Spanish court. Suddenly, when he was already in middle age, Herrera left Spain, came to Amsterdam, and publicly returned to Judaism. He was a man of many-sided philosophical education with a certain inclination toward neo-Platonism. Hence, it is not surprising that when he became familiar with Jewish theological literature, he was greatly interested in the conspicuous affinity between the views of the Jewish mystics and certain fundamental ideas of the neo-Platonists. The greatest influence on his outlook came from his acquaintanceship with the well-known emissary and popularizer of Rabbi Isaac Luria's doctrine Israel Saruk, who came from Italy to Amsterdam and found in Herrera the most devoted disciple and admirer. After Saruk had inducted him into the mysteries of Luria's Kabbalah, Herrera decided to expound philosophically the system of the mystics of Safed from the neo-Platonic standpoint in a special work.[33] Since Herrera did not have full command of Hebrew, he wrote his work in Spanish under the title *Puerta del Cielo* and before his death (1639) requested his friend Isaac Aboab to translate it into Hebrew and publish it at the first opportunity. Aboab, himself a devoted mystic and connoisseur of Kabbalist literature, fulfilled his friend's request in superlative fashion. All the theosophical-philosophical concepts and tags that are to be found in such profusion in Herrera's work are rendered clearly and distinctly in the translation. *Shaar Ha-Shamayim*, which appeared in 1655, provided for the first time the possibility of obtaining some knowledge of Luria's Kabbalah, not in the chaotic and unsystematic reports of Vital and his associates but in the clear form of a philosophically schooled systematizer. It is quite possible that in the manner and external form in which Herrera reports Luria's system, a certain role was played not only by his competence in neo-Platonic philosophy but also by his knowledge of Christian theological literature. This, in our view, is especially noticeable where the author of *Shaar Ha-Shamayim* reports one of the basic ideas in Luria's system, the divine "emanations" and the appearance of the *partzofin* (faces). Herrera ingeniously explains to the reader the problem of the divine attributes, which must have a negative character, and how one must

33. *Shaar Ha-Shamayim*, Book II, Chapter 6.

come, at first blush, to paradoxical conclusions when dealing with the question of the nature of the "First Cause": without name, without limit, beyond time and space—and yet everything is in it and nothing outside; without form and structure—and yet the primordial source of all structures and forms; single and indivisible—and yet the source of all the infinitely varied forms and phenomena; above all human conceptions of lovingkindness and mercy, of beauty and justice—and yet the measure and highest symbol of loveliness, grace, and righteousness.[34]

But the rich variety of being, Herrera insists, is not the *direct* product of the First Cause. The *maaseh bereshit* (work of creation) was produced through the *Ein Sof*'s single radiation or emanation which the other Kabbalists named *Keter Elyon* (High Crown) but which is called by Rabbi Isaac Luria (who faithfully follows the "bright pillar," the godly Rabbi Simeon ben Yoḥai) *Adam Kadmon* (Primal Man), the primordial structure of man, which is also the *Sechel Ha-Ne'elam*, the hidden divine thought.[35] This first and perfect divine emanation is the cause of all further causes, the fashioning power of creation, of worlds and beings. It is also the first name of the *Ein Sof*, for the *Ein Sof* Himself transcends all names.

According to Herrera's interpretation, this "cause of all further causes"—*Adam Kadmon*—occupies a more important place in Luria's system than Vital reports. The author of *Shaar Ha-Shamayim* even speaks, for this reason, not merely of five *partzofin* or "faces" which were created after "the breaking of the vessels" but of six. Not the three-headed *Arich Anpin* (Long Face) is the first among the *partzofin* but the *Atika Kadisha* (the Holy Ancient One), the *partzof* or "face" of the first divine emanation, *Adam Kadmon*. To be sure, Herrera explains further that the two *partzofin* are merged and the *Arich Anpin* is indivisible from the *Atika Kadisha*, for it is His external vestment.[36]

With the extremely important role of *Adam Kadmon*, which is so sharply stressed in *Shaar Ha-Shamayim*, the comparison that Herrera makes between "the heavenly man" and earthly man is highly interesting. Just as earthly man surpasses with his perfection all other creatures, whose goal and model he is, so the heavenly man (*He-Adam Ha-Elohi*) is higher and more perfect than all the other emanations and heavenly powers, whose cause and origin he is. Earthly man is the closing link and final goal of all the created worlds, and the heavenly man is their beginning. Earthly man is

34. *Ibid.*, Book VI, Chapter 6.
35. *Ibid.*, p. 91; *cf.* p. 11.
36. See also the last chapter of *Shaar Ha-Shamayim*.

the focus receiving from everything and everywhere the scattered sparks, while the heavenly man spreads light and radiates. Earthly man is the midpoint of the reflected light which strives towards the heights to its primordial source; the heavenly man is the source of light which illuminates and animates everything. As earthly man raises everything to the First Cause, so the heavenly man, who is a radiation of the First Cause, unifies and embraces all levels, from the highest to the lowest. Earthly man is the resting place of the *Shechinah*, the tent of the *Malchut Kadisha* (holy kingdom), and the heavenly man is the temple of the *Ein Sof*.[37] And the highest representative, the incarnate symbol of earthly man, the tent of the *Malchut Kadisha*, is the Messiah, the redeemer of the world, who will liberate all the good seeds from the *kelipot* or shells and lift all the holy sparks from the valley of weeping and sin to the celestial heights, the source of infinite light.

Soon after Isaac Aboab had published his translation of *Shaar Ha-Shamayim* tidings came to him that the long-awaited Messiah had already appeared, that he was marching with royal steps, and that his agents were proclaiming in all corners of the world: The day of great judgment is at hand!

"I, your Messiah, Shabbetai Tzevi!"

We have observed several times previously that precisely at the time when a new era in European history commenced and the shadows of the Middle Ages began to disappear, the Jewish ghetto became ever darker and more melancholy. Filled almost to the brim was the cup of suffering, and the only hope and consolation of the homeless people was their firm belief in speedy redemption: soon the Messiah the son of David would appear, the fortunes of the exiled nation would revive, the troubles and sorrows would pass away like a shadow, and grace and lovingkindness would again flow over the chosen people.

But the day of redemption did not come. The cup of suffering was not yet completely filled. In the middle of the seventeenth century, just when the works of Menasseh ben Israel and Herrera appeared, a violent new storm broke out which cruelly laid waste hundreds of Jewish communities. On the bloody forestage appeared Bogdan Chmielnitzki with his bands, and the terrible deeds of the era of the Crusades and the years of terror of the Black Plague were reenacted. Almost a quarter of a million Jews perished in the course of the frightful decade 1648–58. The despairing people was permeated with a single thought: To go on living in this way is beyond human powers! Something *must* happen and make

37. *Ibid.*, Book VI, Chapter 4.

an end of the indescribable sufferings! The people waited for redemption, waited impatiently, with the anger and frantic trust of which only a grieved, homeless, and mystically minded human soul is capable.

At that critical moment there appeared on the arena of Jewish communal life two antithetical personalities—extreme representatives of diametrically opposed worlds and world outlooks which fought with great stubbornness for dominance throughout many generations and each of which wished to place its stamp on Jewish culture. One of these was a giant in the realm of philosophical thought, a man for whom seeking and knowing was the only goal, the greatest joy in life; the other was an imaginative dreamer, an exalted mystic, who lost the boundary between the real and the unreal, between dream and reality. These men were Baruch Spinoza and Shabbetai Tzevi.

The spirit of free investigative thought and the thirst for knowledge so characteristic of the Spanish Jews in the heyday of the Arabic period were not entirely extinguished even in later times when mystical and orthodox currents occupied the entire foreground of Jewish cultural life. This was noticeable in the new center in Holland, where the refugee Marranos felt liberated from the leaden pressure of the Catholic Church and the fear of the hellish Inquisition with its executioners. Men had a chance to breathe freely, to follow their own consciences, to cast off the yoke that inquisitorial hands had placed upon them. In this intellectually excited environment appeared, soon after the restless, weak-charactered freethinker and rationalist Uriel Acosta,[38] the magnificent, calm and sedate figure of Spinoza, whose critical thinking refused to take account of any tradition or authorities.

The influence of this great philosopher on Judaism and its culture was slight and insignificant. Ordinarily the attempt is made to explain this by citing the fact that the Jewish community in that era of decline was at too low an intellectual level to be able to accept the ideas of its brilliant son. This may, indeed, be true in regard to German-Polish Jewry, but one cannot say it of the community in which Spinoza himself grew up. We have observed that in Amsterdam there were men of encyclopedic knowledge. There were also those who listened carefully to the teaching of their great contemporary. Yet at the decisive moment they placed themselves not on his side but on the side of his antipode and, together with thousands of their brethren, greeted with turbulent cries of joy, with dancing and singing, the happy tidings that the

38. For a discussion of Acosta, see our article in the *Russian-Jewish Encyclopedia*, Vol. I (1908).

redeemer was coming. Other motives and conditions apparently made it impossible for Spinoza's ideas and views to find resonance in the Jewish environment. Above all, the question must be raised: What could Spinoza's profound and harmoniously complete doctrine really give at that time to the grievously suffering people, drowning in their own blood? Could it assuage their sufferings? Could it heal their wounds? To answer this question it is sufficient to recall how Spinoza regarded Jewish culture and its bearer, the Jewish people.

One must first take into consideration that Spinoza is not only one of the greatest philosophic thinkers of the West but also the founder of scientific Biblical criticism. Even the great Jewish rationalists Maimonides and Gersonides take the position that the Torah is a divine revelation of eternal significance. Spinoza, however, tears the mantle of sacredness from the Torah. He considers it a product of human civilization whose worth and significance is valid only for a definite time.[39] Furthermore, Spinoza is not content with purely scientific criticism; polemical notes are also heard in him. "He who lives under the guidance of reason," he teaches in his *Ethics*,[40] "endeavors as far as possible to reply to another's hatred, anger, and contempt with love or kindness." "He who endeavors to avenge wrongs with hatred is assuredly wretched." In another place Spinoza says further, "The man of strong character[41] and noble soul bears no hatred toward any one, comes to no anger, knows of no pride, and has contempt for no one."[42]

Unfortunately, however, Spinoza himself—the remarkably noble, crystal-pure personality who so profoundly and thoroughly investigated and analyzed human passions—did not always conduct himself as, in his view, a man "who lives under the guidance of reason" should. He refused to forgive the members of his community their hostility toward himself. He forgot his own principle that one must respond to hatred and anger with love and magnanimity. He could not overcome his feeling of indignation and hatred for the spiritual leaders of his people stemming from the fact that the rabbis of Amsterdam had excommunicated him. His hostility extended even to historical Judaism and Jewry. Just as did Acosta, so Spinoza called the rabbis nothing other than "Pharisees." He speaks with particular contempt of the "chosen-

---

39. In his *Theologico-Political Treatise*.
40. *Ethics*, Part IV, Proposition 46.
41. "By a strong character" Spinoza declares (*Ethics*, Part III, Proposition 59), "I understand man's effort to preserve his own being solely according to the dictates of the understanding."
42. *Ethics*, Part III, Note to Proposition 73.

ness" of the Jewish people and endeavors to show that the Jews are in no respect superior to other peoples. He emphasizes that among other peoples also there were prophets,[43] and that the apostles of Christianity were at a much higher level than the Hebrew prophets.[44] It is true that the Torah was received only by the Jewish people; but in this, Spinoza asserts, there is nothing of which to be so proud, for the laws of the Torah are for everyday, material existence. These laws were suited to the political life of the Jews of Palestine. At present, however, they are superfluous. The laws of the Torah, Spinoza is persuaded, have no greater value than the laws of any other people. They are not required for their truth and justice but for their utility. The supreme goal of life and true morality consists in knowing God, and this can be attained not through fulfilling commandments but through studying the universal laws of nature.[45]

But Spinoza is not content with fighting against Jewish "chosenness" and endeavoring to show that the Jewish people has no greater merits than any other people. He has still another intention: he wishes to *degrade* this people, whose spiritual leaders expelled him, the free thinker, from their midst. He poses the question: Why is it that the Jewish people so frequently forsook the laws of the Torah, when the goal of these laws was presumably to maintain the people in its land? Why was Israel so often subjected to foreign nations and its land finally destroyed?[46] To this Spinoza gives an extraordinary answer: God, out of hatred for and anger at the Jewish people, deliberately gave it laws whose purpose was not to sustain the people but to destroy it as quickly as possible. "The more I delve into this problem," says Spinoza,

the more the idea is confirmed in me that God at that time was not at all concerned about its [the Jewish people's] happiness and security but was endeavoring to punish it for all its evil qualities, as Tacitus already noted in his day. And it is, indeed, quite astonishing that the divine wrath against the Jewish people was so great that God bestowed upon it laws that were not suited to serve the people but must be considered punishment and revenge for evil deeds.[47]

Many Spinoza scholars stress the influence that the Kabbalah had on his philosophical system.[48] This influence can certainly not

43. *Theologico-Political Treatise*, 188.
44. *Ibid.*, 203–4.
45. *Ibid.*, 198–202.
46. *Ibid.*, Chapter 17.
47. *Ibid.*, 384.
48. Johann Georg Wachter first pointed to this influence already at the end of the seventeenth century (1699).

be denied, but it was not of such great significance as is commonly thought. First of all, it must not be overlooked that the influence of the Kabbalah is discernible only in the metaphysical, speculative part of Spinoza's system. Like the Kabbalah, Spinoza teaches that God is the absolutely single primal substance from which everything that exists, every individual and concrete being, derives. "All that is is God, and outside of God nothing can exist or even be thought."[49] In opposition to his teacher Descartes, and in consonance with the *Zohar*, Spinoza carries through the strictest monism in his system. He does not consider matter and mind two independent substances, completely different in their nature, which are united only in divinity; matter (extension) and mind (thought) are, according to the Spinozist system, merely two of the infinite attributes of the First Cause. Extension, in Spinoza's view, is embodied thought which may be seen with the senses, and thought is the hidden extension that we cannot see; both are identical in divinity.

Agreeing with the *Zohar* in the basic idea that God is one and all, that *omnia in Deo esse* (everything is in God), Spinoza, however, diverges from it in the chief point, which is in fact the most valuable core of the *Zohar*, its teaching about ethics. The fundamental idea that is the backbone of the philosophy of the *Zohar* consists in considering the world as having an enormously powerful moral element, in whose development and final victory a supremely important role is played by the human personality. In Spinoza's system, however, the function of the human personality is virtually nil. With great brilliance the philosopher develops the idea that nature knows of no accidental phenomena, for everything is the result of iron necessity, every phenomenon is a link in the infinite chain of causes and effects.[50] Good and evil, the perfect and imperfect, beauty and ugliness—all these are notions which, from the objective standpoint, have no meaning, for these qualities do not belong to objects themselves; they are merely emotional impressions of our way of thinking.[51] Objective knowledge has to do only with the constant, regular connection of entities among themselves. Good, beautiful, and the like are merely subjective notions and, depending on one's point of view or mood, the beautiful may be considered ugly, the useful harmful, the good evil, etc. All these opinions and valuations produced by thinking and feeling persons have, in Spinoza's view, merely a subjective and relative valence, not an objective and absolute one.

49. *Ethics*, Part I, Proposition 15.
50. *Ethics*, Part I, Proposition 29.
51. *Ibid.*, Part I, Appendix to Proposition 36.

This is also true with regard to morality. In the infinite chain of being and becoming, the same place belongs to the moral as to the immoral. From the objective view, both alike denote nothing more than the association or connection of various demands, wishes, and inferences. Both are included in the great chain binding all forms of being to their everlasting foundation.[52] Into this general union of all forms of being with their eternal foundation Spinoza sets his teaching about morality, purely *intellectual* morality. Not without reason does he teach that "the will, like the intellect, is only a certain mode of thinking."[53] We must regard all things, Spinoza repeats, not as accidental but as necessary. The necessity of all things in nature is the necessity of God's eternal essence itself. Here we touch upon the major point in which the world view of the *Zohar* is in complete opposition to Spinoza's philosophical system. The *Zohar* teaches that the First Cause, divinity, is *above* the world and completely *free* in creating it. But Spinoza, relying on Hasdai Crescas,[54] gives divine "freedom" an altogether unique interpretation. He takes the position that "God acts only according to the laws of His own nature and is constrained by no one."[55] And because "all that is is God and outside God nothing can be," everything is predetermined by the necessity of the divine nature. It is not only predetermined to be but, indeed, to be and to behave in a specific way, and there is nothing whatever that is accidental.[56] "Everything is foreseen"—from this it logically follows that "the [divine] will cannot be denoted as a free cause but as necessity." And from this, Spinoza forthwith declares, "it follows first that God does not act according to free will."[57] For His being and acting follow necessarily from the essence of His nature. The dispassionate search for the universal connections among all things and phenomena—this, according to Spinoza's doctrine, is the supreme level, the true essence of morality. Rational thought, correct inquiry, is the sole consequence that follows with genuine, harmonious necessity from the spiritual or intellectual essence. To devote oneself entirely to rational inquiry, to the proper understanding of everything that surrounds us—in this consists the only bliss, the only joy, of man. "In life," Spinoza teaches, "it is more useful than anything else to perfect, as far as possible,

52. See Jodl, *Geschichte der Ethik*, I, 250–51 (we quote according to the Russian translation).
53. *Ethics*, Part I, Proof to Proposition 32.
54. See Vol. III of this work, pp. 202–26.
55. *Ethics*, Part I, Proposition 17.
56. *Ibid.*, Proof to Proposition 29.
57. *Ibid.*, Proposition 32.

the understanding, or wisdom; and in this alone does man's happiness or beatitude consist."[58] In calm, quiet philosophical inquiry, Spinoza, like Maimonides and Gersonides in their day, sees the only goal and the supreme flowering of man's spiritual powers.

Spinoza's idea that the concepts of good and evil have no absolute but only a relative significance is certainly quite correct. However, he does not draw from it the logical conclusion that the value of these concepts is not at all thereby diminished among men, because they reflect *human* and *social* relationships. Like his contemporary Thomas Hobbes, he perceives in human society only the "war of all against all." And, again like Hobbes, he refuses to take account of the social tendencies of man and gives very little attention to the role and significance of the group. As Maimonides had done in his day, so Spinoza tore man out of his social bonds and considered him merely as an abstract "mode" of divinity and not as a member and product of the social and cultural community. Hence, he sees the essence of morality, of man's happiness and virtue, only in intellectual knowledge. "The highest good (*summmum bonum*) of the mind," Spinoza teaches, "is God-knowledge, and the supreme virtue is to know God."[59] "In him," the moral philosopher Jodl quite properly notes, "appears very clearly the idea that the truly ethical can preserve its specific content only when it separates itself from the sentiments and subjective inclinations of man's heart and creates, so to speak, with its own means a world of pure reason and logical deduction." One must also not forget, in this connection, that Spinoza who, like Maimonides, saw in pure thinking alone the supreme task of morality himself recognized that this task can be fulfilled only by the elect few.

It is clear that Spinoza's doctrine was even more foreign and inimical to the traditional Jewish world view than the doctrine of Maimonides in his day. In the *Guide for the Perplexed*, which was produced in the most glorious period of Arabic-Jewish civilization, the problems for which a significant part of the contemporary Jewish intelligentsia so impatiently sought a solution found a clear resonance, but the teaching of the great philosopher of Amsterdam could not find any reverberation in the Jewish community of the seventeenth century. The objective cultural historian can therefore not free himself from the doubt whether he has the right to judge the orthodox rabbis of Amsterdam harshly for excluding from their midst their brilliant son, the great freethinker, because they saw in him a serious threat to their national

58. *Ibid.*, Part IV, Fourth Appendix to Proposition 73.
59. *Ibid.*, Part IV, Proposition 28.

heritage, for the sake of which they had just endured so many troubles and sufferings.

The thinker expelled from the community led a solitary life, immersed in his world of philosophic ideas. He lived and died alien to the Jewish people and its needs. At that time, however, another personality appeared whose entire soul was permeated with the longings and hopes of his suffering brethren. He gave a clear, categorical answer to the cardinal questions burning in the grieved heart of his homeless people, and the people surrendered itself to him with blind faith and ardent love.

This other was Shabbetai Tzevi.

CHAPTER SEVEN

The Shabbetai Tzevi Movement

HABBETAI Tzevi, the extraordinary man who knew of no barriers between the imaginary and the real and whose spirit wavered between the normal and the abnormal, proclaimed with definite assurance to all corners of the Diaspora that the cup of suffering was already overflowing and that the day of redemption had arrived. Even the determined opponents of the Shabbetai Tzevi movement who lived in that era were compelled to admit that in this man there was a powerful attraction that literally enchanted all who came into contact with it.[1] Something in this young man with the melodious, richly resonant voice and dreamy eyes, flashing with mystical ardor, won people over.

From his early years Shabbetai Tzevi had been engrossed in the Kabbalah of Rabbi Isaac Luria. He afflicted his body with mortifications and fasts[2] in order to attain the level of separation from corporeality, and lived constantly on the boundary between two worlds. The young Kabbalist from Smyrna declared relentless war against the *Sitra Aḥara* (the "other side"), for he felt that on him lay the obligation to liberate the holy "sparks" imprisoned in the sinful *kelipah* or shell. The mystic lived in a milieu which was overburdened with messianic hopes. With bated breath men awaited the "end," the redeemer, the symbol of glory and beauty who would make an end to the dark rule of Samael. The melodies

1. See, for example, the testimony of Shabbetai Tzevi's contemporary published in Yaabetz' (Jacob Emden's) *Torat Ha-Kenaot*, 3 (1870).
2. *Ibid.*

of Israel Najara's fervent, mystical songs resounded everywhere,[3] and men waited impatiently for the fulfillment of the prophetic words of the holy *Zohar* to the effect that in the year 1648 the redemption would come.[4] From his own father, an agent and representative of an English firm,[5] the young Shabbetai Tzevi learned that in certain Christian circles men were also sure that the redeemer must soon appear. They relied on a verse in the Revelation of St. John (13:18) for their conviction that in the year 1666 the fate of the people of Israel would be determined: either all Jews would pass over into the bosom of the Christian church or their Messiah would appear and reestablish a Jewish state.

And now the year 1648, about which the *Zohar* had uttered prophecies, had arrived. It brought, however, not the long-awaited redemption but fearful destruction, a new page of blood and terror which Bogdan Chmielnitzki inscribed with his Cossack sword in the history of Jewish suffering and persecution. In the terrible catastrophe which struck the major Jewish community, the youthful mystic perceived a promise that the "pangs of the Messiah" were beginning. These were the great woes of the coming redemption that must soon be revealed before the whole world. Gradually there ripened in the depths of the soul of Shabbetai Tzevi, who was surrounded by a circle of fervent disciples and admirers, a seductive thought: perhaps he himself, Shabbetai ben Mordecai Tzevi, was the chosen one, the long-awaited redeemer. He disclosed this intoxicating secret to his associates, and the latter with enchantment confirmed the idea and removed all his doubts. It has happened! He for whom men have waited so long has finally appeared! He will redeem the homeless people from their sorrow, bring them back to the land of their fathers, and there recompense them for their vast sufferings with exceeding joy and splendor.

Not without reason did the young Kabbalist twice resist temptation and refuse to enjoy woman's love.[6] He, the chosen of God, was united with another mate; his bride and destined one was the

3. Testimony about the great influence of Najara's poems on the messianic hopes and expectations of that era is given by the prominent adherent of the Shabbetai Tzevi movement, Raphael Sofino, in his letter to Jacob Sasportas (see *Kitzur Tzitzat Novel Tzevi*).
4. For the passage in question see the *Zohar*, I, 139.
5. For a discussion of Shabbetai Tzevi's father, see *REJ*, LVIII, 270–72.
6. Mordecai Tzevi married his eighteen-year-old Shabbetai to the beautiful daughter of a wealthy merchant of Smyrna. Shabbetai, however, refused to have sexual relationships with his wife, and her parents thereupon demanded that he give her a divorce. Mordecai Tzevi then married off his son again, but the second woman also had to be divorced by Shabbetai for the same reason (see *Torat Ha-Kenaot*, 3).

sacred Torah, the incarnate *Shechinah*. In 1657 he came with a group of his devoted followers from Smyrna to Salonika, there arranged a great wedding feast and went under the canopy, embracing with both arms a scroll of the Torah. This was a symbol that the Messiah had bound himself forever with his celestial bride, the sacred Torah. To her, his bride, the one destined for him by heaven, Shabbetai Tzevi sang mystical love songs permeated with the burning pathos of the Song of Songs:

From the peak of the mountain I descended to the valley and there met the princess Meliselda. She has just come out of the fresh waters; from her tresses black as night drops still fall. Like a sharply honed sword does her face shine, her brows are like hardened steel, her lips like coral, and her body whiter than milk.

To report the details of the Shabbetai Tzevi movement is no part of our enterprise. Our task is merely to provide an account of the literature which the movement elicited and produced. The first shoots of this literature appeared after Shabbetai Tzevi came to Constantinople and the popular preacher Abraham Ha-Yachini there joined him.

It is difficult to give a proper estimate of this doubtless talented man, since the necessary material is lacking. In any case it is very hard to believe that Yachini was really such a base swindler and deceiver as David Kahana, the author of *Even Ha-To'im*, portrayed him. It is common knowledge that this scholar of the Haskalah period has only one color for mystics and Kabbalists— soot black; hence, one must utilize the works of this diligent but biased investigator with great caution.

An excellent stylist[7] and talented preacher, Abraham Ha-Yachini was extremely popular among the masses of the Jewish populace, and it was said of him that he was as wise as King Solomon. This "wise Yachini" was a fervent mystic, an ardent follower of Isaac Luria's Kabbalah. He suffered from hallucinations, frequently saw fantastic prophetic dreams which he later wrote down in typical apocalyptic style. We present here in translation two of his mystic "visions."

I

In the year 1652 in the month of Ḥeshvan I had a dream: An enormous camel was pursuing me and I fled from it in deathly terror. I entered

7. Especially interesting in this respect is Abraham Ha-Yachini's *Hod Malchut* (1655), which consists of one hundred and fifty chapters written in the style of the Psalms. On Abraham Ha-Yachini's other works, see *REJ*, LVIII, 273-83.

a room and bolted the door firmly behind me. But the door could not withstand the camel, so I had to flee to another room and from there to a third, where lay a mantle light as a wave. From the room steps led directly to the sea. In this room leading to the sea, I was no longer afraid of the camel. Before me appeared a maiden of marvelous beauty who embraced and kissed me. This extraordinary beauty began to adjure me not to forget her, for she knew that I would marry a princess who was still temporarily on the moon and is covered by the sun. The princess will descend from the sun and the moon and I will wed her. And I swore to the lovely maiden that I would not forget her, and I had great compassion for her and she surrendered herself to me. Immediately thereafter another virgin appeared. The sun and the moon rose, and on them the princess who was to be my bride appeared, shining and radiant as the sun. In great terror and fear I awakened and saw that it was only a dream. How wondrously all this occurred. I swear by the Torah that I have reported everything faithfully, word for word.

II

In the same month of Ḥeshvan I saw another dream: In the room where I was lying an old man of medium height and fearful appearance appeared. The old man approached me, and deathly terror fell upon me as I saw him coming to me. He took me by the hand, and I understood that he wished to lead me to judgment. So I fell on my knees before him and begged him not to lead me anywhere but himself judge me on the spot. He sat down and did not lead me anywhere. I then said to him: "Know, my lord, that it is now fully twenty years that I have withdrawn from this world and occupied myself solely with the Torah. Perhaps I have nevertheless sinned, but I am, after all, no more than flesh and blood, and the evil inclination sometimes triumphs." The terrible old man rose at once and I pleaded with him: "I have sinned, I have done perversely, I have transgressed." I confessed before him not only in Hebrew but in the vernacular as well. Then I asked him: "Who are you, my lord?" He answered me: "I am the Mishnah that punishes men. I am the Torah that loved you much and bound you firmly to herself. Take heed, and speak such words no more." But out of great fear I continued to confess before him, until suddenly the old man was transformed into a marvelously beautiful virgin. I took her and embraced her. And when the fearful old man uttered his words, he constantly embraced and kissed, embraced and kissed. . . . In great fear, with raised hair, I awakened. A cold sweat fell upon me, and I wept bitterly when I remembered my dream. Only God knows and understands what this marvelous vision can mean. Let Him grant that my portion may be among those who occupy themselves with the Torah for its own sake, Amen.[8]

8. *Ibid.*, 283–84.

This mystic became one of Shabbetai Tzevi's most devoted followers and played a major role in the latter's remarkable life.[9] Indeed, the opponents of the Shabbetai Tzevi movement charge Abraham Ha-Yachini with being the author of the falsified "document" (*Ketav*) with which Shabbetai Tzevi's appearance as Messiah and redeemer is so closely associated. A skilled scribe and copyist of old manuscripts, he declared that he found an old parchment deriving from an ancient manuscript, and in this parchment it is related:

And I, Abraham, who was locked up fully forty years and found myself in great affliction because of the power of the great sea monster which crouches in the river of Egypt, always thought: When will the wondrous end come? And now a voice is heard: "Know that in the year 1626 a son will be born to Mordecai Tzevi, and the name Shabbetai will be given to him. And he will subjugate the great sea monster, overcome the fearful rattlesnake, the furious dragon. And he is the true Messiah. Not with strength of hand will he go to war, and he will ascend the ladder on an ass.[10] His kingdom will rule to all eternities, and beside him there is no redeemer for Israel. Stand on your feet and hear what is recounted of the power of this man who appears outwardly so weak and poor. He is My beloved and as precious to me as the apple of My eye. . . . And he will sit on My throne and his hand will be on God's footstool.

Further on there is an account in obscure, fantastic expressions of a "man of a cubit upon a cubit and with a beard of a cubit." In the hands of this dwarf is a hammer with which he is breaking down an enormous mountain. This "vision" ends with the following prophetic words:

A month later this fearful man [the dwarf] again appeared to me and said: "My son, how great is your power, that I reveal to you mysteries such as are hidden even from the ministering angels. Now write down this vision and conceal it in an earthen pot so that it may be preserved for many years. And know that this man of whom I now tell you will make great efforts to attain the heavenly faith, and of him the prophet Habakkuk prophesied: *Ve-tzaddik be-emunato yihyeh* ["the righteous shall live by his faith"—from the Hebrew words the acronym Tzevi is easily derivable]. For Israel will serve false gods for many years, but *he* will return to the true faith. Many

9. Very interesting in this respect is Abraham Ha-Yachini's letter to Nathan of Gaza after Shabbetai Tzevi had converted to Islam (published in *REJ*, XXVI, 209–19).
10. A mystical-symbolic expression, which is interpreted in various ways.

of his contemporaries, however, will issue forth against him with blasphemy and scorn, for these blasphemers are descended from the 'mixed multitude,' despite the fact that they stand at the summit of their generation and are considered the 'heads and sages of the generation.' But he will perform fearful wonders and sacrifice himself for the sanctification of God's name."[11]

Shabbetai Tzevi was soon familiarized with this "document," and it made a colossal impression upon him. His last doubts were destroyed. Yes, he is the true Messiah, the beloved and chosen of God. This must be announced in all the dispersions of Israel, the joyous tidings must be proclaimed to all corners of the world. This role of spreading the news through all lands was brilliantly fulfilled by Shabbetai's Tzevi's two associates, the "chief secretary of the king Messiah," Jehudah Samuel Primo, and the Messiah's "prophet," the twenty-year-old Nathan Benjamin of Gaza. With great pride and self-assurance Nathan of Gaza stepped forth in the role of Elijah the prophet, the emissary and harbinger of the Messiah who will soon appear in all his splendor. He distributed proclamations and announcements, written in the feeling, exalted style of the Biblical prophets, to numerous Jewish communities. "Know ye, all our brethren of the house of Jacob," we read in one of these proclamations,

God has accepted His people and sent to us the redeemer and protector, Shabbetai Tzevi our king, whom the prophet Nathan of Gaza has anointed at God's command. Now, at the order of our king and his prophet, you must declare days of fasting and repentance. Turn away from your evil ways, gather together, and come to bow down before your king.

Nathan of Gaza circulated the following letter to many cities:

My brethren of the house of Israel, know that our Messiah was born in the city of Smyrna and his name is Shabbetai Tzevi. Soon his kingdom will reveal itself. He will take away the royal crown from the king of Ishmael and set it upon his own head. The king of Ishmael will serve him as a Canaanite slave, for to him the kingdom belongs. Afterwards our Messiah will disappear from the eyes of Israel and no one will know where he has gone, whether he is alive or dead. And our Messiah will go to the other side of the river Sambatyon where the daughter of our teacher Moses, Rebecca, whom our Messiah will take to wife, lives. And Moses waits for the advent of the Messiah

11. See *Even Ha-To'im*, pp. 61–62; *Inyanei Shabbetai Tzevi* (1912), p. 99.

and will go to meet him, together with the Rechabites and the ten tribes, to bring him across the River Sambatyon which, as is known, no mortal man has yet succeeded in crossing in peace. For every day of the week the river casts tremendous stones with terrific impact, resting only on the Sabbath day. But if anyone attempts to cross the river on the Sabbath, then, as soon as he comes to the ten tribes, they stone him, because he has desecrated the Sabbath rest and violated the law of our sacred Torah. But when our Messiah will have to cross the river along with Moses our teacher and the ten tribes, the river will be calm and will not cast any stones until all will have crossed in peace. . . . Then a lion, out of whose mouth fire spurts forth and whose bridle will be a seven-headed serpent, will come down from heaven. On this lion our Messiah will ride and bring Moses our master with all the Jews to Jerusalem. On the way Gog and Magog will come to meet them with their people, which is as numerous as the sand of the seas, and will want to wage war against our Messiah. And our Messiah Shabbetai Tzevi will not fight with the sword or the spear, but with the breath of his mouth will he slay the wicked and with the word of the living God will he smash them to the ground. And when our Messiah will come to Jerusalem with Moses our teacher and the people of Israel, God will let down from the heavens the Temple, constructed of gold and precious stones that will illumine the whole city of Jerusalem. Then our Messiah will bring sacrifices to God, and the resurrection of the dead will take place over the whole world. . . . What more will occur may not be revealed, for all this must still be veiled in secrecy. But all will see these things with their own eyes as soon as God brings the exiles back to Zion. I inform you of all this so that you may know that you will soon have the privilege of being redeemed. Thus says Nathan Benjamin Ashkenazi.[12]

At the same time that Nathan of Gaza, the Messiah's prophet, distributed his proclamations and urged Jews to fast and repent in order to be worthy of the advent of the Messiah, the "chief secretary," Samuel Primo, sent solemn orders to all communities with the proud subscription: "David, the son of Jesse, the Messiah of the God of Jacob, Shabbetai Tzevi."

"I, your Messiah, Shabbetai Tzevi"—this solemn, jubilant cry was carried to all Jewish congregations and communities, and everywhere evoked a wild, fervent, literally intoxicating joy. Anyone who reads even the dry, protocol-like reports of that time in which is described the "mass psychosis," as the stormy messianic movement called forth by the mystic of Smyrna is regarded by some psychological investigators, experiences a feeling of profound

12. Nathan Benjamin's father, Ḥayyim Elisha, was descended from Ashkenazic Jews.

tragedy and heartfelt woe. It has finally happened! He has come—the long-awaited emissary of God! God has heard the cry of His people, and now great consolation and joy are in store as recompense for the incomparable agonies and trials. A tumultuous happiness filled deeply tried hearts. Yes, it was a "mass psychosis," an epidemic of madness. But in this madness the burning and thirsty longing for life, the longing which always flickered in the depths of the grieved soul of the people, disclosed itself with special power. The most fearful trials and catastrophes could not extinguish among the people the belief in better times, in the bright and beautiful day that must and will come. Only a miracle, a great and astonishing wonder, would save the miserable people and liberate it from its oppressors. And the people, which stubbornly clung to life with all its powers, believed and waited for the miracle. It was firmly convinced that God's agent would come and transform the great sorrow into great joy, lamentation and weeping into triumphant jubilation. The Messiah and redeemer *must* come—and he *has* come! "I, your Messiah, Shabbetai Tzevi!"

A mad joy seized the entire people, the whole Jewish community—great and small, from simple water carriers to great scholars of the generation and renowned rabbis. From the smallest, remote towns in far-off corners of Moravia to the wealthy Sephardic community of Amsterdam, from Smyrna to Hamburg to London—everywhere in the Jewish quarter people danced in circles and sang on the streets and in the synagogues to music. In the Portuguese synagogue of Amsterdam participants in the wild, jubilant dance around the platform included not only the Kabbalist and mystic Jacob Aboab but also the *parnass* and "grandee" Abraham Pereira; the learned philologist and follower of Spinoza's philosophy Benjamin Mussafia;[13] the court physician of the Swedish queen Christina, Benedict de Castro (Baruch Nehamias); the wealthy minister and friend and advisor of the same enlightened queen Manuel Teixeira; and many others.

In Hamburg the whole community gathered in the synagogue, the scrolls of the Torah were taken out of the holy ark, a band of musicians played spirited tunes, and all the people danced. The rabbi himself was supervisor of the dance. As in ancient Greece lots were cast to determine which of the citizens should have the privilege of participating in the dramatic performances, so in the synagogue of Amsterdam lots were cast to decide who should participate in the dance around the platform. The enthusiasm, how-

13. The author of a whole series of scientific works. Especially popular was his lexicographical work *Zecher Rav*, which was reprinted a number of times.

ever, was so tremendous that, despite the supervising rabbi, the order of the dance quickly broke down and the whole congregation turned and twisted with wild fury in the singing circle. At the great clamor, many Christians came running, and the Jews told them the news that the Messiah, the Jewish redeemer, had come and that they were no longer slaves.[14]

As in the time of King Saul "bands of prophets" appeared in many Jewish communities, so now hundreds of men and women suddenly felt in themselves "the spirit of God" and uttered "prophecies." They would fall to the ground in ecstasy, a shudder would seize their limbs, and with glazed eyes they would cry out sentences, all of which had one and the same purport: "Shabbetai Tzevi is the Messiah of the God of Israel!"[15] In Constantinople there were over five hundred such "prophets" and "prophetesses," among them the gray-headed rabbi Mordecai Ḥasid. He had always wished to see with his own eyes the emissary of God, but the face of the redeemer, the aged Mordecai later related, shone with such dazzling light that he, Mordecai, almost became blind. He only observed that above the "head of the Messiah" glistened a royal crown of pure fire which flared up to the heavens. The old man fell to the ground in terror. Then he began running through the streets and crying in ecstasy: "He, he is our lord! There is no king beside him!"

People from distant lands disregarded all difficulties and dangers and set out on the long, hard journey to have the privilege of seeing the Messiah.[16] Spinoza's childhood friend, the head of the Amsterdam Talmudic academy Isaac Naar, and Abraham Pereira set out with their households for Turkey to greet Shabbetai Tzevi. Benjamin Mussafia, together with other prominent representatives of the Amsterdam community, dispatched a letter of greeting to the "king of kings," the "Messiah of the God of Jacob," "our king and redeemer," the "ruler of Judah, the beauty of Israel"— Shabbetai Tzevi. With artful rhetoric and Oriental similes the *parnassim* of Amsterdam express their submissiveness and great enchantment, then beg their "lord and king" that he not turn his

---

14. See Jacob Sasportas, *Kitzur Tzitzat Novel Tzevi*, 10.
15. *Ibid.*, 13; *Torat Ha-Kenaot*, 5; *Inyanei Shabbetai Tzevi*, 49–50, where several of these "prophetic" speeches are given.
16. See *Maaseh Tovyah*, Book IV, Chapter 3: "And some of the sages and rich men of Germany and Poland and Italy left their land and their birthplace and travelled a great distance, crossing rivers and seas and enduring many perils and troubles. And they travelled to this land, the land of Turkey, to see the face of the Messiah and to go up with him to Jerusalem."

bright countenance away from them but teach them what they must now do: whether they should set out on the way and "fall at his feet," or sit and wait for the great day of the "gathering of the exiles." "Not only for ourselves do we beseech you, our lord," write the Amsterdam *parnassim* at the end of their letter, "but also for all your servants, the exiles from Spain who now live here with us. All of us together bend the knee and bow before your royal throne. Praised and revered be your royal name forever and forever!"[17]

We have quoted these lines to give the reader some notion of the flood of letters and proclamations which literally inundated the Jewish community in that historic year 1666, with its three mystical sixes, of which there is a prophecy in symbolic language in the apocalyptic Revelation of Saint John. All of Jewry was in ferment, all were in a state of strained expectation. They were always waiting for new information, impatiently expecting the command to set out on the way to welcome the Messiah. The distant communities pelted the leaders of the communities in Constantinople, Jerusalem, and Smyrna with letters. Typical is the reply which the rabbis of Venice received from Constantinople to their question whether it is really true that speedy redemption is to be awaited. The letter of the Venetian rabbis came into the hands of Shabbetai Tzevi's ardent followers in Constantinople, and the reply was composed by none other than Abraham Ha-Yachini. The letter is written in a disguised allegorical form:

You seek information and inquire about the little goat that Israel Yerushalmi the son of Abraham purchased in Constantinople. Among those near to him there is a difference of opinion, for some think that the purchase is an erroneous purchase and they will lose their money. Therefore, know that we have thoroughly investigated and searched out this purchase, and we have become firmly convinced that the merchandise is of the highest quality and is current in all lands, and that whoever utters a slander against it will have to give account therefor. Competent merchants believe that this business will bring great profit. One must wait for the great fair which will take place, God willing, a year hence.

This letter passed from hand to hand. It was disseminated in numerous copies and read before the people in the houses of study and the bourses in various cities. All waited impatiently for the "great fair." An interesting portrayal of this impatient mood of ex-

17. The letter is published in *Kitzur Tzitzat Novel Tzevi*, 56–57, and in *Inyanei Shabbetai Tzevi*, pp. 112–13, where another letter of the Amsterdam community to Shabbetai Tzevi is also printed.

pectation in which the Jewish populace then found itself has been preserved in the famous memoirs of Glückel of Hameln who lived at that time in Hamburg:

When I remember the penance done by young and old—it is indescribable, though it is well enough known in the whole world. O Lord of the Universe, at that time we hoped that You, merciful God, would have compassion on Your people Israel and redeem us from our exile. We were like a woman in travail, a woman on the labour stool who, after great labour and grievous pains, expects to rejoice in the birth of a child, but finds it is nothing but wind. This, my great God and King, happened to us. All Your servants and children did much penance, recited many prayers, gave away large amounts in charity, throughout the world. For two or three years Your people Israel sat on the labour stool—but nothing came save wind. We did not merit to see the longed-for child, but because of our sins, we were left neither here nor there, but in the middle. Your people still hope every day that You, in Your infinite mercy, will yet redeem them and that the Messiah will come, if it be Your divine will to save Your people Israel. The joy, when letters arrived, is not to be described. Most of the letters were received by the Portuguese. They took them to their synagogue and read them aloud there. The Germans, young and old, went into the Portuguese synagogue to hear them. The young Portuguese on these occasions all wore their finest clothing and each tied a broad green silk ribbon round his waist—this was Shabbetai Zevi's livery. So all, "with kettledrums and round dance" went with joy like the joy of the Festival of the Bet Ha-Shoevah to hear the letters read. Many people sold home, hearth, and everything they had, hoping for redemption. My father-in-law, peace unto him, who lived in Hameln, moved from there, leaving things standing in the house just as they were, and went to Hildesheim. He sent us here, to Hamburg, two big barrels of linenware. In them were all kinds of food—peas, smoked meat, all sorts of dried fruits—that would keep without spoiling. The good man thought they would leave from Hamburg for the Holy Land. These barrels were in my house for more than a year. At last, afraid that the meat and other things would be spoiled, he wrote that we should open the barrels and take out all the food, so that the linen underneath should not spoil. They remained here for three more years, my father-in-law always expecting to need them at a moment's notice for his journey. But this did not suit the Almighty.[18]

Not without reason does Glückel mention that "young and old" repented at that time. We have already observed that the "prophet" Nathan of Gaza summoned Jews to penitence and fast-

18. *Zichronot Marat Glikel Hamil*, 80–82.

ing in order to hasten the "end" and so that the redeemer might come as quickly as possible after the "pangs of the Messiah." The words of the "prophet" found the strongest reverberation among the people. Young and old turned to repentance, fasted every Monday and Thursday with brief intermissions, rolled in the snow in the winter time, bathed in icy water, and slept on prickly thorns.[19]

But nerves were overly strained and men lost their psychic equilibrium. Thus, one must not be greatly surprised that just after the severest penance, after all the mortifications and fasts, the "purified" penitents surrendered themselves with wild enthusiasm to debauched joy in circles of dancing and singing which not infrequently passed all bounds of decency.

This mood was strengthened in very significant measure by Shabbetai Tzevi himself and his associates. The "days of the Messiah" had already come, and so it was time to liberate the wearied people from the heavy yoke of the commandments, to take away all the fences and strictures with which the rabbis in the course of generations surrounded the individual at every step. Shabbetai Tzevi even decided to abrogate the fast days long accepted among Jews. In the name of "the only son and first-born of the Lord the God of Israel, Shabbetai Tzevi, the Messiah of the God of Jacob and the redeemer of His people Israel," the "chief secretary," Samuel Primo, distributed to all the larger Jewish communities the following proclamation:

To all the children of Israel, peace. I hereby inform you that, as you have been privileged to see God's great day and to hear God's word from His faithful servants the prophets, your lamentation must be changed into joyous dance and the day of fasting into a day of happiness and rejoicing. Let the fast of the Tenth of Tebet from this day on be among you a day of jubilation and happiness, for your redeemer lives and your king and protector has already come!

Shabbetai Tzevi decided to declare even the day of national sorrow, the anniversary of the destruction of Jerusalem, the Ninth of Av, a festival of joy and delight. Several congregations received from "the king, the Messiah" the following command:

I, your king, decree that you shall make the ninth day of Av that is approaching into a day of great joy. On that day you shall prepare a great banquet with the best foods and finest liquors, with much light and illumination and many songs and melodies, for it is the birth-

19. See *Tzitzat Novel Tzevi*, 2; *Torat Ha-Kenaot*, 6.

day of Shabbetai Tzevi, your king, who rules over all the kings of the earth.

Further on in this command the order of prayer for this new Jewish festival is given. In the Eighteen Benedictions the festival must be mentioned in the following way:

And the Lord our God in love has given us appointed seasons for rejoicing, festivals and times for happiness, this day of consolation, this season of the birth of our king, our Messiah, Shabbetai Tzevi, Thy servant and Thy first-born son, as a holy convocation, a memorial of the exodus from Egypt.

And this "decree" was signed and sealed by Shabbetai Tzevi with the following title:

The saying of David, the son of Jesse, the fearful one of the kings of the earth, the man raised above all blessings and praise, the Messiah of the God of Jacob, the lion of the exalted house and the deer of the exalted house, Shabbetai Tzevi."[20]

Many congregations obeyed the decree. Into the order of the prayers a special "May He who blessed" was inserted for the "king of kings," Shabbetai Tzevi. This insertion was constructed according to the familiar style:

May He who gives salvation to kings and dominion to princes bless, guard, keep, help, exalt, and raise to the supreme heights our lord, our king, the holy teacher, the righteous and saved, the sultan Shabbetai Tzevi, the Messiah of the God of Jacob. May his glory rise and his kingdom be exalted. May God bestow power and splendor upon him. Let all nations and tongues be subject to him and fulfill his command. Let his power rule forever and his kingdom be unshakeable. . . . May his name be blessed at all times. May he be the pride of all peoples, and may our eyes have the privilege of seeing the building of the Temple. . . . So may it be Thy will. Amen.[21]

An entire literature of hymns and songs of praise in honor of the "King Messiah" who had come forth from Smyrna was created.

20. See *Kitzur Tzitzat Novel Tzevi,* 57–58; *Inyanei Shabbetai Tzevi,* 57–58.
21. *Kitzur Tzitzat Novel Tzevi,* 5b; especially *Inyanei Shabbetai Tzevi,* 56, 113–14, where several versions of this prayer are given. In one of them Shabbetai Tzevi is crowned with the following title: "Our lord the great king, Shabbetai Tzevi, the Messiah of the Lord, the Messiah the son of David, the Messiah the eternal king, the Messiah the redeemer, the Messiah the savior, the Messiah our righteous one, the Messiah of the God of Jacob."

We present as illustrations two of these songs. One was composed by Abraham Ha-Yachini and the other by the "prophet" Nathan of Gaza.

I

I will praise and sing to the God who is tremendous in power. The only and fearful One has illumined His people with light. From the best fragrances and spices the Holy One of Israel has created a form and anointed it for the kingdom of glory and beauty. Swift as a deer[22] is he to lend beauty to the Torah. With his wondrous wisdom he assuages wrath. Great is he and exalted—the firm protector of truth. He is adorned with the crown of dominion; the darling of the *sefirot* is he. All the secrets of the Torah are wondrously revealed to him; he will build up the chosen house. With God's breath is he beautified; his soul derives from the highest holiness. He has received his light from God Himself, with Him is he firmly bound up. God's bloom has Tzevi received, and all power is on his shoulders. Tzevi flourishes! Risen has the king, risen has the king over the persecuted little lamb![23]

II

How fearful, how highly exalted, are you, Tzevi's light! Priests and prophets does he beautify. In him is hidden the awaited gift. Who is like unto you, light of my heart, O great king, Shabbetai Tzevi?

I praise God my father who has sent to us on earth the deer [Tzevi]. He bestows upon me the great power to sing his praise in hymns and prayers. Thou eternal One above all worlds! My Messiah—he is my support! My king, my crown, my pride—Shabbetai Tzevi!

Overflowing with great joy is my heart! My loveliest hope has already come, has already arrived, and God has chosen me to sing a hymn of praise. Thou eternal One above all worlds! My Messiah—he is my support! My king, my crown, my pride—Shabbetai Tzevi!

He has seen my sufferings, taken me under his protection, cast my enemies and oppressors at my feet. I gape and am astonished. . . . Thou eternal One above all worlds! My Messiah—he is my support! My king, my crown, my pride—Shabbetai Tzevi![24]

Many of these songs of praise were sung with special melodies, as, for example, Solomon de Oliveyrra's "Piyyut Le-Motzaei Shabbat," of which the opening verse

Eliyahu ha-navi, Eliyahu ha-navi, Eli Yah
Lanu yavo, im melech ha-mashiah, im melech ha-mashiah

22. An allusion to the name Tzevi.
23. See *REJ*, LVIII, 289–90.
24. Published in *Even Ha-To'im*, p. 72.

was sung to the melody of the prayer "Agil Ve-Esmaḥ Be-Levavi."[25]

Several of these songs even have, by reason of their melody, an altogether unique rhythm, as, for example, the following hymn:

> *Yatza ḥoter mi-geza Yishai*
> *Shabbetai Tzevi darei darei shir*
> *Tenaḥ tenaḥ le-Eli Eli*
> *Darei darei shir . . .*[26]

It was not only Shabbetai Tzevi's associates who created these songs. Even in distant countries many of the common folk were so inspired by the appearance of the Messiah of Smyrna that they celebrated him in hymns and poems.[27]

But all this was not enough. Some Jews also undertook to rework the prayerbooks. Numerous prayers were remade and many new ones inserted. The presses in Amsterdam and Constantinople were busy day and night in the year 1666, working to produce as quickly as possible all the new prayerbooks and prayer arrangements which are designated with the following characteristic date: "The first year, in the month of priesthood and royalty."[28]

The year 1666, after all, was the "apocalyptic" year, in which Shabbetai Tzevi publicly declared himself the Messiah and redeemer before the whole world. On the title page of one of these prayerbooks, *Ateret Tzevi* (put together by the prophet Nathan of Gaza) Shabbetai Tzevi is portrayed sitting on a throne with four angels holding over his head a royal crown with the inscription "*Ateret Tzevi*" (the crown of Tzevi). On both sides of these stand Shabbetai's disciples and around them lions, the emblem of the tribe of Judah.

In this liturgical literature a special place is occupied by the three-volume *Ḥemdat Yamim*, a large collection of ethical instruction, prayers, customs, commandments, and laws for the Sabbath, the festivals, and the whole year. The first and most important part of this work, a thickly packed volume of more than six hundred pages, appeared in print for the first time in 1731 in Smyrna.

---

25. See *Inyanei Shabbetai Tzevi*, p. 115.
26. Published by Moritz Güdemann in *MGWJ*, 1868, p. 118.
27. Such poems were also composed in Judeo-German, or Yiddish. One of them was published by Dr. Weinreich (see his *Bilder fun der Literatur-Geshichte*, 219–53). For more about this, see the volume of our work on Old Yiddish literature.
28. David Kahana gives in his *Even Ha-To'im* (p. 89) a whole list of these *tikkunim* or prayer arrangements that were printed in 1666.

The author is not indicated. The publisher, Jacob Algazi, simply informs us that the manuscript of the work was obtained by him in upper Galilee, where the anonymous author spent his life. A year later the same publisher issued the remaining two volumes of *Ḥemdat Yamim*, the second dealing with the laws and customs of the Sabbath, and the third with the customs associated with Ḥanukkah, Purim, Ḥamishah Asar Be-Shevat, and Rosh Ḥodesh.

Ḥemdat Yamim was extremely popular in its day. It was several times reprinted (not completely and in changed order). Many of the prayers printed in it entered various prayerbooks. But it also had fierce opponents who saw heresy and illegitimacy in it and therefore placed it under the ban and forbade Jews to take it into their hands. The first to cast suspicion on *Ḥemdat Yamim* was the zealous Jacob Emden, the bitter fighter against the followers of Shabbetai Tzevi. He declared that this work is full of "blasphemies" and that it teems with the "idolatry" of Shabbetai Tzevi's accursed band.[29] Emden was also the first to declare that the author of this work is none other than Shabbetai Tzevi's prophet, Nathan of Gaza. Of all the arguments that have been given from Jacob Emden on to David Kahana[30] to prove that Nathan of Gaza is the author of *Ḥemdat Yamim*, only a single one deserves to be taken seriously: in the work several poems bearing the name of Nathan of Gaza are printed. Into three poems written in Aramaic the name Nathan ben Elisha[31] is woven in acrostic form. In all

29. Jacob Emden (Yaabetz), *Migdal Oz*, Part II, end of *Yiḥud Ha-Maaseh*, 16: "And in fact the accursed sect that drew pure souls to believe in a banished deer, a stinking corpse . . . who enchanted, misled, and seduced Israel to break from off their necks the yoke of the Torah and the commandments . . . and he left after him a curse, a root bearing the fruit of spreading leprosy. . . . They established for him prayers and supplications and devoted all their works to him, as I recently saw with my own eyes. They composed for him a special work called *Ḥemdat Ha-Yamim*, filled with abominations and blasphemies. They placed the unclean cross in the holy sanctuary, and they clothed the petitions and the holy names with the name of this abominable man, may the name of the wicked rot! Woe to us for what has happened in our time, for there is no one who gives heed to uproot this idolatry completely! Let the Holy One, blessed be He, be zealous for His name and take compassion upon His people which walks in its sincerity and uproot the sins from the land of the living, *selah!* Let Him remove the spirit of uncleanness from the land!"
30. *Even Ha-To'im*, pp. 149–52.
31. See *Ḥemdat Yamim*, I, 29, 64, and 75. In two cases the acrostic reads: *Ani Binyamin Natan ben Elisha Ḥayyim Ḥazak;* in the third poem, *Ani Avraham Natan Binyamin ben Elisha Ḥayyim Ḥazak*.

three cases, however, the author of these poems is spoken of in the third person and, in addition, is magnified with the laudatory title "the holy one." But may one properly conclude, on the basis of these three poems,[32] that the whole work was composed by the prophet of Gaza? In *Ḥemdat Yamim* are also found in complete form the three hymns of Rabbi Isaac Luria (II, 68–72, 124–25, 146–47) and two poems of the poet and Kabbalist Menaḥem Lonzano (I, 288; II, 85–86).

We believe that every objective reader who takes the trouble to familiarize himself more precisely with this three-volume work will come to the conclusion that Nathan of Gaza was not its author. David Kahana has rightly pointed out that *Ḥemdat Yamim* was written in 1670, because it is mentioned incidentally that 1602 years have passed since the destruction of the Temple (*ibid.*, 5). But at just that time, in 1670, Nathan of Gaza, whom the rabbis has excommunicated and declared a dangerous seducer and misleader, was being pursued from city to city and could nowhere find rest.[33] It is extremely difficult to believe that under such circumstances the wanderer could have had the leisure required to write such an immense work.[34] The following point is also important: in matters of religious law or ethical questions the author refers very frequently, as to a great authority, to his teacher, whom he does not name but mentions as the rabbi of a congregation and the head of a Talmudic academy. So, "in the house of study of my teacher";[35] "and my teacher taught me";[36] "and this was the custom of my teacher and his congregation";[37] "and in the house of study of my teacher they used to read";[38] "and my teacher's custom was";[39] etc. In one place, where Solomon Alkabetz' "document" with the account of how the heavenly *maggid* visited him

32. One of them is also found in the *Maḥzor Minhag Kaffa*.
33. See *Tzitzat Novel Tzevi*, 44, 50, and 92.
34. In modern times the question of the authorship of *Ḥemdat Yamim* has also been intensely debated in orthodox circles. In 1896 the Kabbalist M. M. Heilpern published in Jerusalem his *Kevod Ḥachamim*, in which he endeavors to show that Nathan of Gaza was not the author of *Ḥemdat Yamim*. The author of *Derech Tzaddikim* agrees completely with the conclusions of *Kevod Ḥachamim*. Against them M. Luria issued forth in his *Milḥemet Yaabetz* (first edition, 1914, second edition 1924), in which he accepts the view of Jacob Emden. Unfortunately, we have not been able to see these works and know them only from *Kiryat Sefer*, 1924, pp. 17–18.
35. *Ḥemdat Yamim*, I, 72.
36. *Ibid.*, 74.
37. *Ibid.*, 105.
38. *Ibid.*, 191.
39. *Ibid.*, 201; cf. II, 15, 17, 19, 21, etc.

and Joseph Karo on the night of Shavuot is mentioned, the author of *Ḥemdat Yamim* remarks that he found this account "among the documents of my teacher."[40] But Nathan's teacher was Jacob Hagiz, who later was one of the most bitter opponents of the Shabbatai Tzevi movement. Indeed, he himself excommunicated Shabbatai Tzevi and his own former pupil Nathan, and the latter therefore publicly issued forth with a sharp protest against his erstwhile teacher.[41] It is clear that if Nathan of Gaza were the author of *Ḥemdat Yamim*, he would not rely at every step on his former teacher with whom he carried on a life-and-death struggle. Furthermore, in 1670, when *Ḥemdat Yamim* was written, Jacob Hagiz was still alive (he died in 1674), but the author of the work speaks of his teacher as of someone long deceased. Along with this, it must also be taken into consideration that in 1670 Nathan of Gaza was all of twenty-six years old, but whoever reads *Ḥemdat Yamim* and acquaints himself with its manner and style can have no doubt that the author of this work is an older man who has wandered far[42] and experienced much in his years. From numerous comments it may be conjectured that the author of the work served as a rabbi and preacher in a congregation for many years. The author says of himself: "And I was accustomed in my congregation . . . "; "and many times it happened in my congregation . . . before the sermon that I preached on Sabbaths"; "and when I preached this with the other admonitions to penitence in my congregation."[43]

To be sure, it might be said that this is nothing more than the pretense of a swindler and mystifier who wishes to dazzle our eyes. But not everything lends itself to mystification; there are realms into which it is exceedingly difficult for the swindler to penetrate. Many of the most prominent anti-Sabbatians, e.g., Jacob Sasportas, Jacob Emden, and others, assure us that Shabbetai Tzevi's young prophet from Gaza was a wretch and an outcast. The historian Heinrich Graetz depicts Nathan as an insignificant man with very slight knowledge in the realm of Talmudic literature, besides being

40. *Ibid.*, I, 101. We have noted (Chapter 3) that Alkabetz' document was first published in one of the editions of *Shenei Luḥot Ha-Berit* (Amsterdam edition, p. 180). This perhaps permits the conjecture that the teacher of the author of *Ḥemdat Ha-Yamim* was Isaiah Horowitz, the author of *Shenei Luḥot Ha-Berit*, who spent the last years of his life in Safed and died there around 1630.

41. See *Kovetz Al Yad*, 1885, p. 126.

42. Of the cities which he visited he mentions Salonika, Antioch, Brusa, and various "German cities."

43. *Ḥemdat Yamim*, I, 98; cf. *ibid.*, 113, 142, 138, 196, and 266; II, 140, 84, 52, and 138; III, 68, 77, 93, and 100.

a stutterer and afflicted with a speech impediment; and this defect could barely be covered by his nimble pen, for his style, Graetz asserts, was an inflated one and the empty rhetorical flourishes could not conceal the poverty of thought.[44] For his part, David Kahana sees in Nathan the vilest of men, a shameless liar and terrible swindler. Hence, it is literally astounding that it is precisely Kahana who most strongly insists that the author of *Ḥemdat Yamim* was none other than Nathan. This is amazing not only because *Ḥemdat Yamim* testifies that its author was a true scholar in Talmudic and rabbinic literature;[45] whoever familiarizes himself with the work also sees before him a man with genuine literary talent who was permeated with the pathos of an enthusiastic preacher, with a profound feeling of strict moral responsibility. Indeed, we are so much concerned with *Ḥemdat Yamim* precisely because it is the most important book of ethical instruction produced in the circles of the Palestinian Kabbalists; even the extremely popular *Reshit Ḥochmah* cannot be compared to it.

The author of *Ḥemdat Yamim* is an ardent mystic and devoted follower of Rabbi Isaac Luria's Kabbalah. Luria for him is the "wondrous light,"[46] "our teacher and our master, our holy teacher,"[47] the "lord of the earth,"[48] the deserving heir of Rabbi Simeon ben Yoḥai.[49] Many prayers in *Ḥemdat Yamim* are filled with "combinations of letters," with wild-sounding "names" and incomprehensible incantations. The irksome feeling which these prayers full of "names" arouse is strengthened by the fact that together with them are to be found also some extremely beautiful, heartfelt prayers, as, for example, "Yehi Ratzon Milfanecha," (*ibid.*, 65) "Ribbono Shel Olam Male Mishalotenu" (*ibid.*, 66), "Ribbono Shel Olam Baal Ha-Raḥamim Veha-Seliḥot" (*ibid.*, 199), and many others. And the pious, Godfearing men who reprinted several of these prayers in various prayerbooks thereby showed more taste than David Kahana, who sees in this a desecration of God's name.

As a true follower of the "holy" Rabbi Isaac Luria, the author of *Ḥemdat Yamim* also preaches a severely ascetic life. He recog-

44. Graetz, *Geschichte der Juden* (S. P. Rabinowitch's Hebrew translation), VII, 239.
45. The author of *Ḥemdat Yamim* frequently quotes Hai Gaon, Maimonides, Rabbi Mordecai, Rabbi Asher ben Yeḥiel, Rabbenu Nissim, the author of *Ha-Ittur*, Rabbi Jacob ben Asher, and many others.
46. *Ḥemdat Yamim*, I, 57, 103.
47. *Ibid.*, 142, 252.
48. *Ibid.*, 224.
49. *Ibid.*, 284.

nizes only one joy in the world—the joy of performing the commandments.[50] His greatest concern is that the "princess," the heavenly soul, is held captive by so many wolves—the sinful desires.[51] He therefore earnestly summons his readers to repentance, fasting, and mortification of the flesh. In this he perceives the surest way leading to redemption.[52] But in this book so permeated with the mystical spirit are also heard quite strongly social tones reflecting actual, earthly life. The temperamental preacher and reprover frequently triumphs over the fervent mystic. He castigates the powerful and the rich not only because they have forgotten the Torah but also because they are deaf to the sorrows of the people and do not take part in "the troubles of Israel." In fiery words of reproach he pours out his wrath on the rich men and officials who think only of dazzling luxury, deck themselves in the richest clothing, and when a poor man appears at the door drive him away and avoid him like the plague. They allow poor Torah scholars to fall but are great patrons of all kinds of magicians and tricksters who prompt to mockery and derision.

"How can you let it happen," the author wrathfully exclaims,

that on festival days, on days of joy, poor persons perish of hunger and suffer from misery and distress? How dare you call out loudly on the night of the Passover *seder*, "Let all who are hungry come and eat" when you close the doors before the poor and let them wander in the streets?

The author, in this connection, incidentally relates a story "that happened in former times in Jerusalem," where a "pious man and modest sage" who lived in great poverty was left without means for Passover. He cried with a bitter heart and prayed before God. His cries reached Him and He was, as it were, extremely angry and wished to punish the entire city for mercilessly letting an ordinary man, a pious man, perish of hunger. But thanks to the prophet Elijah, who prayed before God, the community was saved from divine punishment.[53]

Anecdotes in general are an organic part of the tapestry of *Hemdat Yamim*. As a skilled orator and preacher, the author very frequently adorns his ethical instruction with various anecdotes and

50. *Ibid.*, 225: "The *Shechinah* does not dwell amidst sadness, nor amidst sloth, nor amidst laughter and levity, nor amidst profane things, but only amidst the joy of performing a commandment."
51. *Ibid.*, 174.
52. *Ibid.*, I, 7, 10–11, 280; II, 17–18.
53. *Ibid.*, 11.

legends and understands how ingeniously to render them in their own rhythm and typical popular style. Very interesting in this respect are the tales of the exodus from Egypt,[54] the legend about Moses,[55] the story about the seven elders who came to the *sukkah* of a famous rabbi,[56] the story of the Jew and the Spanish king,[57] the stories of Judith[58] and Esther[59] and many others.

No less interesting than the legends are the authentic pictures of the contemporary way of life which are braided into the preaching and moral instruction of *Ḥemdat Yamim*. When, for example, the author indicates how a Jew ought to conduct himself in the synagogue on the Sabbath and the Day of Atonement he turns with emotive words of reproof to his audience and portrays in clear, vivid colors how the congregation gathers on festivals or on the Sabbath in the synagogue, carries on conversations about politics, listens to rumors, exchanges gossip, and speaks all kinds of evil, one man of another. "Woe to the ears that listen to this, woe to the eyes that look on this!" the pious author feelingly exclaims. Of significant ethnographic interest are also the passages in which the author tells of the masquerades and merry performances on the days of Purim and Ḥanukkah.[60]

The author of *Ḥemdat Yamim* is not only a strict reprover, uttering wrathful words of punishment, but also a beloved friend and close comrade. He addresses the reader as "my brother," "my deeply beloved brother." He calls those whom he addresses "my children," "golden children, beloved of God."[61] Filled with tender simplicity are his words about a pure moral life, about pious conduct, how one must approach God's house with a broken spirit and a heart filled with humility and penitence, how every person must think above all of peace and harmony. In this connection it must be remembered that this book was written in an agitated milieu in which not peace and harmony but controversy and hatred reigned. Shabbetai Tzevi and his associates had converted to the Mohammedan faith, and the Sabbatians had been declared "troublers of Israel." But not all had yet lost their belief in the Messiah of Smyrna and because of this, sharp conflicts, which in some places passed over into bitter struggle, broke out in many com-

54. *Ibid.*, in the chapter on the Seventh Day of Passover.
55. *Ibid.*, 79.
56. *Ibid.*, 248.
57. *Ibid.*, III, 96–97.
58. *Ibid.*, 78–82.
59. *Ibid.*, 98, 112–15.
60. *Ibid.*, 119, 122; cf. *ibid.*, 75–76.
61. *Ibid.*, 114, 137, 173, 204, 205, etc.

munities. It is for this reason that our author speaks so emotionally of peace and harmony and warns against controversy and warfare.

"Woe to us, that we have no peace in our midst," laments the author,

Woe to us who, by reason of this great sin, have brought so many misfortunes and troubles upon ourselves with our own hands and still languish in exile. . . . Listen to me, my brethren, you holy scions of God's blessed patriarchs. I will teach you true piety. I will remind you how God's honor is desecrated among the peoples. They babble in His sanctuary, and God's own children have been driven away from His table. The chosen people are in fearful distress, and everyone brings them new troubles and afflictions. Do you know why God's judgment is so harsh, why we go from fall to fall and descend ever lower, why we drown in a sea of misery and distress and there is no day that does not bring new afflictions of which the previous day did not know? God is no doubt just, but we have done evil. We are guilty, and from our hands does all this come, for controversy and discord rule in our midst.

The author cries out,

Why is there among you, O holy children of Jacob, no harmony? Are you not the offspring of one people, one father? Has not one God created us? Why should we not live at peace among ourselves, O children of Israel? How can we forget that we are in the land of our enemies, like a lamb among millions of wolves? Is it not enough for us that all peoples hate us, that we magnify enmity among ourselves, with our own controversies intensify the fire that ruthlessly consumes us from day to day?[62]

"We must create harmony in Israel"—this principle is repeated by the author many times, and he devotes a number of heartfelt pages in his thick volume to it. "Forgiveness," he stresses, "is to be requested not only of friends but of enemies as well." And he himself composes a prayer to be recited for the "sinners of Israel," so that they may repent.[63]

One further point is interesting. Like all other mystics, the author of Ḥemdat Yamim underscores the tremendous power inherent in prayer. But for prayer to be exalted with great devotion and concentration it must be in a comprehensible language. "Hence," he writes, "he who does not understand Hebrew may pray in the language he understands, and his prayer will certainly be accepted."[64] "We see," he adds, "that on the Ninth of Av one

62. *Ibid.*, I, 178; see also *ibid.*, the section on Shavuot, Chapter 2.
63. *Ibid.*, 133–34.
64. *Ibid.*, 105.

lamentation read aloud in the vernacular makes a far more power-ful impression even on those who understand Hebrew than ten in the holy tongue." "Even a common man of the people," the author notes, "can make an enormous impression in the upper world with his heartfelt prayer." In this connection he relates a story of one of the "dumb souls" that I. L. Peretz celebrated with such marvelous beauty in his *Folkstimliche Geshichtes*. Somewhere in a city lived, quietly and unnoticed, a poor, simple Jew who could barely translate a passage of the Pentateuch. He died in ripe old age and soon after his death appeared in a dream to an honor-able, pious man of the city, dressed in a shroud with a little book in his hand. The pious man asked him, What book are you holding? The deceased replied that it was a little Book of Psalms and that he had come to him so that he might admonish the Jewish inhabi-tants to flee the city at once and save their souls, for as long as he lived he protected them by the fact that for many years he would recite the entire Book of Psalms each week. In the merit of his Psalm-saying the whole community lived in peace, but now that he was dead there was no one to protect them, and so they must quickly leave the city. In the morning the pious man rose in great dread and at once informed the community of the terrible danger impending. Some forthwith fulfilled what the deceased commanded and were in fact saved, but others who refused to listen to the pious man's dream perished.[65]

The author violently attacks that "segment of the scholars and well-educated persons" who waste their time on hair-splitting and overrefined explanations and subtleties.[66] He speaks with great in-dignation of the preachers who merely wish to show off their learning and mental acuity. They confuse the people with barbaric, silly questions, do mental gymnastics, perform all kinds of tricks like magicians and sleight-of-hand artists. The author adds that since the method of *pilpul* (hairsplitting dialectic) has become so popular in the Ashkenazic communities[67] and, instead of following the straight paths of studying Torah, men have entered upon crooked and tortuous ways leading to falsehood and delusion, it has grown pitch black in these lands. God has turned away from them. One misfortune after another has pursued them, one ca-tastrophe after another has struck them. Hundreds of thousands of souls have perished, their corpses have rolled about in the streets, and there was none to bury them.[68]

65. *Ibid.*, 111.
66. *Ibid.*, 209.
67. The author here means the German-Polish communities.
68. *Ibid.*, 70.

This mystic and Kabbalist summons Jews to return to the classic source of simplicity and clarity, the Bible. He quotes the lines of Profiat Duran[69] in which Duran marvels at the wondrous beauty of Holy Scripture. The author of *Hemdat Yamim* insists that even scholars and experts in the sea of the Talmud are obliged to read the Bible every day and to go through it in its entirety at least once a year.[70]

Was the anonymous author of this interesting book of ethical instruction a believer in Shabbetai Tzevi at the time he wrote his work,[71] i.e., after Shabbetai Tzevi had already converted to Islam and the "Messiah of the God of Jacob" had been transformed into Mohammed Effendi? Many consider this a proven fact, but we have our doubts. Even if some not altogether clear expressions may arouse suspicion that the author inclined toward the Sabbatians, it must be remembered that before the work appeared in print it sustained major transformations in the course of several decades and passed through many strange hands. Hence one cannot be certain whether it was not such a hand that, for some reason, altered the text in places. In any case, it is difficult to believe that a Sabbatian, a man who was convinced that the redeemer, the long-awaited Messiah, was living in his generation, would lament "that our generation is an orphaned generation; we all grope in the darkness, for there is no leader, no protector."[72] Like all other Kabbalists, especially those who grew up under the influence of the mystics of Safed, so the author of *Hemdat Yamim* waits impatiently for the advent of the Messiah and implores God in heartfelt prayers to bring the end near "and to grant us the privilege of seeing the face of Thy holy anointed one, and that our eyes may behold the king in his beauty." He waits for the Messiah who is yet to come and has still not appeared.[73] The miracle has *not* yet happened.

69. Vol. III, of this work, 186–93.
70. *Hemdat Yamim*, 112.
71. The author very frequently mentions two other works of his which, however, were not preserved: *Hemdah Genuzah* and *Mahamad Ayin*.
72. *Hemdat Yamim*, 154.
73. *Ibid.*, 65, 224, 275, etc.

CHAPTER EIGHT

Pro- and Anti-Sabbatians

E have referred to the large number of paeans, poems, and hymns filled with praises and laudations of the greatness of the "Messiah of the God of Jacob," the redeemer Shabbetai Tzevi. Mystical enthusiasm attained the highest level. All boundaries of the normal and the possible were wiped away. The labyrinth in which the sick and strained imagination, the soul grieved and worn out by vain expectations, trembled so convulsively became ever more tortuous, confused, and hazy.

The pathological and frantic confusion was especially intensified after the great hope was not fulfilled, and the figure in whom the people saw the redeemer, the "Messiah of the God of Jacob," adopted the Islamic faith.

In the circles of Shabbetai Tzevi's followers a unique apocryphal literature, consisting of a mass of mystical legends and miracle stories, was produced. All of these are permeated with the same tendency: to set forth the apostate Messiah, who had converted to Mohammedanism, as the *suffering* Messiah, the "holy" Messiah, who takes upon himself in love the greatest suffering and shame in order to atone for the sins of the whole people.[1]

---

1. Typical in this respect are the memoirs *Zikkaron Le-Venei Yisrael* of the Sabbatian Baruch ben Gershom of Arezzo (*Inyanei Shabbetai Tzevi*, pp. 41–69), and also the well-known *Meoreot Tzevi*.

"Know all of you who seek the truth and are filled with compassion for the people of Israel," feelingly exclaims the anonymous author of the leaflet *Sahaduta De-Mehemanuta*

that on the night of the seventh day of Passover God, Blessed be He, invited our glorious and holy Messiah, escorted by twelve thousand angels, and placed a crown upon his head. God also invited to the banquet the patriarchs of the world, the fathers on whom the world rests. During the banquet, the Holy One, blessed be He, posed the following question: What is the law regarding a child who is still in his mother's womb and is already so strong and big that he kicks with his feet and strikes his mother in the womb? What is to be done with such a child? The fathers answered: The child must be made smaller, his powers must be weakened so that he will not be able to kick. Then the face of our lord, the Messiah, became dark and displeased. He understood at once that this was an allusion to the people of Israel, who rebuff him, the Messiah, and desecrate his honor. So our lord answered: One should ask the mother of the child; perhaps she is willing to suffer the child's beating and kicking, as long as he comes forth beautiful and strong. Only then did the fathers understand that the people of Israel was spoken of here. Then they blessed our lord and said: Blessed may you be, O faithful guardian![2]

Even the old Midrash *Zerubbabel*[3] was enriched in the Sabbatian circles with new variants which purportedly testified that Shabbetai Tzevi was, indeed, the true Messiah. A legend was created to the effect that in an old parchment *Zerubbabel* manuscript the following prophecy is to be found: Zerubbabel fasted all of forty days and adjured the angel Metatron to come to him. Metatron then appeared and asked: Son of man, what is your wish? Zerubbabel answered: When will the time of the great miracles come? Metatron replied: The secret must remain hidden; you may not know it. Zerubbabel then fasted still another forty days but received the same answer. Only after the third time did Metatron reveal to him that in the fifth century of the sixth millenium, between the twentieth and the thirtieth year, the Messiah will appear, the people of Israel will repent greatly but afterwards turn away from the Messiah because a rumor that he has become an apostate will be noised abroad. Nevertheless, he is the true Messiah, even when he converts to another faith; for so it must be.[4]

In the Sabbatian circles, however, there were also men who saw in Shabbetai Tzevi not merely the Messiah the son of David. We

2. *Inyanei Shabbetai Tzevi*, pp. 85–86.
3. See Volume II of our work, pp. 157–59.
4. *Inyanei Shabbetai Tzevi*, p. 98.

have already observed[5] that Shabbetai Tzevi's chief secretary, Samuel Primo, circulated a proclamation to all the larger Jewish communities in the name of "the Messiah of the God of Jacob and the redeemer of his people Israel." Shabbetai Tzevi, who was also called by him the "only son and firstborn of the Lord the God of Israel," is not only "a shoot from the stock of Jesse, the Messiah the son of David;" he is also the divine emanation, the corporeal revelation of God's *Shechinah*.

Unfortunately we lack the sources necessary to give us an accurate and objective portrait of the unique religious-mystical conceptions that developed in the Sabbatian circles after Shabbetai Tzevi's apostasy, when the movement called forth by him lost its broad national-mystical-political character and took on limited and narrow sectarian forms. The sectarian Sabbatians avoided public appearances as far as possible. They used to express their views in a disguised way, through allusions and hints only. In the years when the persecutions of the Sabbatians were intensified, the rabbis and their assistants very diligently burned and destroyed all the books and manuscripts about which there was some suspicion that they smacked of Sabbatian heresy. One mystical-philosophical work that undoubtedly derives from Shabbetai's associates, *Raza De-Mehemanuta*, was preserved only in the talentless interpretation and commentary of a very suspicious adventurer and swindler, Nehemiah Ḥayon. Even this commentary, *Oz Le-Elohim*, was so diligently cleared out by the opponents of the Sabbatian movement that the work is now extremely rare and we have had the opportunity to employ only Ḥayon's *Raza De-Yiḥuda*, which is an abridged extract of *Oz Le-Elohim*.[6] Only one document published for the first time in the second half of the nineteenth century brings a little light into this dark, still so little investigated, realm, the confusion surrounding which was significantly magnified by such zealots and enemies of the Sabbatians as Jacob Emden with their biased attacks and accusations. Henrich Graetz was the first to point out that this document is closely associated with an extremely interesting person, Abraham Michael (Miguel) Cardozo.

Such bitter anti-Sabbatians as Jacob Sasportas and the author[7]

5. See above, p. 143.
6. Ḥayon's major work *Divrei Nehemiah*, a collection of sermons, has no literary value, and from the sea of tedious bombast and babbling it is impossible to obtain any original idea.
7. More correctly the composers or authors, for the author, Elijah Kohen, himself notes that he utilized a polemic work of Isaac Roman, and *Merivat Kodesh* was edited by Yomtov Roman.

of the lampoon *Merivat Kodesh*[8] portray Cardozo as a "vile swindler"[9] and "terrible seducer and misleader."[10] Naturally, David Kahana[11] also judged that Cardozo was a wicked man and an "impostor." However, we doubt very much whether such a unique, restless, constantly seeking nature as Cardozo's really deserves this harsh verdict. A child of a Portuguese Marrano family, Miguel Cardozo spent his youth in Spain, where he studied medicine. A happy, life-loving young man with a sparkling wit, Cardozo led a carefree and frivolous life at night in the company of playboys like himself under the windows of beautiful young women.[12] But suddenly a very unexpected transformation took place in his life. With his elder brother, Fernando,[13] he fled from Spain to Italy, where both brothers returned to Judaism. Miguel, who was now called Abraham Michael, became a penitent, sat "in the tent of Torah" and studied the Hebrew language and literature with such diligence that Graetz, who first gathered precise biographical information about him, is compelled to admit that this frivolous dandy who used to sing serenades under the windows of the beauties of Madrid became far more competent in Hebrew style than many rabbis of his time. In Leghorn he became acquainted with one of Shabbetai Tzevi's associates and the latter familiarized him with the secrets of the "hidden wisdom." The mystical world of the Kabbalah made a tremendous impression on Cardozo. Night after night "glorious visions" revealed themselves before him and he uttered prophecies that the "end" was already near and that the Messiah would soon come.[14]

Cardozo was living in Tripoli, where he was a doctor at the court of the local pasha, when Shabbetai Tzevi declared publicly before the world that he was "the Messiah of the God of Jacob." Cardozo became one of the most energetic propagandists of the Sabbatian movement. He declared Shabbetai Tzevi the Messiah the son of David, and himself the Messiah the son of Ephraim.[15]

8. Published in *Inyanei Shabbetai Tzevi*, pp. 1–40.
9. See *Tzitzat Novel Tzevi*, 94.
10. Moses Hagiz in *Sefer Eleh Ha-Mitzvot*.
11. *Even Ha-To'im*, p. 112.
12. *Tzitzat Novel Tzevi*, 45.
13. He later assumed the Hebrew name Yitzḥak (Isaac) and obtained renown as a thinker and physician with his works *Philosophia libela* (Venice, 1673) and *Las excelencias caluminas de las Hebreas* (Amsterdam, 1679).
14. See Cardozo's interesting letter to his brother (*Inyanei Shabbetai Tzevi*, pp. 87–92).
15. For a discussion of this, see the previously-mentioned tract *Merivat Kodesh* and Moses Hagiz' *Sefer Eleh Ha-Mitzvot* (Zolkiev, 1785).

He remained Shabbetai Tzevi's faithful disciple even after the latter
had gone over to Islam. At that time he wrote to his brother:
"I believe with perfect faith, without any hesitation or doubt, that
the true Messiah is Shabbetai Tzevi, may his majesty be exalted."
In this connection he adduces arguments from the prophet Isaiah,
who predicted that the Messiah, who is more exalted than the
angels on high, would in the beginning be "despised and rejected
of men, a man of sorrows and acquainted with grief . . . and we
reckoned him smitten of God . . ." (Isaiah 53:3–4). "We do not
understand," says Cardozo, "that he bears our sins, that he takes
upon himself our sufferings and wounds, and is punished for all
of us, for our vanity and evil."[16]

A man of multifaceted culture and a talented orator, Cardozo
propagandized very energetically through sermons and proclamations among the Jewish communities in North Africa. When the
persecutions of Shabbetai Tzevi's followers were intensified, the
rabbis especially pursued the tireless Cardozo and publicly burned
his papers and proclamations in Smyrna.[17] Of the character and
content of these writings we may obtain some notion through one
of them which was accidentally preserved. This is a long letter,
Be-Inyan Sod Ha-Elohut, on the subject of the mystery of divinity, which Cardozo sent to the Sabbatian Samuel de Foges.[18] This
work tells us not only of Cardozo's world view but also gives us
a notion of the new mystical-philosophical tendencies which dominated Sabbatian circles.

We have observed[19] that the Kabbalist Herrera, who was learned
in Christian theological literature, emphasised that *maaseh bereshit*,
the creation of all worlds and existences, was realized through the
one and only emanation of the *Ein Sof* which bears the name *Adam
Kadmon* (Primal Man) and also *Sechel Ha-Ne'elam* (Hidden, Divine Thought).[20] We also cited the most characteristic passage in
Herrera in which the comparison between the heavenly man and
the earthly man is carried through. While the former is the temple
of the *Ein Sof*, the latter is the dwelling place of the *Shechinah*,
the tent of the *Malchut Kadisha* (Holy Kingdom), which is the
Ze'er Anpin, the child of the first two *partzofin*, *Abba*, the father
and primal source of the active-masculine, and *Imma*, the mother
and foundation of the passive-feminine. And the highest repre-

16. See the letter cited above (*Inyanei Shabbetai Tzevi*, pp. 88–89).
17. See *Torat Ha-Kenaot*, 68 (1870 edition).
18. Published by N. Brüll in *Bet Ha-Midrash* (Vienna), 1865, pp. 63–71,
    100–3.
19. See above, Chapter Six.
20. See above, pp. 128 ff.

sentative, the incarnate symbol of earthly man, the tent of the *Malchut Kadisha*, is the glorious Messiah. Hence, it is no wonder than when the hoped-for Messiah appeared and the triumphant cry, "I, your Messiah, Shabbetai Tzevi!," resounded over the entire Diaspora, there were among his followers and associates men who perceived in the Messiah of Smyrna not only the scion of David's house but also the bodily "garment" of the heavenly *Ze'er Anpin* and *Malchut Kadisha*.[21]

Cardozo was a determined opponent of these views, but he admits that they found ardent followers among those who were closest to Shabbetai Tzevi. Among these associates of his the mystical idea that the Messiah Shabbetai Tzevi is the incarnate, six-angled *sefirah* known as *Tiferet* (Beauty), the human form of the third letter of the Ineffable Name of God,[22] was very popular. There were even those who declared that God assumes, as it were, human form and that His features are similar to those of the Messiah Shabbetai Tzevi.[23] "This means," Cardozo angrily exclaims, "that these men have lost God entirely." There was even one—Cardozo calls him the "accursed Jacob Israel Duchan"—who went further. He asserted that God had isolated Himself in His heights and no longer ruled the world; His place is now taken by Shabbetai Tzevi. Duchan's view, Cardozo informs us, gained numerous adherents.[24]

Cardozo was enraged, more than by anything else, by the fact that such blasphemous ideas were spread abroad in the name of Shabbetai Tzevi himself and all were assured that they had been heard from his own mouth. This, Cardozo asserts, is utterly false, for "this man from childhood on was a righteous, pious and holy man, and all attest that he [Shabbetai Tzevi] always had the greatest respect for the Talmud and the Midrashim, and the Tannaim and Amoraim were his true teachers and guides in the secret wisdom."

After rejecting these "false and mendacious views,"[25] Cardozo

21. Herrera's term *Malchut Kadisha* was transformed in these Sabbatian circles into *Malka Kadisha*.
22. According to Isaac Luria's mystical system, the third letter of the Ineffable Name of God is the symbol of the *Ze'er Anpin* (see *Raza De-Yihuda*, 14, 19, 23).
23. See *Bet Ha-Midrash*, 1865, p. 65: "And the other great sages sat with our lord, our king, may his glory be exalted, and the king of Turkey listened and at the end said to them that the Holy One, blessed be He, is a splendid young man like him."
24. *Ibid*. This view found many adherents especially among the Kabbalists in Salonika.
25. Cardozo even asserts that he polemicized against these views in many of his works.

endeavors to give in his letter to Samuel de Foges his own religious-philosophical outlook. Cardozo rests, first of all, on Moses
Cordovero's basic principle concerning the double nature of the
sefirot. We already know[26] how the author of *Pardes Rimmonim*
resolved the difficult question concerning the true nature of the
sefirot—whether they are separate, independent existences or are
to be considered merely vessels of the divine emanation. Cordovero
attempts to effect a compromise between these two views. As
God's emanation, the *sefirot*, he urges, are dynamic, creative
powers, all of which are combined in divinity in perfect unity.
But the *sefirot* are also the soul, the dynamic power, of their external dress, of the "vessels" that are the bearers of the names
wherewith we designate each individual *sefirah*. And it is the "vessels" and external "garments" that disclose themselves before man's
eye in finite and bodily forms. This idea of Moses Cordovero about
the dual character of the *sefirot* is employed by Abraham Michael
Cardozo also in relation to the First Cause, God Himself.

The First Cause, too, has two aspects. One aspect is the "channel
of light," as it is called by Isaac Luria, the dynamic power, the
soul of all the *sefirot* and of their complete unity, through which
everything is created and imbued with life. Only in this aspect
can the First Cause be clothed with names and attributes; only
to it can man turn with prayers and petitions.[27] But besides this
aspect there is another—not only the "channel of light," the
emanation of light that is confined in the "vessels," but also the
luminosity that embraces everything, that has no boundary and
no shore. This is the First Cause in its true essence, the actual
Ein Sof, which it is impossible to attain and which cannot be designated by any name and effect.[28] The first aspect, the "channel
of light," is the God of Israel, the *Abba Kadisha* (Holy Father),[29]
the creator of the universe, the ruler of the world, but not the
First Cause in its incomprehensible, infinite essence. When we say
"the Holy One, blessed be He," this is in regard only to the God
of Israel but not the First Cause, which is beyond all names and
concepts and cannot be addressed with blessings and praises.[30] Even
the Ineffable Name is not borne by the First Cause but by the
God of Israel. He, the Holy One, blessed be He, is the source,

26. See above, p. 55.
27. *Bet Ha-Midrash*, 1865, pp. 67–68.
28. *Ibid.*
29. *Abba Kadisha* is actually the same concept as *Adam Kadmon*. They
  are identical in their initial letters.
30. *Bet Ha-Midrash*, 1865, p. 70.

the essence of the Ineffable Name, and this name is the soul, the dynamic power, of all the *sefirot* and all the *partzofin*.[31]

Thanks to Cardozo's letter we obtain a more or less adequate notion of the religious-mystical views and currents that appeared in the Sabbatian circles and were especially strengthened after Shabbetai Tzevi's apostasy and more particularly after his death, when the whole Sabbatian movement took on a strictly sectarian character. The doctrine of the *du-partzofin*, of the double character of divinity, and the declaring of the converted Messiah to be a human incarnation of the *Malka Kadisha* (Holy King)—this of necessity greatly disturbed the pious rabbis and orthodox leaders of the people. They saw in these views, which smack of Christian dogma, a dangerous "heresy" and declared a bitter struggle against them—a struggle that found, as we shall later see, a certain echo in literature.

But considerably earlier, when Shabbetai Tzevi had just publicly come forth as the Messiah and redeemer, and when the enthusiasm of the messianic movement reached its zenith and the whole Jewish community jubilantly recognized in the Messiah of Smyrna the "King of Israel," there were some—to be sure, only a few—who at once perceived in this stormy messianic movement a great danger that might bring enormous harm to the Jewish people. These individuals had the courage to issue forth against the tide and to raise their admonitory voices amidst the joyous cries, even though they knew that they would be like men crying in the wilderness and that they would be met with anger and mocking laughter. There is an immense tragedy in the situation of these admonishing and incredulous persons—to be the only sober ones in a sea of psychotic mass intoxication; to sit like "mourners among bridegrooms"; to be the only melancholy persons in a frenzied circle of dancing joy; to understand their utter powerlessness and yet not be able or willing to remain silent witnesses; courageously to protest and warn and cry about the impending danger in the full knowledge that this involved martyrdom, that the exulting mob might pour out all its rage on them and simply trample them with its feet. Thus, these individuals grew into tragic, heroic figures, and their protesting voice certainly deserves to be noted in the literary history of the Jewish people.

The most interesting among these first fighters against the Shabbetai Tzevi movement are the two Frances brothers and Rabbi Jacob Sasportas. Jacob and Immanuel Frances came from Mantua[32]

31. *Ibid.*, pp. 70–71.
32. See *Kol Ugav*, 78.

which, as we noted earlier, was an important center of Jewish culture in the Renaissance era. The elder and more gifted of the brothers, Jacob, was born in 1615 and spent most of his life in Florence. A strict rationalist, he was more interested in philosophic problems than in anything else and regarded everything that smacked of mysticism and "hidden secrets" with contempt. "The Kabbalists occupy themselves with foolishness," he would always say.[33] He publicly declared that the *Zohar* was falsified and not written by the Tanna Rabbi Simeon ben Yoḥai and his disciples. The erotic motif discernible in the Kabbalist books was especially repugnant to this sober rationalist. "Let those read the *Zohar*," he declares, "who are not disgusted by vile language."[34] Jacob Frances composed a caustic satire in verse, *Ashrei Ha-Goy*, in which he pours out all his scorn and anger on the Kabbalists and their teaching. "I cannot be silent," the poet asserts in the introduction,[35] "for my sufferings are bitter as death. Even when I cry, my woe is not alleviated. My Muse, however, cannot lock her lips but must openly and unafraid raise her voice before men and instruct them concerning God's ways." Jacob Frances further declares in his satire:

Over all the streets and market places the voice of the Kabbalah is heard. Men without knowledge men whose eyes see nothing more than did King Zedekiah[36] in prison, speculate about the emanations and the mysteries of the Torah. Schoolchildren, persons who grope in the darkness and are utterly devoid of wisdom, empty and arrogant fools—all babble about *sefirot and maaseh merkavah* [the work of the Throne or Chariot].

Jacob Frances correctly foresaw that his poem would be cursed "with sharp curses at the head of all the streets." As soon as his satire was published in Mantua, the local rabbis ordered that the entire edition be immediately burned;[37] and when some decades later, in 1704, the young Samson Morpurgo reprinted Frances' satire at the end of *Etz Ha-Daat*, the Kabbalist Aviad Sar-Shalom Basilea violently attacked him[38] because he published this "filthy poem."

33. See *Emunat Ḥachamim* (Johannesburg edition, p. 34).
34. *Ibid.*, p. 35.
35. The introduction to the satire is reprinted in Morpurgo's work *Etz Ha-Daat* (a commentary to *Beḥinat Olam*).
36. Both of King Zedekiah's eyes were struck out and afterwards he was put in prison.
37. See *Metek Sefataim*, 74.
38. In his *Emunat Ḥachamim*, Chapter 22.

It is quite understandable that when the exhilarating news came to Italy that the long-awaited Messiah had finally appeared and would soon reveal himself in all his glory, Frances was the only nay-sayer, the stubborn non-believer who with all the ardor of his militant temperament issued forth against the enthusiastic messianic movement. With great courage he hurled one lampoon after another against the *tzevi muddaḥ* (the banished deer), Shabbetai Tzevi. "One may not be silent when the whole people begins to sin." "Ah," the poet exclaims in one of his poems of reproof, "you should all weep, cover your heads out of great sorrow. Only Lilith and her legions rejoice, for God's people—old and young, great and small—have gone mad. They are punished with the plague of insanity which has no boundary or limit."[39]

Frances decided to fight against the "plague of folly" which had seized the entire people, to fight with the weapon of indignation, with the armor of fiery protest. "If the fire has gone out in hell, I will again bring it to burning with the flame of my wrath," he proudly proclaims, "I will disclose the shame of the banished deer—this wolf who disguises himself as a lamb! I will expose his baseness, and all will realize that this deer brings not redemption but enslavement. This deer is a fly, not a lion."[40]

Jacob Frances had to suffer greatly in consequence of his courageous struggle. The enraged mob attacked his residence and threw stones at him.[41] This, however, did not frighten him, and when Shabbetai Tzevi's followers and the hosts of "prophets" who then appeared sang songs and praises before the "king Messiah," Frances in his lampoons and epigrams mocked the Messiah and his prophets. "This man who is like a prickly thorn—will he be the redeemer of the whole generation? This petty man, this shameful pygmy—is he God's chosen, and does he stretch forth his hand to the royal mantle?"[42] With bitter laughter the poet speaks of the miracles and wonders which the exultant mob believed the Messiah had performed. He mockingly refers to the abovementioned legend that the Messiah will ride on a lion and drive with a seven-headed snake. "I realize very clearly," Frances concludes,

that Tzevi's defeat is unavoidable. He is the certain victim of Ashmodai. I would laugh over his doglike downfall, but I am distressed

39. In *Kovetz Al Yad*, 1885; *Tzevi Muddaḥ*, p. 116.
40. *Ibid.*, p. 101.
41. The poet mentions this several times in his poems. See *Kovetz Al Yad*, 1885, pp. 114, 116.
42. *Ibid.*, p. 104.

by the fate of my people. I fear that this plague of a deer will bring upon my people ruin after ruin and exile after exile. Some he will bring to heresy, others he will lead to apostasy. I mourn for my people. This false Messiah will be a stumbling block for them. He will not bring redemption but make their chains even stronger.[43]

"I see," the poet bitterly says, "that the pangs of the Messiah are already here, but there is no hope for redemption." And to the enraged mob he declares proudly:

All you who thirst for vengeance, who laugh at me and are angry with me, you will not silence me! Even if you shed my blood, I will expose your shameful deeds before the people. I will remain on watch and will not allow free thought to fall asleep.[44]

The poet is encouraged by the thought that his heroic deeds will not be forgotten. "I am certain," he declares, "that my song will not be forgotten and that men will eagerly gather my verses that are now trampled under foot."[45]

In all of Italy Jacob Frances had only one collaborator in his obdurate struggle, his brother Immanuel. Immanuel Frances as a poet was strongest in epigrams and lampoons. After his brother's poem against the Kabbalists was burned by order of the rabbis of Mantua, Immanuel issued forth with an angry lampoon, *Vikkuaḥ Livni Ve-Shimi*, in which he charges these rabbis with being worse than Korah and his band because "they trample under foot the pride of the people and destroy the foundations of the true faith." Like his brother, Immanuel also wrote lampoons against Shabbetai Tzevi and his associates, and for later generations composed a brief description of the Sabbatian movement, *Sippur Maaseh Shabbetai Tzevi Ve-Natan Ha-Azzati Be-Kitzur.*[46] After the death of his brother,[47] Immanuel collected all the poems and epigrams that Jacob Frances had written against Shabbetai Tzevi, adding his own to them, and made of them a complete work under the title *Tzevi Muddaḥ*, a work which has been published in modern times.[48]

43. *Ibid.,* p. 105.
44. *Ibid.,* p. 115.
45. *Ibid.* His hope that his poetry would be published was only partially fulfilled. His collection of poems (the largest part still unpublished) is in the library of Oxford University (see *Serapis,* 1840, p. 27).
46. Published in *Kovetz Al Yad,* 1885.
47. Immanuel Frances survived his brother by many years and died at the beginning of the eighteenth century.
48. In *Kovetz Al Yad,* 1885, pp. 97–128. There also is Jacob Frances' rather small piece which he composed for the Jewish musical society

Of a different stripe was the previously mentioned third opponent of the Shabbetai Tzevi movement, Jacob ben Aaron Sasportas. Born in Oran around 1610, he led a wandering life and served as a rabbi in Fez, Sali, and Tlemcen. In 1646 he was imprisoned but was soon ransomed and in 1651 was already in Amsterdam. In 1655 he accompanied Menasseh ben Israel on his journey to London and four years later was sent by the sultan of Turkey on a diplomatic mission to the Spanish court. In 1664 he occupied the post of *ḥacham* in the Portuguese community of London and a year later, when the Shabbetai Tzevi movement was at its peak, he was serving as rabbi in Hamburg. Only the last twenty-five years of his long life[49] were quietly spent in Amsterdam.

Sasportas was an ardent follower of Luria's Kabbalah and believed with perfect faith in all the miracles and wonders recounted in *Shivḥei Ha-Ari*. As the first corrector and proofreader of Menasseh ben Israel's *Nishmat Ḥayyim*, he expressed in an epilogue his great enthusiasm over the fact that the author of the book had so ingeniously disclosed "the hidden secrets of wisdom and the doctrine of transmigration of souls."

Nevertheless, in 1666, when in all communities men were dancing, rejoicing and happily greeting the "king Messiah," Sasportas was the only rabbi in Europe who did not lose his head and who courageously raised his warning voice. "And I, in my distress, saw how the leaders of the people were wandering in error," he bitterly relates.[50] Himself a mystic and Kabbalist, he nevertheless recalled the sorrowful facts of history—how "so many gave themselves out to be Messiahs but were finally changed into seducers." He saw in Shabbetai Tzevi "the stumbling block for the whole people of Israel." Sasportas' situation was even more difficult than that of the Frances brothers. He could not, like they, reply with mockery and laughter to all the miracles and wonders which people related about the Messiah and his prophets. He did not deny these, but merely endeavored to show that this is magic which takes place

---

"Anelanti" in Florence. In it the following appear as personages or actors: a cappella singers, a child, the *yetzer ra* (evil inclination) and *yetzer tov* (good inclination), a group languishing in Hell and another group resting in Heaven. Immanuel Frances also composed a work on Hebrew meter, *Metek Sefataim* (published by H. Brody in 1892, together with some of Immanuel's still-unpublished poems). Several poems of the Frances brothers were published by Abraham Baruch Paperna in the collection of poetry entitled *Kol Ugav* (1846).

49. Sasportas died in ripe old age in 1698 (see the introduction to the first edition of his *Ohel Yaakov*).

50. *Kitzur Tzitzat Novel Tzevi*, 4b (1867 edition).

with the aid of the *Sitra Aḥara* (the Other Side).[51] Precisely because Shabbetai Tzevi and his colleagues based themselves on the Kabbalah and the *Zohar*, Sasportas perceived in this messianic movement the greatest threat to the "secret wisdom" that was so precious to him. "These wicked men," he laments, "sully the words of the *Zohar* with falsehood. Their babbling deeds they adorn with quotations from holy books."[52] And he steps forth, one against all; himself a mystic, he fights against the intoxication of mystical illusions. His own community persecuted him. He was mocked in the synagogue. He was compelled to rise when they recited the prayer "May He who blessed" for the "king Messiah." It was demanded of him that he publicly acknowledge that Shabbetai Tzevi was the true redeemer and Messiah. Nevertheless, Sasportas did not lose courage. With great energy he circulated letters and proclamations to all the prominent rabbis and heads of communities in various lands.[53] He warned against the serious danger for the entire Jewish community inherent in the Shabbetai Tzevi movement. Among the rabbis to whom he turned, however, a great many were ardent followers of Shabbetai Tzevi, and Sasportas received extremely indignant replies from them. He was reviled, mocked, and laughed at. He was also threatened with severe punishment because he spoke with little respect of the prophet, Nathan of Gaza.[54] "I am like a little lost kernel in the whole land," he laments.[55] With great diligence Sasportas gathered for future generations all the materials and necessary information regarding the "epidemic madness" of "the whole house of Israel," i.e., the messianic movement of his time. This rich material that he assembled and that his son published in Amsterdam in 1737 serves to the present day as one of the major sources for the history of the Shabbetai Tzevi movement.

Following the passionate storm of the "days of the Messiah," the Turkish-Palestinian community began to decline and ceased to play a significant role in the cultural history of the Jewish people. "After the noise, a still small voice." In the years following the exciting clamor and stormy ecstasy of the "days of the Mes-

51. See *Kitzur Tzitzat Novel Tzevi,* in several places. That Shabbetai Tzevi's miracles were performed through magic and trickery is asserted also by the author of the memoirs which Jacob Emden published in his *Torat Ha-Kenaot* (see 5, 8, 9, 10 ff.).
52. *Kitzur Tzitzat Novel Tzevi,* 94.
53. Sasportas himself relates: "I sent letters to Germany, Poland, Italy, Turkey, Egypt, and Syria."
54. See *Kitzur Tzitzat Novel Tzvei:* "And that very night they judged me as a sinner for having despised the words of the prophet Nathan."
55. *Ibid.,* 30.

siah" the Jewish community of the Near East became as silent as a graveyard. The oppressive atmosphere of rigidity and backwardness prevailed; the breath of life was absent; the conflict of ideas died out. Everything became as if petrified in the same old-fashioned posture inherited from ages past. Even the last pathological afterpangs of the Sabbatian messianic movement made themselves noticeable not in the Moslem East, not in the birthplace of the Lurianic Kabbalah, but in the other center of Jewish culture—in the German-Polish community. Sephardic Jewry, after giving birth to two polar opposites—Shabbetai Tzevi in the East and Baruch Spinoza, the brilliant founder of the new philosophical world view, in a cultured corner of Europe—receded into the background. The hegemony of Jewish culture passed over to the Ashkenazim, to German-Polish Jewry. This is the subject of the succeeding volumes of our history.

BIBLIOGRAPHICAL NOTES

The Jewish Center of Culture in the Ottoman Empire

CHAPTER ONE

THE CULTURAL FLOWERING OF TURKISH JEWRY; KARAITE SCHOLARS

On the history of the Jews and Judaism in the Ottoman empire and in some of its major centers, see S. A. Rosanes, *Divrei Yemei Yisrael Be-Togarmah*, six volumes (1907–45), and in three volumes (1930–38); I. S. Emmanuel, *Histoire des Israélites de Salonique* (1936); A. Galanté, *Documents officiels turcs concernant les Juifs de Turkie* (1931); idem, *Histoire des Juifs d'Istanbul*, two volumes (1941–42); J. Nehama, *Histoire des Israélites de Salonique*, five volumes (1935–59); B. Lewis, *Notes and Documents from the Turkish Archives* (1952); M. Franco, *Essai sur l'histoire des Israélites de l'empire Ottoman* (1897); H. Z. Hirschberg, *Toledot Ha-Yehudim Be-Afrikah Ha-Tzefonit*, two volumes (1965); A. Yaari, *Ha-Defus Ha-Ivri Ha-Kushta* (1967); idem, *Sheluhei Eretz Yisrael* (1951); D. Conforte, *Kore Ha-Dorot*, second edition (1842); and I. M. Goldman, *The Life and Times of Rabbi David Ibn Abi Zimra*, based on his *responsa* (1970).

On Mordecai ben Eliezer Comtino and his work, see S. A. Rosanes, *Divrei Yemei Yisrael Be-Togarmah*, I (1930), 25–32; H. J. Gurland, in *Talpiot*, I (1895), 1–34 (in "Toledot Anshei Shem" section); A. Ovadyah, in *Sinai*, VI (1940), 76–80; Silberberg, in *Jahrbuch der jüdisch-literarischen Gesellschaft*, III (1905), 277–92; and N. Menahem, in *Hadorom*, XXVII (1968), 211–20.

On the Karaites, Karaite scholars, and Karaite religious life in Byzantium and later in the Ottoman empire, see Z. Ankori, *The Karaites in Byzantium* (1959), with its extensive bibliography, pp. 461–84; R. Mahler, *Ha-Karaim* (1949); J. Mann, *Texts and Studies*, two volumes (1931–35); P. Grajewsky, *Me-Hayyei Ha-Karaim Be-Yerushalayim* (1922); Z. Cohn, *The Halakah of the Karaites* (1936); idem, *The Rise of the Karaite Sect* (1937); and P. S. Goldberg, *Karaite Liturgy and Its Relation to the Synagogue* (1957).

On Caleb Afendopolo and his work, see S. Bernstein, "Ha-Shirim Le-Hodoshei Ha-Shanah Le-Kalev Afendopolo Ha-Karai,"

Horeb, XI (1951), 53–84; *idem*, "Vikkuaḥ Piyyuti Bein Ha-Meshorer Veha-Yayin Le-Kalev Afendopolo," *Sinai*, XXX (1952), 87–104; *idem*, "Maḥberot Kalev Ben Eliahu Afendopolo Ha-Karai," *Hebrew Union College Annual*, XXIV (1953), 23–83; and J. Mann, *Texts and Studies*, Vol., II (1935), *s.v.* "Index."

On Elijah Mizraḥi and his work, see D. Conforte, *Kore Ha-Dorot*, second edition (1842), *s.v.* "Index"; H. H. Michael, *Or Ha-Ḥayyim: Ḥachmei Yisrael Ve-Sifreihem*, second edition (1965), Nos. 161–64, 306; S. A. Rosanes, *Divrei Yemei Yisrael Be-Togarmah*, I (1930), 70–77; A. Freimann, in *Tziyyon*, I (1936), 188–91; A. Ovadyah, *Ketavim Nivḥarim*, I (1942), 63–198; S. Assaf, *Be-Oholei Yaakov* (1953), pp. 145–96; and M. Steinschneider, *Die hebräischen Übersetzungen des Mittelalters* (1893), pp. 322, 508, 524.

CHAPTER TWO

THE SPANISH EXILES IN TURKEY AND PALESTINE; JOSEPH KARO AND SOLOMON MOLCHO

On the history of the Jewish exiles from Spain in Turkey and Palestine, see S. A. Rosanes, *Divrei Yemei Yisrael Be-Togarmah*, six volumes (1907–45) and in three volumes (1930–38); I. Ben-Zvi, "Eretz Yisrael under Ottoman Rule, 1517–1917," in L. Finkelstein, ed., *The Jews: Their History, Culture, and Religion*, third edition (1966), I, 602–89; and other works on the history of the Jews in the Ottoman empire listed under Chapter One above.

On Isaac Akrish and his work, see N. Brüll, in *Jahrbücher für jüdische Geschichte und Literatur*, VIII (1887), 53 ff.; I. Davidson, *Sefer Shaashuim* (1925), pp. 67 ff.; C. Roth, *The House of Nasi: The Duke of Naxos* (1948), pp. 173 ff.; A. Yaari, *Meḥkerei Sefer* (1958), pp. 212–13, 235 ff., 279; *idem*, *Ha-Defus Ha-Ivri Be-Kushta* (1967), pp. 118 ff.; and D. H. Dunlop, *History of the Jewish Khazars* (1954), pp. 128 ff.

On Obadiah ben Abraham Yare of Bertinoro and his work, see P. Grajewsky, *Rabbenu Ovadyah Yare Me-Bartenura* (1938); S. Sachs, in *Jahrbuch für die Geschichte der Juden und des Judenthums*, III (1863), 193–270; E. N. Adler, *Jewish Travellers*, second edition (1966), pp. 209–50; A. Yaari, *Iggerot Eretz Yisrael* (1943), pp. 98–144; M. A. Shulvass, *Roma Ve-Yerushalayim* (1944), pp. 31 ff.; Ch. Albeck, *Mavo La-Mishnah* (1959), pp. 249 ff.; and I. Ben-Zvi, *Eretz Yisrael Ve-Yishuvah* (1963), pp. 139 ff.

On Jacob Berab and the *semichah* or "ordination" controversy of the sixteenth century, see J. Newman, *Semikhah (Ordination):*

A Study of Its Origin, History, and Function (1950), which includes a bibliography; M. Benayahu, in *Sefer Yovel Le-Yitzḥak Baer* (1960), pp. 248–69; and Z. Dmitrovsky, in *Sefunot*, VI (1962), 117–23; VII (1963), 41–102; and X (1966), 113–92.

On Jacob ben Solomon Ibn Ḥabib, see D. Conforte, *Kore Ha-Dorot*, second edition (1842), pp. 32a, 33a–b; S. A. Rosanes, *Divrei Yemei Yisrael Be-Togarmah*, I (1930), 84–85, 101–5; A. Ovadyah, *Ketavim Nivḥarim* (1942), pp. 97, 101; I. S. Emmanuel, *Histoire des Israélites de Salonique* (1936), pp. 85–86; and A. Marx, *Studies in Jewish History and Booklore* (1944), pp. 85, 89, 91.

For a list of the many editions of Joseph Karo's *Shulḥan Aruch*, see *Kovetz Rabbi Yosef Karo* (1969), pp. 89–120. On Karo and his work, see the excellent study by R. J. Z. Werblowsky, *Joseph Karo: Lawyer and Mystic* (1962); idem, "Le-Demuto Shel Ha-Maggid Shel Rabbi Yosef Karo," *Tarbitz*, XXVII (1958), 310–21; I. Twersky, "The *Shulḥan Aruch*: Enduring Code of Jewish Law," *Judaism*, XVI (1967); J. J. (L.) Greenwald, *Ha-Rav Rabbi Yosef Karo U-Zemano* (1954); Z. Dmitrovsky, in *Sefunot*, VI (1962), 71 ff., and VII (1963), 58–62; D. Tamar, *Meḥkarim Be-Toledot Ha-Yehudim Be-Eretz Yisrael Uve-Italyah* (1970); idem, in *Kiryat Sefer*, XL (1964–65), 65–71; H. Tchernowitz, *Die Entstehung des Schulchan Aruch* (1915); and idem, *Toledot Ha-Posekim*, III (1947), 1–36.

On David Reubeni and Solomon Molcho, see A. Z. Aescoly (ed.), *Sippur David Ha-Reuveni Al Pi Ketav Yad Oksford Be-Tzeruf Ketavim Ve-Eduyyot Mi-Benei Ha-Dor* (1940); idem (ed.), *Ḥayyat Kaneh* (1938); idem, *Ha-Tenuot Ha-Meshiḥiyyot Be-Yisrael* (1956); R. J. Z. Werblowsky, *Joseph Karo: Lawyer and Mystic* (1962); A. H. Silver, *A History of Messianic Speculation in Israel* (1927); D. Kaufmann, in *REJ*, XXIV (1897), 121–27; H. Vogelstein and P. Rieger, *Die Geschichte der Juden in Rom*, Vol. II (1895); J. H. Greenstone, *The Messiah Idea in Jewish History* (1906); Y. Baer, in *Kiryat Sefer*, XVII (1940), 302–12; A. S. Yahuda, in *Ha-Tekufah*, XXXIII–XXXIV (1940), pp. 599–625; C. Roth, in *Midstream*, IX (1963), 76–81; M. D. Cassuto, in *Tarbitz*, XXXII (1962–63), 339–58; and S. Simonsohn, in *Tziyyon*, XXVI (1961), 198–207.

CHAPTER THREE

MEIR IBN GABBAI; THE KABBALISTS OF SAFED

On Safed as a major center of Jewish mysticism in the sixteenth century, see I. Ben-Zvi and M. Benayahu, eds., *Sefer Tzefat*

(*Sefunot*, Vols. VI and VII, 1962–63), and the bibliography given there; S. Schechter, "Safed in the Sixteenth Century: A City of Legists and Mystics," in his *Studies in Judaism*, second series (1908), pp. 202–306; M. Benayahu, in *Sefer Assaf* (1953), pp. 109–25; *idem*, in *Sefer Ha-Yovel Le-Yitzhak Baer* (1960), pp. 248–69; *idem*, in *Sinai*, XLIII (1958), 35–113; and Y. Raphael, ed., *Rabbi Yosef Karo* (1969), pp. 7–18.

On David ben Solomon Ibn Abi Zimra, see H. Y. D. Azulai, *Shem Ha-Gedolim* (1852), pp. 44–45, No. 16; H. J. Zimmels, *Rabbi David ibn abi Simra* (German, 1932); I. M. Goldman, *The Life and Times of Rabbi David Ibn Abi Zimra* (1970); and E. Ashtor (Strauss), *Toledot Ha-Yehudim Be-Mitzrayim Ve-Suryah Tahat Shilton Ha-Mamlukim*, II (1951), 458–70.

On Solomon Alkabetz and his work, see S. A. Horodetzky, in *Sefer Ha-Shanah Shel Eretz Yisrael* (1935); R. J. Z. Werblowsky, in *Sefunot*, VI (1962), 135–82; *idem*, *Joseph Karo: Lawyer and Mystic* (1962); S. Bernstein, *Be-Hazon Ha-Dorot* (1928), pp. 14–21; and M. Benayahu, in *Sefunot*, VI (1962), 14–17.

The publication of Moses ben Jacob Cordovero's complete commentary to the *Zohar* has begun in Jerusalem, and several volumes have now appeared. His *Tomar Devorah* was translated into English by L. Jacobs under the title *The Palmtree of Deborah* (1960). On Cordovero and his thought, see S. A. Horodetzky, *Torat Ha-Kabbalah Shel Rabbi Mosheh Kordovero* (*Mahadurah Hadashah Im Tosafot*) (1952), and J. Ben-Shlomo, *Torat Ha-Elohut Shel Rabbi Mosheh Kordovero* (1965).

On Elijah de Vidas and his work, see M. Steinschneider, *Catalogus Librorum Hebraeorum in Bibliotheca Bodleiana* (1852–60), pp. 950–52, No. 4973; H. H. Michael, *Or Ha-Hayyim: Hachmei Yisrael Ve-Sifreihem*, second edition (1965), Nos. 184–85; M. Wilensky, in *Hebrew Union College Annual*, XIV (1939), 457–69; and S. A. Horodetzky, *Olei Tziyyon* (1947), pp. 69–82.

CHAPTER FOUR

ISAAC LURIA AND HIS DISCIPLES

On Isaac Luria and the Lurianic Kabbalah, see H. Y. D. Azulai, *Shem Ha-Gedolim* (1852), Part I, Index; S. Schechter, "Safed in the Sixteenth Century: A City of Legists and Mystics," in his *Studies in Judaism*, second series (1908), pp. 202–306; D. Kahana, *Toledot Ha-Mekubbalim Ha-Shabbetaim Veha-Hasidim*, I (1913), 22–42; S. A. Horodetzky, *Torat Ha-Kabbalah Shel Rabbi Yitzhak*

Ashkenazi Ve-Rabbi Ḥayyim Vital (1947); *idem*, in *Encyclopedia Judaica*, X (1934), cols. 1198–1212; I. Tishby, *Torat Ha-Ra Veha-Kelipah Be-Kabbalat Ha-Ari* (1942); G. Scholem, *Major Trends in Jewish Mysticism*, revised edition (1946), pp. 244–86, 407–15; *idem*, *Shabbetai Tzevi Veha-Tenuah Ha-Shabbetait Be-Yemei Ḥayyav*, I (1957), 18–60; *idem*, *Kitvei Yad Ha-Kabbalah* (1930), pp. 103–6, 115–43; *idem*, "Shetar Ha-Hitkashrut Shel Talmidei Ha-Ari," *Tziyyon*, V (1940), 133–60; *idem*, "Yisrael Sarug-Talmid Ha-Ari?," *Tziyyon*, V (1940), 214–43; *idem*, "Ketavav Ha-Amitiyyim Shel Ha-Ari Be-Kabbalah," *Kiryat Sefer*, XIX (1943), 184–99; *idem*, in *Kiryat Sefer*, XXVI (1950–51), 185–94; *idem*, "Lyrik der Kabbala?," *Der Jude*, VI (1921), 55–69; "Der Begriff der Kawwanah in der alten Kabbala," *MGWJ*, LXXVIII (1934), 492–518; M. Wiener, *Die Lyrik der Kabbala* (1920); Ph. Bloch, *Die Kabbala auf ihrem Hohepunkt und ihre Meister* (1905); A. Berliner, *Randbemerkungen zum täglichen Gebetbuche*, I (1909), 30–47; A. I. Schechter, *Lectures on Jewish Liturgy* (1933), pp. 39–60; M. Benayahu, *Sefer Toledot Ha-Ari* (1967); *idem*, in *Areshet*, III (1961), 144–65; *idem*, in *Sefer Ha-Yovel Le-Ḥanoch Albeck* (1963), pp. 71–80; *idem*, in *Sefunot*, X (1966), 213–98; and D. Tamar, *Meḥkarim Be-Toledot Ha-Yehudim* (1969).

Hayyim ben Joseph Vital's autobiographical notes, which he entitled *Sefer Ha-Ḥezyonot*, was published from an autograph manuscript by A. Z. Aescoly (1954). On Vital and his work, see G. Scholem, in *Encyclopedia Judaica*, XVI (1971), cols. 171–75; *idem*, "Shetar Ha-Hitkashrut Shel Talmidei Ha-Ari," in *Tziyyon*, V (1940), 133–60; M. Benayahu, in *Sinai*, XXX (1952), 65–75; *idem*, *Sefer Toledot Ha-Ari* (1967), Index; and D. Tamar, in *Tarbitz*, XXV (1956), pp. 99 f.

CHAPTER FIVE

ISRAEL NAJARA AND SHALEM SHABBEZI

On the Gavison family, see A. Cahen, *Les Juifs dans l'Afrique septentrionale* (1867), pp. 104 ff.; S. A. Rosanes, *Divrei Yemei Yisrael Be-Togarmah*, III (1938), 246, 247, 250 ff.; and H. Z. Hirschberg, *Toledot Ha-Yehudim Be-Afrikah Ha-Tzefonit*, II (1965), 46–47.

On Saadiah Longo and his circle, see J. Patai, *Mi-Sefunei Ha-Shirah* (1944), pp. 86–125, A. M. Habermann, *Toledot Ha-Piyyut Veha-Shirah* (1970), pp. 232–34; and H. Brody, *Minḥah Le-David* (1935), pp. 205–20.

On Menahem de Lonzano, see A. L. Frumkin and E. Rivlin, *Toledot Hachmei Yerushalayim*, I (1928), 134–45; G. Scholem, *Kitvei Yad Be-Kabbalah* (1930), pp. 115–16, 152, 156; S. A. Rosanes, *Divrei Yemei Yisrael Be-Togarmah*, II (1938), 182–86; M. Wander, *Derech Ha-Hayyim* (1931), introduction, pp. 1–29; I. Sonne, in *Kovetz Al Yad*, V (1950), 197–204; and S. H. Kook, *Iyyunim U-Mehkarim*, I (1959), 241–45.

A new scientific edition of Israel Najara's *Zemirot Yisrael*, edited by I. Pris-Horev and vocalized by A. Avrunin, appeared in 1946. His collection of 120 poems, *Pizmonim*, was edited with an introduction and notes by M. H. Friedlander (1858). On Najara and his work, see I. Davidson, *Parody in Jewish Literature* (1907), pp. 34–36; *idem*, in *Sefer Ha-Yovel Le-Shemuel Krauss* (1937), pp. 193–270; *idem*, in *Sefer Ha-Shanah Le-Yehudei Amerikah*, IV (1939), 282–94; A. Ben-Yisrael, *Shirat Ha-Hen* (1918), pp. 23–58; M. D. Gaon, "Rabbi Yisrael Nagarah U-Zemirotav," *Mizrah U-Maarav*, V (1930), 145–67; D. Yellin, in S. W. Baron and A. Marx, eds., *Jewish Studies in Memory of George Alexander Kohut* (1935), pp. 59–88 (Hebrew part); I. Mendelson, in *Horeb*, IX (1946), 50–58; A. Mirsky, in *Kiryat Sefer*, XXV (1948–49), 39–47; *idem*, in *Sefunot*, V (1961), 207–34; VI (1962), 259–302; G. Scholem, in *I. Goldziher Memorial Volume* (1948), pp. 41–44 (Hebrew part); and *idem*, in *Behinot*, VIII (1955), 85–86.

On the history and life of the Jews of Yemen, see M. Zadoc, *Yehudei Teiman-Toledoteihem Ve-Orhot Hayyeihem* (1967); E. Brauer, *Die Ethnologie der jemenitischen Juden* (1934); S. D. Goitein, *Studies in Islamic History and Institutions* (1966); and H. Z. Hirschberg, *Yisrael Ba-Arav*. A bibliography of the literature of the Yemenite Jews was published by Y. Ratzhavi in *Kiryat Sefer*, XXVIII (1952), 255–78, 394–409.

On Shalem Shabbezi, see W. Bacher, in *Jahresbericht der Landes-Rabbinerschule in Budapest*, XXXIII (1909–10); A. Z. Idelsohn and H. Torczyner, *Shirei Teiman* (1930), pp. 88–221; A. Z. Idelsohn, in *Mizrah U-Maarav*, I (1929), 8–16, 128–40; and Y. Ratzhavi, in *Sefunot*, IX (1965), 135–66; and *idem*, in *Kiryat Sefer*, LXIII (1967–68), 140–59 (contains bibliography).

CHAPTER SIX

THE CULTURAL CENTER IN AMSTERDAM

On the history and life of the Spanish-Portuguese Jews and Marranos in the Netherlands, see H. Brugmans and A. Frank, eds.,

Geschiedenis der Joden in Nederland (1940); *Encyclopedia Sefardica Neerlandica* (1949); H. I. Bloom, *The Economic Activities of the Jews of Amsterdam in the Seventeenth and Eighteenth Centuries* (1937, reprinted 1969); C. Roth, *A History of the Marranos*, second edition, revised (1959); E. Rivkin, *The Shaping of Jewish History* (1971); J. S. da Silva Rosa, *Geschiedenis der portugeesche Joden te Amsterdam, 1593–1925* (1925); S. Wijnberg, *Joden in Amsterdam* (1967), with English summary and bibliography; and J. Melkman, *David Franco Mendes* (1951).

On Joseph Penso de la Vega and his work, see C. Roth, *A History of the Marranos*, second edition, revised (1959), pp. 336–37; M. B. Amzalak, *Joseph de la Vega e o suo livro Confusión de Confusiones* (1925); *idem, As Operações de Bolsa segundo Joseph de la Vega* (1926); *idem, Trois précurseurs Portugais* (193?–); J. Caro Baroja, *Los Judios en la España moderna y contemporánea*, II (1962), 157–59. Parts of Penso's fascinating book on the Amsterdam stock exchange, *Confusión de Confusiones*, were translated into English by H. Kellenbenz and published under the same title (1957).

On Isaac Aboab de Fonseca, see M. Kayserling, *Biblioteca Española-Portugueza-Judaica* (1890; reprinted 1961), pp. 4–5; *idem, American Jewish Historical Society Publications*, V (1897), 125 ff.; I. Tishby, ed., *Sefer Tzitzat Novel Tzevi* (1954), Index; G. Scholem, *Shabbetai Tzevi Veha-Tenuah Ha-Shabbetait Be-Yemei Hayyav* (1957), Index; A. Wiznitzer, *Jews in Colonial Brazil* (1960), Index, *s.v.* "Fonseca, Isaac Aboab da"; *idem, Records of the Earliest Jewish Community in the New World* (1954), Index; I. S. Emmanuel, in *American Jewish Archives*, VII (1955), 24 ff.; J. S. da Silva Rosa, in *Centraalblad voor Israeliten in Nederland*, XXIX (1913); M. Narkiss, in *Kiryat Sefer*, XV (1938–39), 489–90; A. Marx, *Studies in Jewish History and Booklore* (1944), pp. 209–11; and C. Roth, *A Life of Menasseh ben Israel: Rabbi, Printer, and Diplomat* (1934), Index.

Menasseh ben Israel's *Vindiciae Judaeorum, Or a Letter in Answer to Certain Questions Propounded by a Noble and Learned Gentleman Touching the Reproaches Cast on the Nation of the Jews, Wherein All Objections Are Candidly and Yet Fully Cleared* was published in London (1656). It was translated into German by Marcus Herz, with a preface by Moses Mendelssohn, under the title *Rettung der Juden* (1782). His *Conciliador* was translated into English by E. H. Lindo under the title *The Conciliator of R. Manasseh ben Israel: A Reconcilement of the Apparent Contradictions in Holy Scripture, to Which Are Added Explanatory Notes and Biographical Notices of the Quoted Authorities* (London, 1642; reprinted Edinburgh, 1904, and New York, 1972). His *Esperança de Israel* was translated into English by M. Wall under the title *The Hope of Israel* (London, 1650). Menasseh's pamphlets written between 1649 and 1656 to promote the readmission of the Jews to England were edited, with an introduction and notes, by L. Wolf under the title *Menasseh ben Israel's Mission to Oliver Cromwell* (1901).

On Menasseh, see M. Kayserling, "Menasse ben Israel," in *Jahrbücher für die Geschichte der Juden* (1867), pp. 85–188 (translated by F. de Sola Mendes, in *Miscellany of the Society of Hebrew Literature*, second series, London, 1877); C. Roth, *A Life of Menasseh ben Israel: Rabbi, Printer, and Diplomat* (1934); *idem, Magna Bibliotheca Anglo-Judaica* (1937), Index; idem, in *Transactions of the Jewish Historical Society of England*, XI (1924–27), 112–42; *idem*, in V. Lipman, ed., *Three Centuries of Anglo-Jewish History* (1961), pp. 1–25; R. P. Lehmann, *Nova Bibliotheca Anglo-Judaica* (1961), Index; M. Kayserling, *Biblioteca Española-Portugueza-Judaica* (1890; reprinted 1961), pp. 68–70; M. Wilensky, *Shivat Ha-Yehudim Le-Angliyyah* (1944); and A. Yaari, *Mi-Beit Defuso Shel Menasheh Ben Yisrael: Reshimah Im Mavo* (1947).

On Abraham Kohen de Herrera (or Alonso Nunez de Herrera, or Abraham Irira), see M. Freystadt, *Philosophia Cabbalistica et Pantheismus* (1832), pp. viii, 54 ff.; S. A. Horodetzky, in *Ha-Goren*, X (1928), 120 ff.; H. A. Wolfson, *The Philosophy of Spinoza* (1934), Index; and M. A. Anath (Perlmutter), in *Tarbitz*, XXVII (1958), 322–33.

The best edition of the works of Baruch Spinoza is *Spinoza Opera*, edited by C. Gebhardt, four volumes (1926). Probably the best English translation is R. H. M. Elwes, *The Chief Works of Benedick de Spinoza*, two volumes (1883), many times reprinted. On the life and thought of Spinoza, see H. A. Wolfson, *The Philosophy of Spinoza* (1934); F. Pollock, *Spinoza: His Life and Philosophy*, second edition (1899); H. H. Joachim, *A Study of Spinoza's Ethics* (1901); E. Caird, *Spinoza* (1902), E. Dunin-Borkowski, *Der junge de Spinoza* (1910); A. Wolf, *Spinoza* (1910); K. Fischer, *Spinoza*, fifth edition (1909); L. Brunschvicg, *Spinoza et ses contemporains*, third edition (1923); L. Roth, *Spinoza, Descartes, and Maimonides* (1924); *idem, Spinoza* (1929); J. Freudenthal, *Spinoza: Leben und Lehre* (1927); *idem, Die Lebensgeschichte Spinozas in Quellenschriften* (1899); R. McKeon, *The Philosophy of Spinoza* (1928); M. Frances, *Spinoza dans les pays neerlandais* (1937); V. Delbos, *Le Problème moral dans la philosophie de Spinoza* (1916); D. Bidney, *The Psychology and Ethics of Spinoza* (1940); S. Hampshire, *Spinoza* (1951); J. A.

Gunn, *Benedick Spinoza* (1925); H. F. Hallet, *Benedict de Spinoza: The Elements of His Philosophy* (1957); I. S. Revah, *Spinoza et Juan de Prado* (1959); L. Strauss, *Spinoza's Critique of Religion* (1965); L. Feuer, *Spinoza and the Rise of Liberalism* (1965); W. Bernald, *The Philosophy of Spinoza* (1934); R. Kayser, *Spinoza: Portrait of a Spiritual Hero* (1968); R. J. McShea, *The Political Philosophy of Spinoza* (1968); H. Serouya, *Spinoza: Sa vie et sa philosophie* (1933); J. Klatzkin, *Baruch Spinoza: Hayyav, Sefarav, Shitato* (1923); N. Sokolow, *Baruch Spinoza U-Zemano: Midrash Be-Filosofiah Uve-Korot Ha-Ittim* (1929); and P. Siwek, *Spinoza et le pantheisme religieux* (1937). For other important works on Spinoza, see A. S. Oko, *The Spinoza Bibliography* (1964).

On Spinoza as Biblical critic and scholar, see L. Strauss, *Die Religionskritik Spinozas als Grundlage seiner Bibelwissenschaft* (1930); idem, *Spinoza's Critique of Religion* (1965); and H. Liebeschutz, in *Antike und Abendland*, IX (1960), 39–62.

CHAPTER SEVEN

THE SHABBETAI TZEVI MOVEMENT

Much of the most important work in recent years on Shabbetai Tzevi and the Sabbatian movement has been done by Gershom Scholem. Among his major studies on the subject are the magisterial *Shabbetai Tzevi Veha-Tenuah Ha-Shabbetait Be-Yemei Hayyav*, two volumes (1957); *The Messianic Idea in Judaism and Other Essays* (1971); *Halomotav Shel Ha-Shabbetai R. Mordechai Ashkenazi* (1938); "Perush Mizmorei Tehillim Me-Hugo Shel Shabbetai Tzevi Be-Adrianopol," in *Alei Ayin: Minhat Devarim Le-Shelomoh Zalman Schocken* (1952), pp. 157–211; "Iggeret Natan Ha-Azzati Al Shabbetai Tzevi Ve-Hamarato," *Kovetz Al Yad*, new series, VI (1966), 419–56; "Teudah Hadashah Me-Reshit Ha-Tenuah Ha-Shabbetait," *Kiryat Sefer*, XXXIII (1958), 532–40; "Parashiot Be-Heker Ha-Tenuah Ha-Shabbetait," *Tziyyon*, VI (1941), 85–100; "Beruchiah Rosh Ha-Shabbetaim Be-Saloniki," in *Tziyyon*, VI (1941), 119–47, 181–201; "Le-Yediat Ha-Shabbetaut Mi-Toch Kitvei Cardozo," *Tziyyon*, VII (1942), 12–28; *Be-Ikvot Mashiah* (1944), his edition of the collected writings of Nathan of Gaza; the chapter "Sabbatianism and Mystical Heresy," in his *Major Trends in Jewish Mysticism*, revised edition (1946), pp. 287–324; and his article, "Shabbetai Zevi," in *Encyclopedia Judaica*, IV (1971), cols. 1219–54.

Other significant studies dealing with Shabbetai Tzevi or various aspects of the Shabbatian movement include Y. Tishby, *Netivei Emunah U-Minut* (1964); *idem,* "Le-Ḥeker Ha-Mekorot Shel Sefer Ḥemdat Yamim," *Tarbitz,* XXIV (1955), 441–45; and XXV (1956), 66–92; *idem,* "Mekorot Me-Reshit Ha-Meah Ha-XVIII Be-Sefer Ḥemdat Yamim," *Tarbitz,* XXV (1956), 202–30; *idem,* "Bein Shabbetaut Le-Ḥasidut," *Kenesset,* IX (1945), 238–68; S. Simonsohn, "A Christian Report from Constantinople Regarding Shabbetai Zebi," *Journal of Jewish Studies,* XII (1961), 33–85; R. J. Z. Werblowsky, "Crises of Messianism," *Judaism,* VII (1958), 106–20; J. Sarachek, *The Messianic Idea in Medieval Jewish Literature* (1932); D. Kahana, *Toledot Ha-Mekubbalim, Ha-Shabbetaim, Veha-Ḥasidim,* two volumes (1913–14); I. Sonne, "Le-Toledot Ha-Shabbetaut Be-Italyah," in *Sefer Ha-Yovel Le-Alexander Marx* (1943), pp. 89–104; Ch. Wirszubski, "Ha-Idiologiyah Ha-Shabbetait Shel Hamarat Ha-Mashiaḥ, *Tziyyon,* III (1938), 215–45; *idem,* "Ha-Teologiyah Ha-Shabbetait Shel Natan Ha-Azzati," *Kenesset,* VIII (1944), 210–46; M. Freudenthal, "R. Michel Chasid und die Sabbatianer," *MGWJ,* LXXVI (1932), 370–85; A. Epstein, "Un lettre d'Abraham Ha-Yakhini a Nathan Gazati," *REJ,* XXVI (1893), 209–19; A. Amarillo, "Teudot Shabbetaiyyot," in *Sefunot,* V (1961), 235–74; S. Z. Shazar (Rubaschow), *Sofero Shel Mashiaḥ* (1970, reprinted from *Ha-Shiloaḥ,* XXIX [1913]); M. Benayahu, "Yediot Me-Italyah Ume-Holland Al Reshitah Shel Ha-Shabbetaut," *Eretz Yisrael,* IV (1956), 194–205; *idem,* "Mafteaḥ Le-Havanat Ha-Teudot Al Ha-Tenuah Ha-Shabbetait Be-Yerushalayim," in *Studies in Honor of Gershom Scholem* (1968), pp. 35–45; M. Wilensky, "Arbaah Kunteresim Angliyyim Al Ha-Tenuah Ha-Shabbetait," *Tziyyon,* XVII (1952), 157–72; A. Yaari, *Taalumat Sefer* (1954), on *Hemdat Yamim* (includes bibliography); H. P. Salomon, "Midrash, Messianism, and Heresy in Spanish-Jewish Hymns," *Studia Rosenthaliana,* IV, No. 2 (1970), pp. 169–80.

CHAPTER EIGHT

PRO- AND ANTI-SABBATIANS

On Nehemiah Ḥiyya ben Moses Ḥayon, see A. Freimann, ed., *Inyanei Shabbetai Tzevi* (1912), pp. 117–38; D. Kaufmann, "La lutte de Rabbi Naftali Cohen contre Hayyoun," in *REJ,* XXXVI (1897), 256–82, and XXXVII (1898), 274–83; G. Levi, "La lotto contro N. Ch. Chajjun a Firenze," *Rivista Israelitica,* VIII (1911), 169–85, and IX (1912), 5–29; H. Graetz, *History of the Jews*

(1891–1902), V, 215–31; D. Kahana, *Toledot Ha-Mekubbalim, Ha-Shabbetaim, Veha-Ḥasidim* (1913), pp. 123–27; G. Scholem, in *Tziyyon*, III (1929), 172–79; I. Sonne, in *Kobez al jad*, II (1937), 157–96; and M. Friedmann, "Iggerot Be-Farashat Pulmos Nehemiah Ḥiyya Ḥayon," *Sefunot*, X (1966), 483–619.

Excerpts as well as complete treatises from the writings of Abraham Miguel Cardozo were published by A. Jellinek in the *Bet Ha-Midrash* of A. H. Weiss (1865); by Bernheimer in *JQR*, XVIII (1927–28), 97–127; by G. Scholem, in *Abhandlungen zur Erinnerung H. P. Chajes* (1933), pp. 324–50, in *Tziyyon*, VII (1942), 12–28; and in *Sefunot*, III–IV (1960), 245–300; and by I. R. Molcho and S. A. Amarillo in *Sefunot*, III–IV (1960), 183–241. On Cardozo, see G. Scholem, *Judaica* (1963), pp. 119–46; *idem*, "Abraham Miguel Cardozo," *Encyclopedia Judaica*, V (1971), cols. 163–66; and Ch. Wirzsubski, "Ha-Idiologiyah Ha-Shabbetait Shel Hamarat Ha-Mashiaḥ," *Tziyyon*, III (1938), 215–45.

The poetic works of Jacob ben David Frances were edited by P. Naveh under the title *Kol Shirei Yaakov Frances* (1969); the volume contains a bibliography. The poems of Immanuel ben David Frances were edited by S. Bernstein under the title *Divan Le-Rabbi Immanuel ben David Frances* (1932). His *Metek Sefataim*, on poetry and rhetoric, was published by H. Brody (1892). On the Frances brothers and their work, see G. Scholem, *Shabbetai Tzevi Veha-Tenuah Ha-Shabbetait Be-Yemei Ḥayyav*, II (1957), 425–28; E. Fleischer, in *Kiryat Sefer*, XLV (1969–70), 177–87; and A. M. Habermann, in *Moznayim*, XXIX (1969), 66–69.

The complete version of Jacob Sasportas' *Tzitzat Novel Tzevi* (for a long time known only in the abbreviated version *Kitzur Tzitzat Novel Tzevi*, published in Amsterdam in 1737, in Altona in 1757 [by Jacob Emden], and in Odessa in 1867) was first published by I. Tishby in 1954 from the only complete manuscript in existence. On Sasportas, see G. Scholem, *Shabbetai Tzevi Veha-Tenuah Ha-Shabbetait Be-Yemei Ḥayyav* (1957), and R. Shatz, in *Beḥinot*, X (1956), 50–66.

Glossary of Hebrew and
Other Terms

Acquired Intellect: Among the Jewish and Arabic Aristotelians, the new intellect produced in man when he has acquired abstract concepts through the operation of the Active Intellect (see below).

Active Intellect: Among the Jewish and Arabic Aristotelians, the universal "Intelligence" which serves to control the motions of the sublunar world and especially to develop the human faculty of reason, which, in the infant, is merely a capacity or potentiality (a "material" intellect).

Aggadah (or Haggadah): The non-legal part of the post-Biblical Oral Torah, consisting of narratives, legends, parables, allegories, poems, prayers, theological and philosophical reflections, etc. Much of the Talmud is aggadic, and the Midrash (see below) literature, developed over a period of more than a millennium, consists almost entirely of Aggadah. The term *aggadah*, in a singular and restricted sense, refers to a Talmudic story or legend.

Amora (pl. Amoraim): The title given to the Jewish scholars of Palestine, and especially of Babylonia, in the third to the sixth centuries whose work and thought is recorded in the Gemara of the Talmud (see Gemara).

Ashkenazim: Since the ninth century, a term applied to the German Jews and their descendants, in contrast to the Sephardim (see below). After the Crusades, many Ashkenazic Jews settled in eastern Europe and from there migrated to western Europe and America. In recent centuries they have constituted the overwhelming majority of the world Jewish population.

Bet Ha-Midrash: In the Talmudic age, a school for higher rabbinic learning where students assembled for study and discussion as well as prayer. In the post-Talmudic age most synagogues had a Bet Ha-Midrash or were themselves called by the term, insofar as they were places of study.

combinations of letters: A method of exegesis of Biblical and other texts through combination and permutation of the constituent letters of their words, practiced by many Kabbalists. It was also believed by some Kabbalists that supernatural and miraculous results could be obtained in practical life by the application of this method.

devekut: Literally, "cleaving to." Intense love of God and union with Him. The concept of *devekut* was especially stressed by some of the Kabbalists, among whom it assumed the meaning of "ecstasy."

dybbuk (pl. dybbukim): According to Kabbalist theosophy, the soul of a sinner which has transmigrated into the body of a living person after the sinner's death. The term *dybbuk* literally means "adhesion." According to the Kabbalists, a *dybbuk* could be exorcised by adjurations with various divine names. Such exorcisms were in fact practiced by the followers of the Kabbalah of Rabbi Isaac Luria and later by various Hasidic figures.

Eighteen Benedictions: See **Shemoneh Esreh.**

Ein Sof: Literally, "without end" or "infinite." In Kabbalist thought, the undifferentiated unity of the unknown God, the *deus absconditus* as He is in His own being before His self-revelation through the *sefirot* (see **sefirah**).

Essenes: Perhaps from the Syriac term *Ḥasya,* "pious." A religious sect towards the end of the era of the Second Temple in Palestine. The Essenes were in many respects similar to the Pharisees, but while they believed in the immortality of the soul and in reward and punishment, they rejected the notion of physical resurrection. Living an ascetic life in communes, most of the Essenes practiced celibacy, though some of them married. They were opposed to the animal sacrifices in the Temple and approved only the bringing of offerings of flour and oil.

Gaon (pl. Geonim): The spiritual and intellectual leaders of Babylonian Jewry in the post-Talmudic period, from the sixth through the eleventh centuries C.E. The head of each of the two major academies of Babylonia, at Sura and Pumbeditha, held the title Gaon. The Geonim had considerable secular power as well as religious authority, and their influence extended over virtually all of world Jewry during the larger part of the Geonic age. The title Gaon is occasionally applied in a general honorific sense to a very eminent Judaic scholar.

Gemara: The second basic strand of the Talmud, consisting of a commentary on, and supplement to, the Mishnah (see **Mishnah**).

gilgul ha-nefesh: In Kabbalist theosophy, transmigration of the soul.

Gog and Magog: A king (Gog) and country (Magog) mentioned in the Book of Ezekiel, who predicts the defeat of Gog after his attack on the Land of Israel at the head of the armies of many peoples. According to the Talmud, the wars of Gog and Magog will precede the coming of the Messiah.

Hacham: In Hebrew, "wise man." Originally, an officer of the rabbinic courts in Palestine and Babylonia. Later the term was applied to an officiating rabbi in Sephardic communities.

Halachah: In Hebrew, "law" (derived from the verb *halach*, "to go" or "to follow"). The legal part of Talmudic and later Jewish literature, in contrast to Aggadah or Haggadah (see above), the non-legal elements. In the singular, *halachah* means "law" in an abstract sense or, alternatively, a specific rule or regulation; in the plural, *halachot* refers to collections of laws.

Hamishah Asar Be-Shevat: The fifteenth day of the Hebrew month *Shevat*, celebrated as the New Year of Trees through the eating of various fruits, especially those grown in Palestine.

Hannukah: In Hebrew, "dedication." An eight-day festival commemorating the victory of the Maccabees over Antiochus Ephiphanes in 165 B.C. and the subsequent rededication of the Temple in Jerusalem.

Haskalah: The movement for disseminating modern European culture among Jews from about 1750 to 1880. It advocated the modernization of Judaism, the westernization of traditional Jewish education, and the revival of the Hebrew language.

haskamah (pl. *haskamot*): Approbations or authorizations by respected rabbinic authorities sometimes inserted in Hebrew books. The practice of inserting *haskamot* became particularly widespread after the synod of rabbis in Ferrara in 1554 decided that Hebrew books should obtain prior approval by Jewish authorities in order to prevent suppression or censorship by the officials of the Church. Later a *haskamah* was frequently solicited by the author of a book as testimony of his work's scholarly value and its orthodoxy.

Ineffable Name: YHWH, the Tetragrammaton or *Shem Ha-Meforash*. The particular name of the God of Israel in the Bible. Its original pronounciation is no longer known, though it is generally conjectured to have been Yahweh. By the second century B.C. it was no longer pronounced, except by the High Priest on the Day of Atonement, but read as *Adonai*.

Kabbalah: The mystical religious movement in Judaism and/or its literature. The term Kabbalah, which means "tradition," came to be used by the mystics beginning in the twelfth century to signify the alleged continuity of their doctrine from ancient times.

Karaites: A Jewish sect, originating in the eighth century C.E. in and around Persia, which rejected the Oral Torah or Oral Law and wished to interpret the Bible literally and to deduce from it a code of law without reliance on Talmudic tradition. Major factors in the evolution of the Karaites were their ardent messianic hopes and their ascetic tendencies.

kavvanah (pl. *kavvanot*): In Hebrew, "devotion." The quality of devotion, intention, and spiritual concentration which, according to Jewish teaching, should accompany the fulfillment of religious commandments, especially prayer. *Kavvanah* was particularly stressed by the Kabbalists and the later Hasidim, in whose view prayers uttered with *kavvanah* have a direct influence on the supernal worlds. Many Kabbalists believed that *kavvanah* in prayer is effectuated by various combinations of the letters of the Ineffable Name, and such a combination itself came to be called a *kavvanah*.

kelipah (pl. *kelipot*): Literally, "husk" or "shell." A mystical term in Kabbalah, denoting any of the forces of evil.

kinah: In Biblical and Talmudic times, a dirge over the dead. Later the term came to be applied to a liturgical composition for the Ninth of Av dealing with the destruction of the Temple as well as with contemporary persecutions.

Maḥzor: In Hebrew, "cycle." A term commonly used to designate the Festival Prayer Book. At first the Maḥzor contained prayers for the whole year, including the daily and Sabbath services, but most Ashkenazic *maḥzorim* now contain only the festival prayers.

Marranos: A Spanish term meaning "swine"; in Hebrew, *Anusim,* i.e., those "forced" or "coerced." A term applied in Spain and Portugal to those descendants of baptised Jews who were suspected of continued covert loyalty to Judaism. The class became particularly numerous in Spain after the massacres of 1391 and in Portugal after the forced conversions of 1497. The Marranos achieved high standing socially, economically, and politically, but were frequently persecuted by the Inquisition.

Maskil (pl. Maskilim): An adherent of Haskalah (see **Haskalah**).

Messiah, Pangs of the: In Hebrew, *Ḥevlei Ha-Mashiaḥ.* The woes and troubles, especially those inflicted on the Jewish people, that were expected to precede the advent of the Messiah.

Midrash (pl. Midrashim): The discovery of new meanings besides literal ones in the Bible. The term is also used to designated collections of such Scriptural exposition. The best-known of the Midrashim are the *Midrash Rabbah, Tanḥuma, Pesikta De-Rav Kahana, Pesikta Rabbati,* and *Yalkut Shimeoni.* In a singular and restricted sense, *midrash* refers to an item of rabbinic exegesis.

Minhag Ashkenaz: The prayer customs of the Ashkenazim (see above).

Ninth of Av: In Hebrew, Tishah Be-Av. A fast day commemorating the destruction of both the First and the Second Temples. The day is observed by the reading of the Book of Lamentations and special dirges, many of which were written in the Middle Ages. The Ninth of Av is also traditionally the anniversary of the fall of Betar in 135 C.E. marking the end of the unsuccessful rising of the Jews of Palestine against Rome, the expulsion from Spain in 1492, and other tragic events in the history of the Jewish people.

Oral Torah (or **Oral Law**): The body of interpretation and analysis of the written law of the Pentateuch created in post-exilic Judaism and handed down orally from generation to generation. The Oral Law consists of the Mishnah (see above) and the Gemara (see above), both of which were combined to form the Talmud (see below). Even after the redaction of the Talmud, the body of tradition contained in it continued to be known as the Oral Law because its roots were in an oral tradition.

parnass: From the Hebrew term *parnes*, meaning "to foster" or "to support." A term used to designate the chief synagogue functionary. The *parnass* at first exercised both religious and administrative authority, but since the sixteenth century religious leadership has been the province of the rabbis. The office of *parnass* has generally been an elective one.

pilpul: In Talmudic and rabbinic literature, a clarification of a difficult point. Later the term came to denote a sharp dialectical distinction or, more generally, a certain type of Talmudic study emphasizing dialectical distinctions and introduced into the Talmudic academies of Poland by Jacob Pollak in the sixteenth century. Pejoratively, the term means hairsplitting.

Priestly Blessing: The formula, contained in the Book of Numbers 6:24–26, for the blessing of the people by the priests in the Temple. The priestly blessing passed over into the synagogue service and is still recited by decendents of Aaron in Orthodox congregations as well as in some Conservative ones.

Purim: In Hebrew, "lots." A festival commemorating the saving of Persian Jewry through the efforts of Esther from the threat of destruction on the part of Haman, as recorded in the Biblical Book of Esther. Purim is observed on the fourteenth day of the Hebrew month of Adar.

Rosh Hodesh: The first day of the month, already celebrated in Biblical times as a holiday. At present, Rosh Hodesh is observed only by the addition of a number of prayers to the synagogue service.

Sanhedrin: A Hebrew word of Greek origin designating, in rabbinic literature, the assembly of seventy-one ordained scholars which served both as the supreme court and the legislature of Judaism in the Talmudic age. The Sanhedrin disappeared before the end of the fourth century C.E.

Savoraim: In Hebrew, "reasoners." A term given to the scholars of the Babylonian Talmudic academies between the times of the Amoraim and the hegemony of the Geonim, i.e., between approximately 500 to 700 C.E.

Seder: In Hebrew, "order." The ritual dinner conducted in the Jewish home on the first night (and outside Israel, the first two nights) of Passover. The story of the exodus from Egypt is recounted and a number of symbols related to it are included in the ritual.

sefirah (pl. ***sefirot***): A technical term in Kabbalah, employed from the twelfth century on, to denote the ten potencies or emanations through which the Divine manifests itself.

semichah: In Hebrew, "placing" [of the hands]. The practice of ordination whereby Jewish teachers, beginning in the Talmudic age, conferred on their best pupils the title "rabbi" and authorized them to act as judges and render authoritative decisions in matters of Jewish law and ritual practice.

Sephardim: The term applied to the Jews of Spain (in Hebrew, *Sepharad*) and afterwards to their descendants, no matter where they lived. The term Sephardim is applied particularly to the Jews exiled from Spain in 1492 who settled all along the North African coast and throughout the Ottoman empire.

Shavuot: In Hebrew, "weeks." The last of the three Biblical pilgrim festivals, originally marking the wheat harvest, but after the destruction of the Temple commemorating especially the Covenant between God and Israel and the giving of the Torah on Mount Sinai.

Shechinah: A term used to imply the presence of God in the world, in the midst of Israel, or with individuals. In contrast to the principle of divine transcendence, *Shechinah* represents the principle of divine immanence.

Shemoneh Esreh: The chief prayer, consisting of eighteen benedictions, in the Jewish liturgy.

sukkah: In Hebrew, "tabernacle." A temporary booth erected during the Festival of Tabernacles in which observant Jews are expected to "live" or at least to take their meals.

Talmud: The title applied to the two great compilations, distinguished as the Babylonian Talmud and the Palestinian Talmud, in which the records of academic discussion and of judicial administration of post-Biblical Jewish law are assembled. Both Talmuds also contain Aggadah or non-legal material.

Tanna (pl. **Tannaim**): A kind of teacher mentioned in the Mishnah, or in literature contemporaneous with the Mishnah, and living during the first two centuries C.E.

Tosafists: The French and German scholars of the twelfth to the fourteenth centuries who produced critical and explanatory notes on the Talmud.

yeshivah (pl. *yeshivot*): A traditional Jewish school devoted primarily to the study of the Talmud and rabbinic literature.

Zohar: The chief work of the Spanish Kabbalah, traditionally ascribed to the Tanna Simeon ben Yoḥai (second century) but probably written by the Spanish Kabbalist Moses de Leon at the end of the thirteenth century.

Index

Index

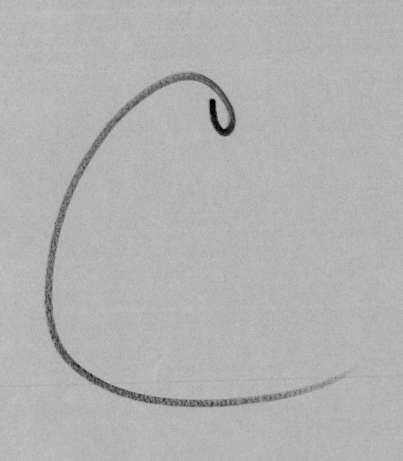